Walks to Churches in Hampshire and the Isle of Wight

41 Walks in Hampshire
9 walks on the Isle of Wight

Diana Pé

Published by ***PP (Pé Publishing)***
Email: Tonype@onetel.com

IS BN: 0-954-36907-6

Maps: John Avenell. Reproduced by permission of Ordnance Survey on behalf of the Controller of Her Majesty's Stationery Office, © Crown Copyright 100041589

Cover Illustration: Audrey Stevens

Photographs: Diana Pé

Artwork production: Den Clarke

Printed by: Downland Print Services Ltd, 2011. Reprinted 2017.

Disclaimer: the information in this book is given in good faith and is believed to be correct at the time of publication. No responsibility is accepted by the author and publisher for errors or omissions, or for any loss or injury howsoever caused. Only you can judge your own fitness, competence and experience.

Preface

Hello Hampshire! I am so happy to have walked over your varied countryside and visited your seaports and little market towns. Hampshire has plenty of coast and miles of rivers. Chalk streams of clear running water rise in the north and make their way to the south to enter the Solent. Naval towns have grown beside the Solent to protect the nation. The English nation was born in Hampshire and Winchester was its capital. King Alfred ruled here, protected his country from the Danes, promoted Christian learning and liberal ideas. Some of the finest old churches include Winchester Cathedral, St Cross, Romsey Abbey, Christchurch Priory and the Saxon, Breamore.

From Hampshire`s shores you look to **the Isle of Wight** and enjoy a ferry ride across the Solent to this fair island. Tennyson made his home here, Queen Victoria built herself a retreat here. The Downs rise above the sea here. The island still has an unhurried pace of life and charming people. With the help of locals, I have found some magnificent walks over downland to remote churches with views far out to sea.

Maps

I am most grateful to John Avenell for stepping in to draw such clear maps. Had he known there would be at least fifty, he might have hesitated!

The Cover

Once again Audrey Stevens has designed the cover, taking as her theme one of the churches in the Meon Valley. Her paintings enliven all my books.

Acknowledgements

My thanks for their help in the preparation of this book go to John Avenell, Christiane Good, Clair Grant, Windy Leung, Gabrielle and Robert Pe, Tony Pe, Pam Shearman, Pam Smith, Karen Standing, Audrey Stevens and, giving encouragement, Peggy Synge.

I dedicate this book to my brother, Stephen Good who so wanted to continue his work on the maps.

Also my thoughts go to fellow ramblers, Doreen Peskett and Kathleen Ramsay.

Hampshire Location Map

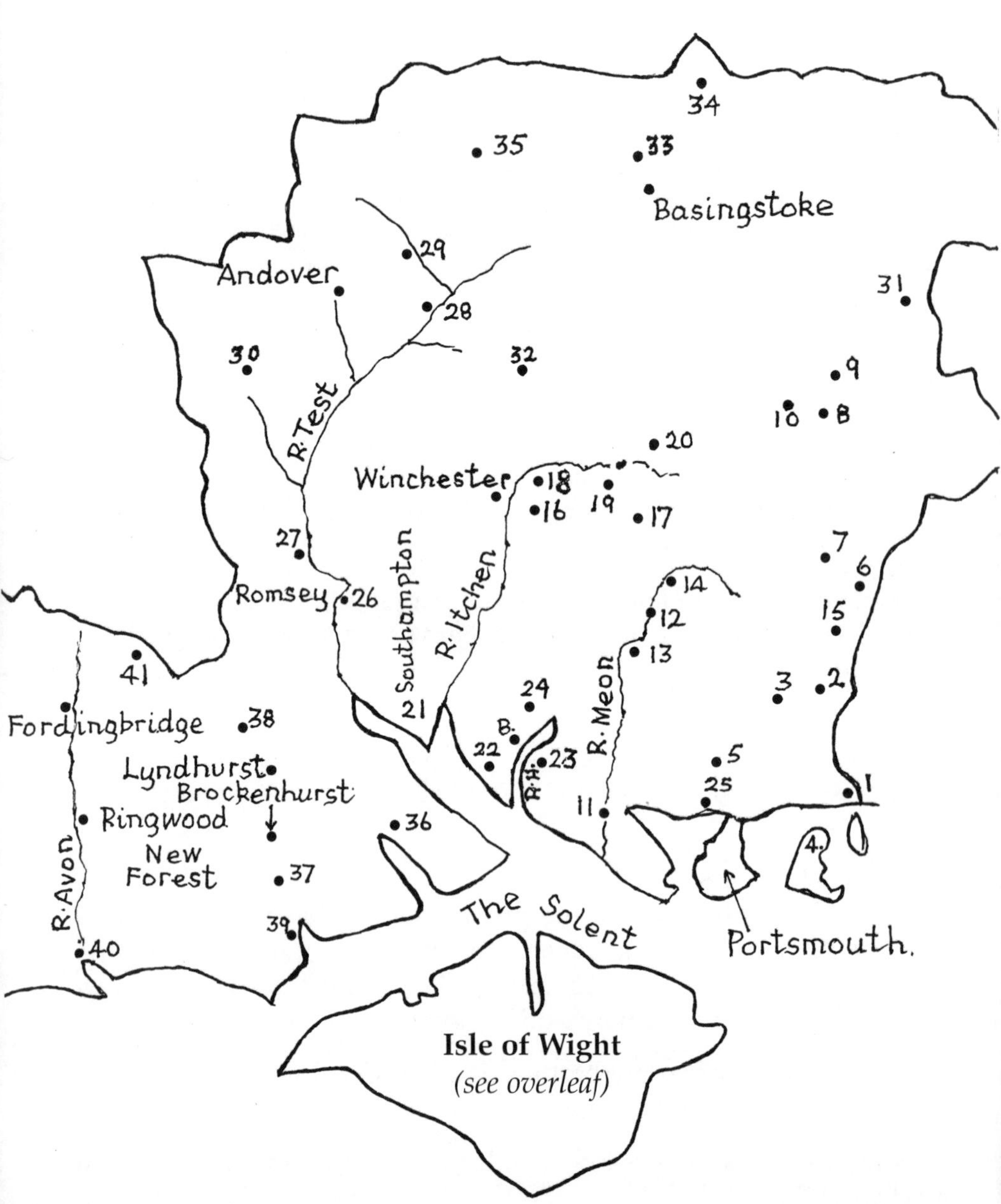

Contents

5 Walks Near the River Test Page

5 Walks Near Basingstoke

6 Walks in the New Forest or near the River Avon

The Solent

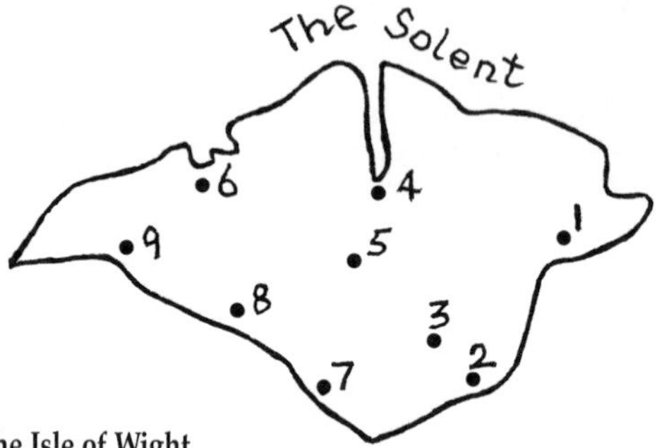

9 Walks on the Isle of Wight

Introduction

'…it was April in its mild air, brisk soft wind, and bright sun, occasionally clouded for a minute, and everything looked so beautiful under the influence of such a sky; the effects of the shadows pursuing each other, on the ships at Spithead and the island beyond, with ever-varying hues of the sea now at high water, dancing in its glee and dashing against the ramparts with so fine a sound, produced altogether such a combination of charms…' –

Mansfield Park by Jane Austen

Hampshire, that most English county, has a great variety of landscape. The Downs stretch from Sussex into east Hampshire. To the north of Petersfield are remote wooded hills with steep sides, known as 'hangers'. Deep lanes from Selborne to Winchester can be compared with Devon. A range of chalk hills dominates in the north and includes 'Beacon Hill' and 'Watership Down'. Below the hills, wide prairies are used for modern agriculture. In the southwest the New Forest is basically sandy heath land, but William the Conqueror decided to plant it with trees. Hampshire is a county of trees: firs and oaks in the New Forest, beeches and yews on the chalk hills.

Hampshire also enjoys a long coastline in the south. Little rivers rise in the north and head to the coast. The Solent waters and harbours on the south coast make Hampshire home to the Navy. Many leisure vessels also ply the waves. From Hampshire coastal waters, the Isle of Wight is a visible charm. 8000 years ago, before rivers formed the Solent, the Island was attached to the mainland. The first hunter gatherers could walk over to the Island. They were invaded by a succession of immigrants from the Continent. The 'Atrebates' settled in Silchester (Walk 27). When the Romans came they named the town 'Calleva Atreban'. Other Belgic tribes settled in the centre of Hampshire at Winchester, later named by the Romans 'Venta Belgarum' (Walk 16). Three chalk streams, the Itchen, the Test and the Meon have clear water to wash the meadows, once occupied by hundreds of mills and now the habitat of wild life.

The First Christians in Hampshire and Dorset

Once Vespasian had captured Maiden Castle, a hill in Dorset, the Romans found little resistance in Hampshire. He took Danebury Hill Fort without apparantly having to attack (Walk 30). The people co-operated with the conqueror to improve their lives. The Romans built good roads, allowing access for travellers including Christian missionaries. Winchester became the focal point. All roads led to Venta Belgarum. Subsequant development in Winchester covered up most Roman remains. Silchester, on the other hand, declined in the Middle Ages, never to recover, giving space for complete excavation. Straight roads of the Roman grid system can be seen here. Shops, offices and houses line the roads. Among the temples, baths and rest houses, over shadowed by the larger forum, there was a small Christian church. One other Christian relic, a Roman coin stamped with the Greek letters 'Chi Rho'. This is a Christian monogram.

Even before the Romans left England, tribes of Angles, Saxons and Jutes invaded from north Europe. West Saxons settled in Wessex. They followed the Rivers Itchen and Test. Jutes populated the New Forest, the Meon Valley and the Isle of Wight. The Romans built castles to repel the invaders, including Portchester (Walk 25) and Carisbrooke (Isle of Wight, Walk 5).

Converting the Saxons

When the Romans withdrew, many of the people of Wessex, mainly Celts were at the mercy of Saxons. Those who escaped massacre or slavery, had to flee to Cornwall or Wales. Saxon cemeteries have been found near Venta Belgarum. Conversion to Christianity began in 635 A.D. Pope Honorus sent Birinus to convert the most heathen Geweissae, West Saxons. This Roman priest landed on the coast, perhaps at Portchester. He converted the Saxon king, Cynegils. The son of Cynegils, Cenwealh made Wini bishop of the West Saxons and Winchester became the centre of the diocese and a royal city. The Old Minster began to be built in 642. Birinus became Bishop of Dorchester on Thames. His body was moved to Winchester in 676.

Only after the conversion of Hampshire was it the turn of the Isle of Wight. Wilfrid (685), his disciple Eoppa and, later Boniface preached on the Island.

The Venerable Bede in consultation with Bishop Daniel of Winchester (705 – 744) is the source of much of this history. He wrote some of his Anglo-Saxon Chronicle in the Old Minster. According to this Chronicle, two Saxon princes Cerdic and Cynric came to Briton in five ships in A.D. 495. It is believed that they landed near Southampton Water and came up the Avon Valley where they settled and cultivated the land.

Despite Royal approval, it took time to convert the whole of Hampshire.to Christianity. Minsters or mother churches were formed at Winchester, Wic (Southampton), Twynham (Christchurch), Wimborne. From these centres, priests went out into the countryside to preach, often under wayside crosses.

By 757 Hampshire was known as 'Hamtunscire', taking its name (as did Southampton) from 'Ham tun' two districts between the Test and Itchen. 'Wintanceaster' became the capital of Wessex. It held three minster churches where music and architecture flourished and two royal monasteries. They were responsible for the style of manuscript, known as the 'Winchester School'. Kings embraced the religious life and endowed minsters. Their sisters and daughters became abbesses. Bishops, abbots and abbesses were men and women of learning. King Alfred was nostalgic for these early days. Many saints were named then. After the middle of 9th century, fewer holy men and women became saints.

The alliance between Church and State strengthened the hand of the warrior kings in their fight against the Danes. Waves of invading Danes or Vikings ravaged the country. When King Offa of Mercia died in 796, the way was open to Wessex to become the leading kingdom, uniting England.

Wessex was fortunate in its kings. Alfred the Great (871 – 899) was a valiant and inspired monarch. He finally overcame the Danes in 877 and made peace with them. Some Danes stayed in Hampshire. Guthran their leader was baptised. In peace time Alfred promoted Christian education. He started a court school to educate the nobility. He encouraged scholars from abroad to come to England. He translated and published 'Bede`s History', Bethuen`s 'Consolation of Philosophy' and Gregory`s 'Pastoral Care'. These are the first works in Anglo-Saxon English. Before then, all books had been in Latin. Alfred is remembered in Winchester where a bronze statue of him dominates the Broadway. It was erected in 1901.

The kings of Wessex and the bishops of Winchester had residences in the countryside and also in Winchester. Between them, they made Winchester.

Minster churches flourished up until the late 10th and 11th centuries. They were at their height around 850. After that, priestly communities prevailed with the local church, manor and farm buildings clustering together.

Both Winchester and Southampton, together with Twynham and Portchester were 'burghs' or fortified places. Alfred probably devised the system and his son, Edward the Elder (899 – 924) put it into practice. Thousands of guards were needed for it to be effective. .

The Normans

William the Conqueror exercised firm power. He appointed new Bishops and new Norman landowners of confiscated estates. The Domesday book was compiled at Winchester. The first Norman Bishop Walkelin rebuilt Winchester Cathedral. The second Norman Bishop William Gifford became Chancellor of England. He also founded Waverley Abbey, a Cistercian order. The third Norman Bishop, Henry de Blois (see Walks 16 and 20) failed to become Archbishop and, to compensate, built Wolvesey, a grand episcopal palace. De Blois drew on his great revenues to give generously to the Cathedral. He supported the building of St Cross in the prevalent Romanesque style and the illumination of the famous Winchester Bible, still to be seen in the Cathedral.

Anglo-Saxon monasteries were retained. Romsey, Wherwell and Winchester already had Benedictine orders. Pamper Priory was founded in 1130. The Bishop had control over the Benedictines. The Bishop and the monks held estates all over Hampshire. New stricter monastic houses were established now. 1132 - 1239 Cistercians came to Quarr on the Isle of Wight, Netley and Beaulieu. They supported themselves from the fruits of their labour. There were also (1128 – 1233) Augustinian 'black' canons at Breamore, Portchester (moved to Southwick), St Denys, Christchurch, Mottisfont, Selborne and white canons at Titchfield.

The Middle Ages

Before disaster struck in 14th century, Hampshire was thriving. Farms owned by the Bishop or Prior, employed theyns and freemen to produce crops. In 1208 Bishop Peter de Roches had manors at Fareham and Bitterne for the distribution of salt and wine. He also went hunting and hawking. Bishop John de Pontoise (1282 –1304) founded a great chapel at Winchester and and licensed private chapels in manor houses. The owner of the Manor at Tichborne distributed dole in the form of flour every year to all his tenants (Walk 18). Bishop Henry Woodlock (1305 –1316), a Hampshire man, rode on his palfreys to perform his duties in the diocese and in Westminster.

War, the Plague and famine depleted towns and villages. Some woodland was saved as a result. The Plague or Black Death killed one third of the population. The clergy suffered. Bishop Edington noted that 30 out of 83 livings were vacant 1348–9. Bishop William of Wykeham threatened excommunication to anyone taking church property. Both valiant bishops rebuilt the Cathedral. Most priests were peasants, who had learnt a little scripture by rote. William Wykeham founded Winchester School to enable the sons of paupers to gain an education and become educated priests. He also arranged for the monks of St Swithun`s to have grammar lessons. Even a few girls were fortunate to have some lessons, taught by nuns in Winchester, Romsey and Wherwell.

The first friars came to England in early 13th century. They were mobile missionaries who cut through diocesan and parochial boundaries. Four friary churches were established in Winchester. Southampton had a friary with a gate in the town walls to their gardens. The friars also maintained a good conduit system.

By the 15th century, Normandy was no longer under the rule of the English King. Most trade had been with France. Power shifted from Winchester to London. The bishops were still exceedingly rich and sat in Parliament. Winchester has retained much of its ancient glory in the Cathedral, the Deanery, the Close, St Cross, the College, the Great Hall and West Gate.

The Reformation

Thanks to the work of William Wykeham, who had already closed inefficient monasteries, such as Mottisfont and Selborne Priory, little fault could be found with the religious institutions in Hampshire. Nevertheless all the monasteries were closed and much of the stone purloined by Henry V111 and his favourites to build castles and grand houses. Even Lord Sandys, owner of the Vyne, Hampshire`s grandest building, was happy to make another home at Mottisfont out of the Priory ruins. Hyde House was built of brick on the site of Hyde Abbey. The Bethell family bought it from Wriothesley, the new Earl of Southampton.

Henry V111 persecuted the last Plantagenets, who were Roman Catholics and, more to the point, might claim the throne. In particular Margaret Pole, aged 69, who had been his friend and a second mother to his daughter, Mary. As a widow, she stayed at Warblington Castle (Walk 1). She was beheaded.

The churches survived the Reformation and not much changed in the Catholic practices until Edward V1 came to the throne in 1547. He was a follower of Luther and made sure to establish the Protestant faith. The Latin missal was replaced with two prayer books in English. Thomas Cromwell ordered the scrapping of the missal. These came in handy as book covers. The earliest parish register at St Michael`s, Southampton and at Southwick are bound in 15th century missals. Similar old bindings were made at Greatham, Brockenhurst and Micheldever.

Bishop Gardiner (1531 – 1555) was in prison in Edward`s reign and released to officiate at Queen Mary`s wedding to Philip of Spain at Winchester Cathedral. Mary tried to reverse the Protestant trend. She was hated for her persecutions of Protestants. Several clerics in Hampshire lost their livings in her short reign (1553 –1558).

When Elizabeth followed her sister to the throne, the situation was again reversed and the Protestants were back. Unfortunately, Winchester now had the dogmatic Bishop Home (1561–80). He destroyed some medieval glass and statues in the Cathedral. He pursued recusants – those Catholics who refused to attend Anglican services. Some managed to avoid penalty. Some escaped to Europe via Portsmouth.

The new landlords after the Reformation included Thomas Wriothesley the new 'Earl of Southampton' (Walk 32). The third earl is mentioned in Walk 11. In Southampton the Mille family, who had been stewards of the priories, became property magnets. In Tudor times Southampton was reckoned to be one of the fairest English towns.

The Marquis of Winchester, William Paulet increased his estates. He said he had survived the religious conflicts by being a 'willow, not an oak'. The family took a firmer stand during the Civil War when Basing House was bastion against the puritans. The Civil War lasted 1642 – 49.

The Restoration

The Restoration of the monarchy in 1660 when Charles 11 came to the throne was very popular in Hampshire. The war had been devastating; Winchester Castle was destroyed and the Cathedral neglected. The Dean and Chapter had been abolished.

St Thomas` Church, Portsmouth was damaged in the Civil War. A new nave with high Tuscan columns was built 1693. This church later became the Cathedral. Portsmouth was already a naval base with a Royal Charter.

In 1662 many laymen and clergy left the Church of England. Some set up Dissenting chapels. In tolerant Hampshire both Dissenters and Catholics were active.

Church building after the Restoration consisted mainly of sculptures, repairs and small additions to existing places of worship. There are some exceptions. Lymington (Walk 39) had a 'makeover' in a style copied from St Paul`s Cathedral in London. The fashionable cupola was added to the tower here and also to St Thomas, Portsmouth. Old Alresford church is early 18th century. Avington is an unspoilt estate church of that period (Walk 19). The tower of Crondall (Walk 31) is a 17th century copy of a church in Battersea. Minstead has had whole rooms added to its church so that the local Georgian gentry and their households could attend services in comfort (Walk 33).

The Jacobian period in early 17th century is most noted for its woodwork in the form of pulpits, panels, screens and communion rails.

The Victorians brought a new zest and vigour to the Church. Their determination to spread the Gospel to every corner is reminiscent of that of the early Christians. Few churches have escaped their Restoration. We have to be grateful to the Victorians for preserving some derelict churches, even if they were heavy handed on occasion. Sometimes they replaced a dilapidated church with one of their own design, some in traditional style, some original.

20th and 21st Centuries are notable for skilled craftsmen and women who have added carvings, beautiful stained and engraved glass windows.

Our contemporaries have been most active in preserving the past. Respect for beautiful church buildings from earlier, holier times has inspired parishioners to care for and tend our inheritance.

5 Walks
Near Havant

Portsmouth Cathedral

Walk 1: Emsworth to Westbourne - Emsworth to Warblington

Two short circular walks can be combined into one long figure of eight:

A. From the harbour town of Emsworth go inland to a Sussex village.
B. From Emsworth follow the harbour to an ancient church and castle ruin. The two outlying churches of this walk have historic links.

Starting Point: Emsworth Train Station **GR**748064
Free parking in ground north of the station **GR**747066
Map: OS Explorer 120 **Terrain:** Mainly flat
Distances: Emsworth to Westbourne 2½ Miles
Emsworth to Warblington 5 Miles
Local Information: Warblington Castle was the home (1515–25) of the tragic heroine, Margaret Countess of Salisbury (see Introduction under 'The Reformation'). In 1643 the Parliamentarians seized the castle from the then owner, George Cotton. The Cottons were Catholics who managed to stay loyal to the throne. After destroying the castle, Cromwell`s men abandoned it in 1644. Only the thin turreted tower of the gateway survives. We see it on our walk

The Churches

The Parish Church of Saint John Baptist, Westbourne stands just inside the Sussex border. It is probably one of the two churches mentioned in Domesday under 'Weorbling`s Ton'. The present church originates in 13th century. The nave with north and south aisles were enlarged in 14th century then re-shaped in 16th century. The chancel still has a 14th century piscina. The vestry on the north side has an original door. The tower is early 16th century. In 1770 the Earl of Halifax of Stansted House added the spire. In 1865 the rector the Rev. John Hanson Sperling directed the restoration of the church in true Victorian fashion. Over the centuries the church has grown to the really spacious size we see today. The fine timber roofs of the nave and chancel are early 16th century with trussed rafters. The aisles are roofed in a similar style. The lively village has shops, post office and local bakery.

**The Parish Church of Warblington, St Thomas a` Becket** is a haven from the busy roads to the north and overlooks the harbour to the south. After the Romans left this area, Saxons came to settle here. In Domesday, 'Weorbling`s Ton' had two churches. One of them stands here on this Saxon site. The central part of the tower is Saxon. It has a door facing west into the nave and may have been part of an outdoor pulpit. The priest would address the important people inside the church, the present chancel, then turn to speak to the common people standing outside.

Emsworth to Westbourne - Emsworth to Warblington

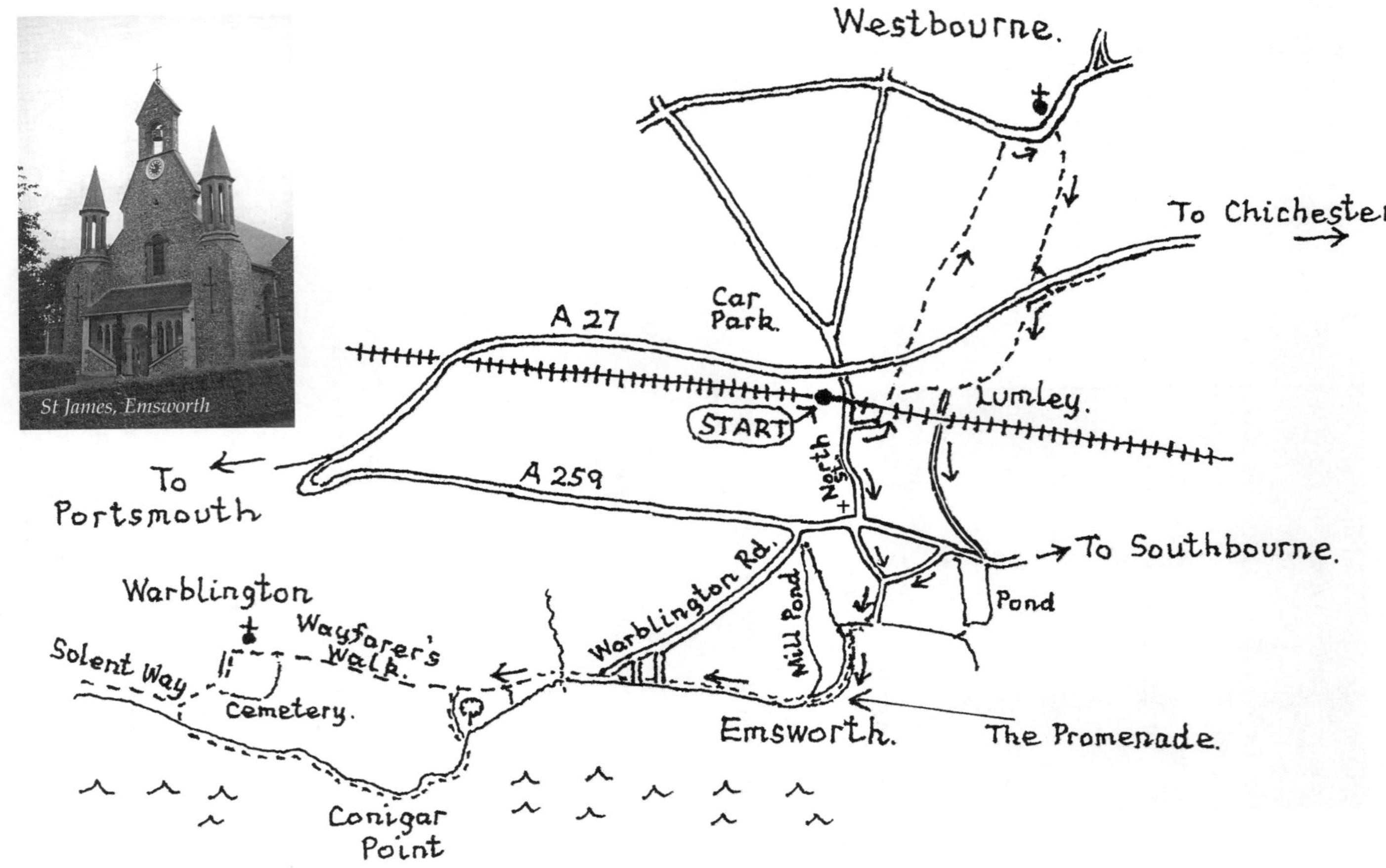

St James, Emsworth

The chancel, 50 feet long was then the entire church. The line of the old roof and the round headed outside pulpit can still be seen from the nave. In 13th century the church was extended westwards beyond the tower to form the present nave. The chancel was rebuilt and a chapel added. The nave still has 13th century stone work; the north and south arcades are of that period. Both have pointed arches. The south arcade is more ornate with leaf carving on the capitals. Then came the north porch in 14th or 15th century. The doorway may be made of ships` timbers. The wood has been skillfully carved. In the chancel some worn medieval caustic tiles are on the altar steps. Other tiles are Victorian. The stained glass throughout is Victorian. The stone memorials in the chancel are mainly to members of the Norris family who have supplied rectors to the church from 1789 to 1929.
Emsworth Church, St James was built in different stages of the Victorian era. I nearly omitted this church after reading Pevsner, but, against expectation, found it attractive. It is firmly locked except for services.

The Walk

A. Emsworth to Westbourne

From Emsworth Station cross the main road, **North Street** diagonally right to Seagull Lane. This is a short road. Turn left at the end then avoid the riverside walk on the right. Instead, follow the enclosed path to the railway line. The path bends right then left to go through a pedestrian underpass.

You come out on the other side to open fields and follow the well marked path northeast for ½ mile to Westbourne. As you approach the village, look out for a gate on the left. Go through to find a short track to the Westbourne Road. Turn right for the church. On the way you pass the village hall and the **footpath** for the return walk.

From the church return to Westbourne Road and cross to

Westbourne

the **footpath** opposite. It goes beside the village hall on the left and a tributary stream of the River Ems on the right. Follow the stream for 200 metres to Mill Lane. Keep on course along this unmade road for 300 metres. You then have to leave the lane to turn left and climb up to a generous bridge over the A27.

At crossways on the other side of the bridge, turn right into a pebble track beside the A27. It veers left away from the road and leads down to cottages then the grand house at Lumley.

Turn left here along the quiet lane, Lumley Road. Go under the railway and continue past terraced houses. Avoid the path off to the right, unless you want to take a short cut to the station. The lane continues southwards past a large pond on the right and detached houses on the left.

You reach the A259 at the edge of Emsworth. Cross with care then turn right. Fork left into Queen Street. This leads up to **the Square,** Emsworth.

To Return to the Railway Station

*Veer to the right, cross A259 at crossroads and walk along **North Street**, passing shops and pubs in the short distance to Emsworth Station.*

B. Emsworth to Warblington

***Note:** Warblington Church is our destination. The thirsty may wish to continue on the harbour path past Warblington to Langstone to find two pubs. See **Note** below.

From Emsworth Station turn right and walk along **North Street** to a roundabout. Cross under the main road, A259 and turn left to **the Square**

From the Square, Emsworth head south past shops, tearooms, pubs and houses to the Harbour.

Continue along the promenade with water on either side. The path curves to the right around the Mill Pond. We join two long distance paths that follow the same route here: Wayfarer`s Walk and Solent Way.

Head due west beside the Harbour on a well established path for ½ mile. You pass harbourside houses on the right.

When the houses end, you come to a natural creek. Cross a stream. Warblington Church is one kilometre away and you have a choice of ways: 1. *Go through Barn Wood then emerge to a path across fields to the church.*

2. You can stick to the edge of the harbour and maintain your view of the water. There is a good path for 250 metres. *At high water you may have to turn inland and in 150 metres you rejoin the main path.*

As the tide recedes, you can walk along the shingle around Conigar Point. A harbour wall is beside you. In 1 kilometre there is a footpath marked to Warblington Church. Turn right here, going back on yourself slightly to walk through the large cemetery.

*****Note** *For Langstone, continue along the harbour path.*

From Warblington Church return on the Wayfarer`s Walk and Solent Way. Follow the signposts with arrows and head east. Pass the church on your left. You are on an enclosed path beside a little road. *Look in the churchyard on the left as you pass to see one of the two guard houses, built 1828. Grave watchers were employed to prevent body snatchers from stealing the new corpses to sell to medical students.*

Keep on course. There are flat fields on the left and you can look back to the tower of Warblington Castle (see Local Information, above).

Warblington

In 300 metres cross a farm track and go straight on to Nore Barn Wood. A hedge on your right obscures the view to the harbour. The main way leads through the wood on a wide straight path. *You can opt again for the harbourside.* Both lead back to the creek at the edge of Emsworth. Re-cross the stream and retrace your steps to Emsworth. *Or veer left into the suburban road and walk for 1 kilometre to A259. The crossing with traffic lights for pedestrians is to your right. Once you have crossed the main road, turn right on the pavement and follow a new wall on your left. A gap in the wall enables you to enter Church Path, a road leading to Emsworth Church on the right. After visiting the Church, continue on the path to North Street.*

Return along **North Street** to Emsworth Station.

Walk 2: Chalton to Blendworth - Chalton to Idsworth

Two walks over the Downs can be combined into one to visit three different churches and the site of a fourth, also a windmill and an old thatched pub.

Starting Point: The public car park next to the pub car park, Chalton
GR733159 **Map:** OS Explorer 120
Terrain: Hilly, a steep descent from Windmill Hill on the Blendworth walk.
Distances: Long Walk to Blendworth and Windmill Hill: 6 Miles
+ 2 Miles if you include Idsworth
Short Walk to Idsworth only: 3 Miles

The Churches

Chalton, St Michael: High on the Downs, this church was an important place of worship and learning in Saxon times. It was the mother church to Idsworth and Clanfield. Early Christians called on St Michael to guard them. They feared Pagan spirits from tumuli and devils not in Hell. The present building, early Norman with a tower in Saxon style, has walls that are three feet thick. The east window has four tall lancets of equal height. Under the blocked lancet on the south side is a window for lepers, allowing them to watch the service without contaminating the church.

Chalton

Chalton to Blendworth - Chalton to Idsworth

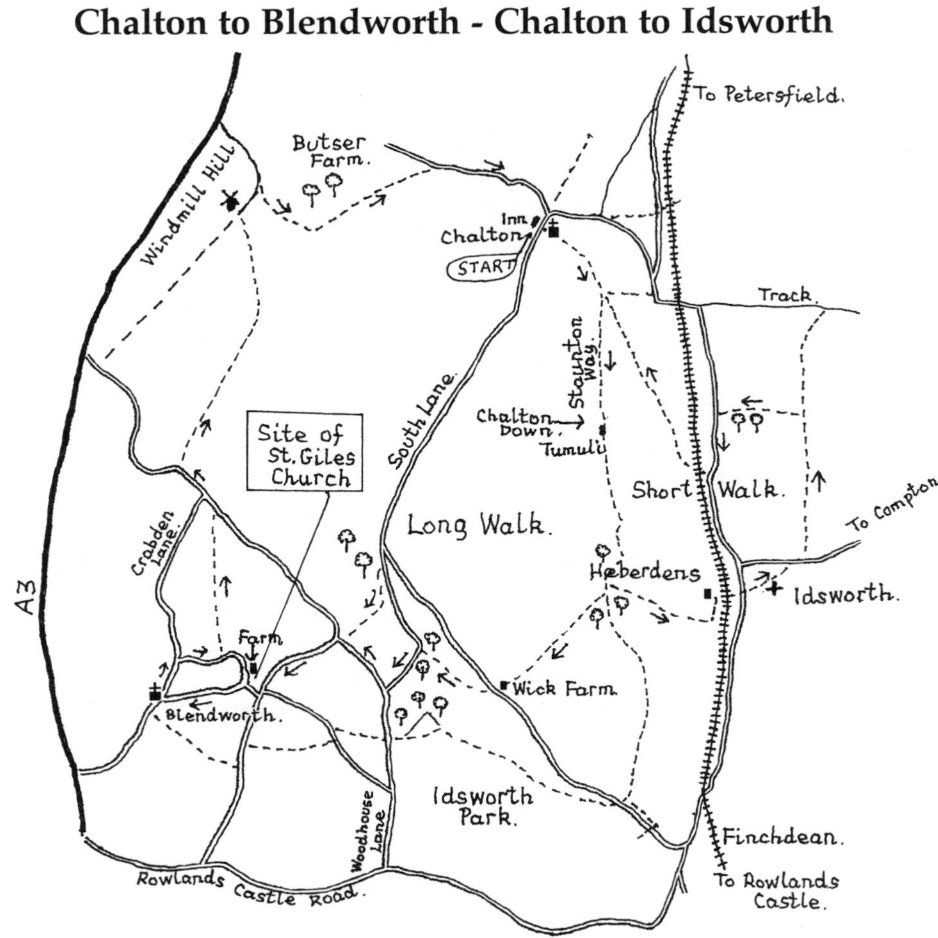

Idsworth, St Hubert: 'The Little Church in a Field' is all that remains of the hamlet of Idsworth, an ancient settlement on fertile soil. The chapel was originally built by Earl Godwin, King Harold`s father. Edward the Confessor would have attended a service here. The nave is in the Norman style which Edward favoured. The Early English chancel, bell turret and porch came later. The chapel contains the only known mural depicting St Hubert. There are other murals of Salome dancing and being presented with the head of St John the Baptist. These murals were made about 1300.

Idsworth

St Giles Church existed in 1303. It was a wayside chapel on the road from Chalton to the Forest of Bere and the Priory of Southwick. Apart from the list of rectors and the garden site, nothing remains. There is no vestige of the medieval chapel. It was rebuilt in 1759. The new building lasted only 100 years. It was then decided to find a new site.

Holy Trinity, Blendworth was built 1851-2 on the new site. It is a happy place that has escaped the urbanization of Horndean, just down the road. The church stands among trees in a small, scattered village. It is free from the heavy handed extravagance of some Victorian buildings. It is a small flint church in Decorated style. The chancel, nave, tower and spire together make a handsome whole. The east window has three lights that depict St Timothy, St Stephen and St Titus. The Italian mosaic was added to the walls of the chancel and nave in 1914.

The Walk

Both Walks

From the pub, Chalton, cross the road to the church. Go through the lychgate and pass the church on your right. Cross the churchyard diagonally right then keep on course across a little field.

When you reach downland, you are presented with three footpaths. Take the one on the right, 'Staunton Way' a long distance path. Heading south, it climbs to the highest point. Then makes a gradual descent, goes under power cables, crosses a stile and passes a tiny copse. Look down to the left to see Idsworth Church alone in a field.

At a gap in the trees you reach **crosspaths**.

Short Walk to Idsworth, see below*

Also the energetic may want to nip down to Idsworth and back up again.

Long Walk to Blendworth: Turn right and go through the wide grassy gap. A track veers left and descends gradually for ½ mile to a byway. On the way you have a distant view of the sea. At the bottom, a cottage, Wick Farm is on your right.

Chalton pub

Cross the road to the footpath opposite. (If this is too muddy, you can turn right on the byway and walk for ½ mile to a turning on the left. Turn left here then look out for a byway on the right. This takes you up over the hanger. At the road, Woodhouse Lane, cross over and keep straight on).

The footpath opposite Wick Farm enters woodland on Wick Hanger. Follow the path as it curves right and takes you uphill to a quiet lane.

Turn left to walk up to a T-junction with Woodhouse Lane. Turn right. At the next junction, turn left.

Follow the lane to a cluster of houses and road junctions. This is the original village of Blendworth. On the corner on the right you will find the site of **St Giles Church.** There is a notice board and a seat here.

Turn right past St Giles Church then immediately left into Blendworth Lane. This brings you down opposite Holy Trinity, Blendworth.

A diversion to the left of ½ mile (and ½ mile back!) finds a pub in Horndean.

At Blendworth Church turn right to follow Crabden Lane uphill for 1 mile to a T-junction. On the way you pass Blendworth House on the left and Duckpond

Lane on the right. At the top, over the road you find New Barn Farm.

At this T-junction turn left. In 100 metres turn right into a track that leads up to Chalton Windmill, seen ahead. This is a steady climb of about 1 mile.

Chalton Windmill

Pass the windmill on your left and you are rewarded with a view over Queen Elizabeth Forest and the A3. Do not go too far on the track. Look out for a footpath just past the windmill. It turns sharp right and you walk back on yourself slightly.

The enclosed path opens onto downland for the prospect of a very steep descent eastwards. You can see the buildings of Chalton village down to your right. Go down carefully, especially in wet or frosty weather. At the bottom you pass a corner of Bascomb Copse on your left, then keep on course to Chalton Lane.

Turn right and walk beside the road for ¼ mile to the village. It has a popular pub – so beware of traffic!

***Short Walk to Idsworth:** At the **crosspath**s turn left and follow the well marked path down to the railway line. Follow this on your right then go under the bridge to come out on the road. Idsworth Church is opposite. Just a footpath leads to this solitary church.*

Pass Idsworth Church on your right. At a distance of 60 metres, a north – south path leads behind the church. Turn left and you come shortly to the road to Compton. Cross diagonally right to a footpath. It passes Old Idsworth Farm on your right.

This is a pleasant path over flat fields with a hedgerow on your left. At a path junction turn left and in ¼ mile you are back on the Idsworth Road. Turn left and walk with care along the road for ¼ mile. Here on the right is a footpath that crosses the railway line then climbs back up Chalton Down to the junction of paths, one of them Staunton Way, and the Church beyond.

Walk 3: Catherington to Hambledon

A varied and hilly country walk to two lovely ancient churches in villages that have managed to stay remarkably unspoilt. We pass three pubs!

Starting Point: Car Park near All Saints Church, Catherington.
GR697145 **Map:** OS Explorer 119 **Distance:** 11 Miles
Terrain: Undulating. A downland nature reserve then fields and tracks that are muddy in places in winter. Some quiet lanes give relief from the mud.

The Churches

All Saints Church, Catherington has a pleasant position among tall trees on a chalk down with fine views south. The first known building here was a late 12th century rectory. At the end of the 13th century it was converted. The flint building was skillfully restored in 1883. The lower part of the tower is Norman and has small round headed lights. The red brick top part of the tower with castellations was added in 1750. Inside, the high timbered medieval roof, the thick Norman walls and small windows create a dim, timeless atmosphere. The arcade columns are also Norman. The earlier south arcade has round columns; the slightly later north arcade has alternate round and octagonal columns. Overlooking the nave there is a restored mural of the archangel Michael weighing souls. A demon tries to weigh down the balance on one side and the Virgin Mary counters the balance on the other side, the work of a fantastical imagination in around 1350. There is no chancel arch. The 13th century frame of the east window has a smaller Perpendicular inset. Go through the low north arch of the chancel to the Hyde

Catherington

Catherington to Hambledon

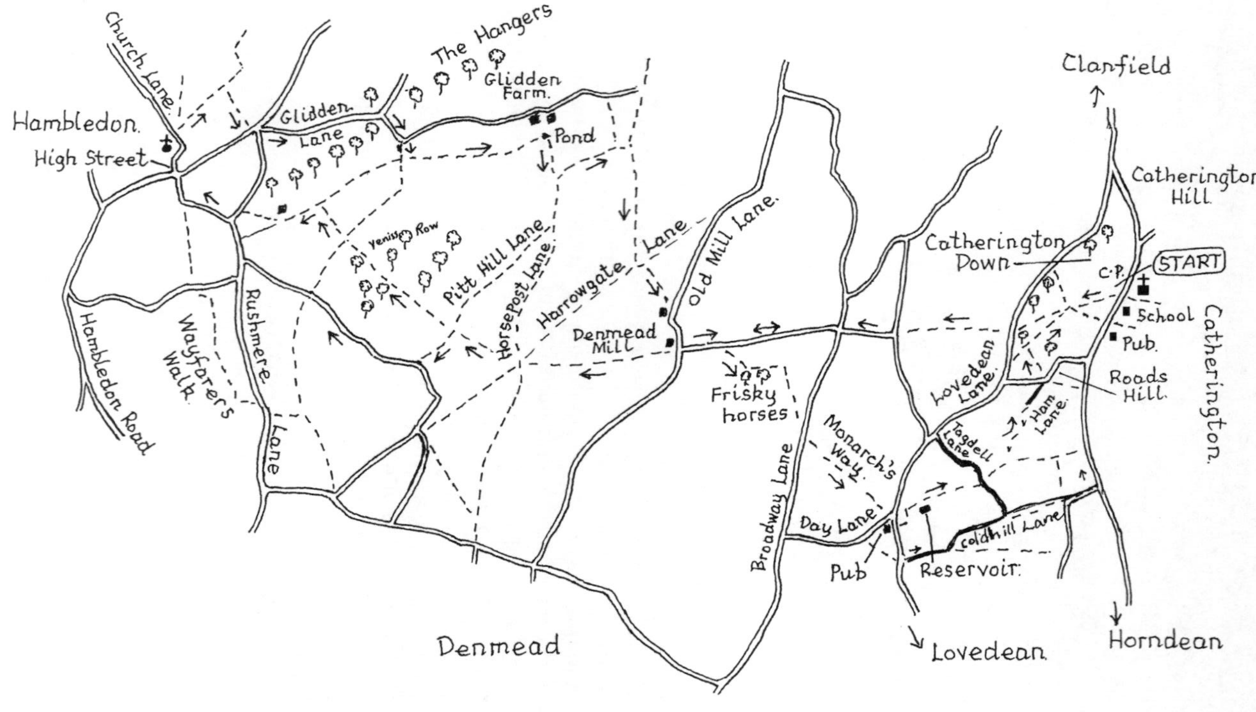

Chapel. The high narrow windows and small round window perpetuate the dim atmosphere. Several memorials in this chapel include a most impressive canopied tomb of Sir Nicholas Hyde and his wife. They are recumbent and life-size whilst their adult children are reduced in size below them. The local manor of *Hinton Daubnay* (see Walk below) came to the barrister, Nicholas Hyde through marriage. The son, Laurence helped plan the last stage of King Charles 11`s escape to Europe. We follow some of this route when we join the 'Monarch`s Way' on our walk below.

Hambledon

St Peter and St Paul, Hambledon started as a small Saxon church in this ancient settlement. It belonged to the Abbey of Winchester. The Saxon building is enclosed within the walls of the present medieval church. The north wall of the Saxon church was made into an arcade in 12th century. The south arcade followed early in 13th century. Saxon pilaster strips are still to be seen on the outer walls of these arcades. Another 13th century feature is the Early English arch in the middle of the nave. It replaced the round Saxon chancel arch and indicates the position of the earlier church. The west wall of this first church was lost when a 13th century tower was added. Much of the tower was rebuilt after a fire in 1794. The present chancel, almost entirely 13th century is large and handsome, a perfect example of its period. In 15th century some of the windows in the church were changed to Perpendicular. The east window of the north aisle is particularly fine. The south porch, added around 1500 has two storeys and may have housed a priest or a hermit. The High Street in front of the church was once the scene of a weekly market, granted to the Bishop of Winchester in 1260. In 1612 James 1 allowed two fairs a year to be held in Hambledon. In 1651 Charles 11, disguised as a yeoman may have spent a night here at a cottage now called 'King`s Rest'.

The Walk

From All Saints Church, cross the road diagonally left. Pass a footpath sign then enter the car park. Two parallel footpaths lead from the back of the car park in a westerly direction. They go gently down the grassy slope. When they reach a rough barrier of trees, you turn left. Walk beside the trees on your right until you come to an opening and a notice board announcing a Nature Reserve. Turn right.

Wooden gates in this opening lead to the expanse of Catherington Down. Ahead is a seat, strategically placed for the view over the valley below. Look across this valley to the slope opposite. You can see the lines of two footpaths, wide apart climbing the slope, one on the left and one on the right. They are in fact nearly 1 kilometre apart. Head for the one on the left.

You have to descend several tiers of Catherington Down to reach another barrier of trees at the bottom and another Nature Reserve notice board. This is your way out to Lovedean Lane. Cross the lane to the footpath opposite (the one you discerned from the seat on high) and start climbing westwards over fields towards a small copse. Go through and keep on course for another ¼ mile. Some uneven steps take you down to a road junction.

Cross to the lane opposite and continue westwards uphill for 250 metres to crossroads. ***Broadway Lane*** *to the left will be your route on the return walk.* Meanwhile you cross to the lane opposite and keep on course for ½ mile. After a while Monarch`s Way, a long distance footpath joins your lane from the left. You then come to a T-junction at **Denmead Mill.**

Cross diagonally left to a footpath and pass the Old Mill, now a private house on your right. This path, still Monarch`s Way continues to head westwards across elevated fields. You have extensive views to Portslade Hill, the Isle of Wight and even to the masts of Fawley Power Station beyond Southampton.

At the third field, the path takes you down Sawyers Hill to crossways in the valley. *Harrogate Lane runs along the base of the valley northeast to southwest. We meet it again on the return walk.* Go straight across the track, Harrowgate Lane, veer slightly left and climb up to a small clump of trees. Pass these on your right and you come to another track, Pithill Lane. **You have a choice of ways here.**

The field route: *keep straight on along Monarch`s Way in a northwesterly direction, gently uphill for 1 kilometre. You pass close to Greasteds Copse on your right, then go through a limb of the woodland known as Veniss Row Pass the rest of this wood and glimpse a deep pit near the edge on your left. Soon after crosspaths you come to a T-junction. Monarch`s Way departs to the right. You turn left. Pass a Stud Farm then continue to* ***Rushmere Lane.***

The road route: at Pithill Lane turn left and in 250 metres you reach a quiet tarmac road. Turn right and walk along the road for 1 kilometre. At first you have a good view to the woods on the right. The lane turns right and goes downhill, up again and passes some cottages on the left. It ends at a T-junction in Rushmere, an outpost of Hambledon.

Both routes turn right **on Rushmere Lane** towards Hambledon. *The field route is much nearer the village.*

You are on the hanger above Hambledon. Avoid the road that branches to the right and start the descent to the left between cottages that enjoy a good view of the village.

At the bottom you reach the main road; the village shop and post office are on the left. The church and High Street are diagonally left opposite. Cross with care to the short High Street that climbs between cottages to the church.

From Hambledon Church return to the High Street and turn immediately left. The road here passes between cottages, curves left and passes the churchyard on the left. The village school is on the right opposite the churchyard.

Turn right and pass school buildings on the left. Enter an enclosed footpath heading northwest. At the first crossing turn right and follow a private lane down to the main road.

Cross with care diagonally left to Back Lane then fork left into Glidden Lane (not named on the ground). You are climbing up through woodland on a hanger or long hill above Hambledon. At the top turn right and continue on the lane for 100 metres. The lane curves to the left. You keep straight on into a field. In 75 metres turn left and you rejoin Monarch`s Way.

Head eastwards across fields with views: to the left to Glidden Farm and on a hilltop away to the right, the buildings of Denmead Mill. In ¼ mile head down to a cattle shed and turn left on the farm track.

Walk up to a nearby pond on the right and you come to a T-junction of tracks. Turn right and pass the other side of the pond, again on your right.

Hambledon High Street

Head southeast uphill on this new track to another T-junction. Turn left and northeast. In 250 metres on this elevated track, you reach a spacious section. Avoid a turning to the left. Follow the track down to the right. In 70 metres at the next junction veer to the right. You are now heading due south.

The track peters out at a field entrance with a stile on the right. Go straight on and keep to the field boundary on your left. At the bottom you have to turn left then immediately right over stiles into Harrowgate Lane *at a higher point than our earlier crossing of this lane.* Cross to the path opposite and climb in the footsteps of other walkers heading towards a copse. This enclosed path passes the copse on your left and climbs more steeply up to tarmac Old Mill Road. Turn right.

After walking for 300 metres along the road you reach the familiar junction at **Denmead Mill**. Turn left, rejoin Monarch`s Way and retrace your steps eastwards along the lane for 150 metres.

You have a choice of routes:

The Field Route *(½ Mile): Monarch`s Way leaves the road and crosses the field to the right. It heads southeast for Mill Copse and passes it on the right. It then goes through several horse paddocks. There are stiles here and a variety of horses; some staid, others frisky. You reach Broadway Lane below and turn right.*

The Road Route (¾ Mile)**:** avoiding the frisky horses above. Keep on the familiar road eastwards to crossroads. Turn right into **Broadway Lane**, a pleasant tree lined lane heading south. Pass the entrance to *Hinton Daubnay (see notes on Catherington Church above). This house was rebuilt in 1868.*

Look out for Monarch`s Way joining us from the right.

Both Routes converge on Broadway Lane and head south. In another 50 metres turn left to follow Monarch`s Way through a fringe of trees into an extensive field. *The Victorian house, Hinton Daubnay is behind you, left.*

Veer right and head southeast over the field for ¼ mile. Go down to the dip in the far right hand corner. You come out to a junction of roads. You have reached Lovedean Lane again and turn right. Pass an alluring pub on the right. Almost immediately you will find a footpath across the road.

See **Note** below.

Turn left into this footpath and climb the slope up to a pit. Do not enter but turn left into an enclosed track that continues the climb up to a reservoir. Pass this on your right and then a pylon stop on the left.

Emerge to an open field and veer left following in the footsteps of others to reach Tagdell Lane, a track. Cross the track to the enclosed footpath opposite. It is muddy but fortunately short and soon comes to a T-junction. Avoid the path on the right and turn left into a welcome track. This bends right and is a pleasant tree-lined way.

Pass a detached house on the left and follow the driveway, Ham Lane to the aptly named, Roads Hill. Fortunately we do not have to go down to the footpath shown on Ordnance Survey map at the bottom of the hill.

Instead, cross the road with care to the stile diagonally left opposite. You are entering woodland on Catherington Down. Go down to meet the path coming up from the bottom and veer right to the open Down. Keep your height and soon you come to the familiar strategically placed seat.

Turn right and go through gates, past the Nature Reserve notice and through the tree barrier to the grassland. You can see the houses on Catherington Lane ahead. Make for the nearest house and go through a metal kissing gate to a twitten leading to the lane. The pub is opposite.

Turn left for the car park and the church.

Note: *a less muddy and more straightforward track back to Catherington can be found. Continue along Lovedean Lane for another 50 metres. Turn left into Coldhill Lane. This track heads northeast for 1 mile to Catherington Lane. You then have to turn left and walk on the pavement for ½ mile.*

Walk 4: Hayling Island Churches and Old Portsmouth Churches

Two separate short walks can be connected by ferry to make one very long seaside walk. The marathon walkers on the long walk return by train.

Note: The Ferry from Hayling to Portsmouth runs every ½ hour; hourly in the evenings.

Starting Point Walk 1: St Peter`s Church, North Hayling (a circular walk on the island) **GR**731033 **Map:** OS Explorer 120
Terrain: Flat, field, park, suburbia and harbourside trail **Distance:** 6 Miles

Starting Point Walk 2: Portsmouth and Southsea Railway Station (a short walk to Portsmouth Cathedral) **GR**642004 **Map:** OS Explorer 119
Terrain: Flat, a walk through the town to the sea. **Distance:** 3 Miles

Starting Point Walk 3: Havant Railway Station
This is the long walk to Langstone Harbour then across Hayling Island to the coast and ferry to Portsea Island. Walk along the promenade to Old Portsmouth then inland to Portsmouth Station for a train back to Havant.
GR718066 **Map:** OS Explorer 120, then 119. **Terrain:** Flat and varied, from cycle track to field paths, seaside to town. **Distance:** 17 Miles

Local Information on Portsmouth:
Old Portsmouth High Street crosses the centre of a medieval defence system that stretched nearly as far as Pier Road to the east. Today, only the sea front defences remain.
The **round tower** (1415) is part of the early defences. The **square tower** (1495) was part of the Governor`s Residence.
Also 1495 Henry V11 chose Portsmouth with its deep channel for his dockyard
Southsea Castle was part of Henry V111`s scheme to defend the Solent (see also Walk 39).
In 1545 he watched a sea battle against the French and was aghast to see the Mary Rose sink.
In 19th century the ring of forts around the Solent were to protect the dockland.
In 1860 then 1879 **Clarence Pier** then **South Parade Pier** were built for passenger ships to the Isle of Wight.
Spinnaker Tower (2005) is an iconic landmark, 558 ft high.

Local Information on Hayling:
Hayling Billy (Walk 1) is the name affectionately given to the train that ran along

Walk 1: Hayling Island Churches

Walk 3: Hayling Island Churches and Old Portsmouth Churches

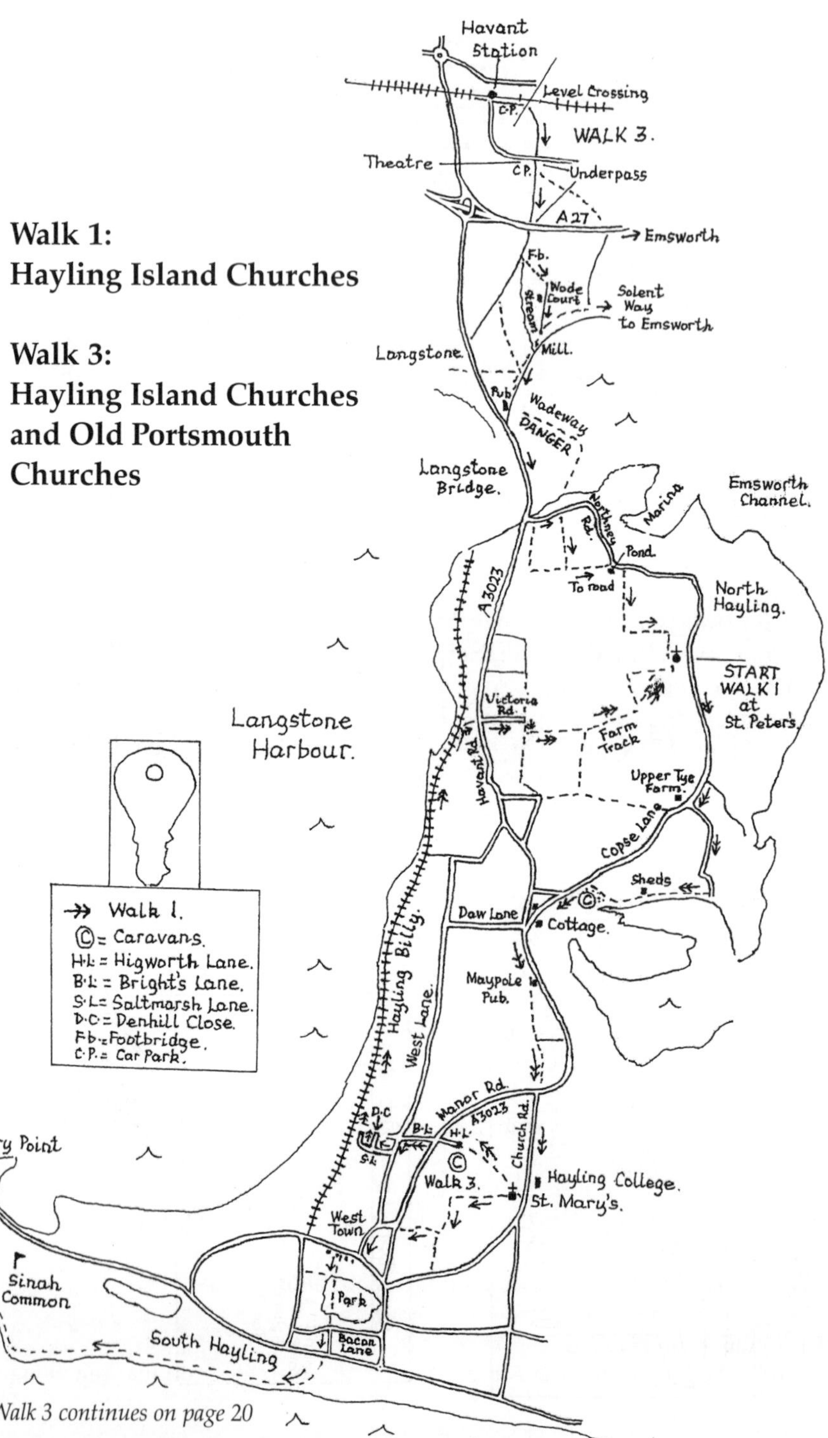

Walk 3 continues on page 20

Portsmouth and Southsea

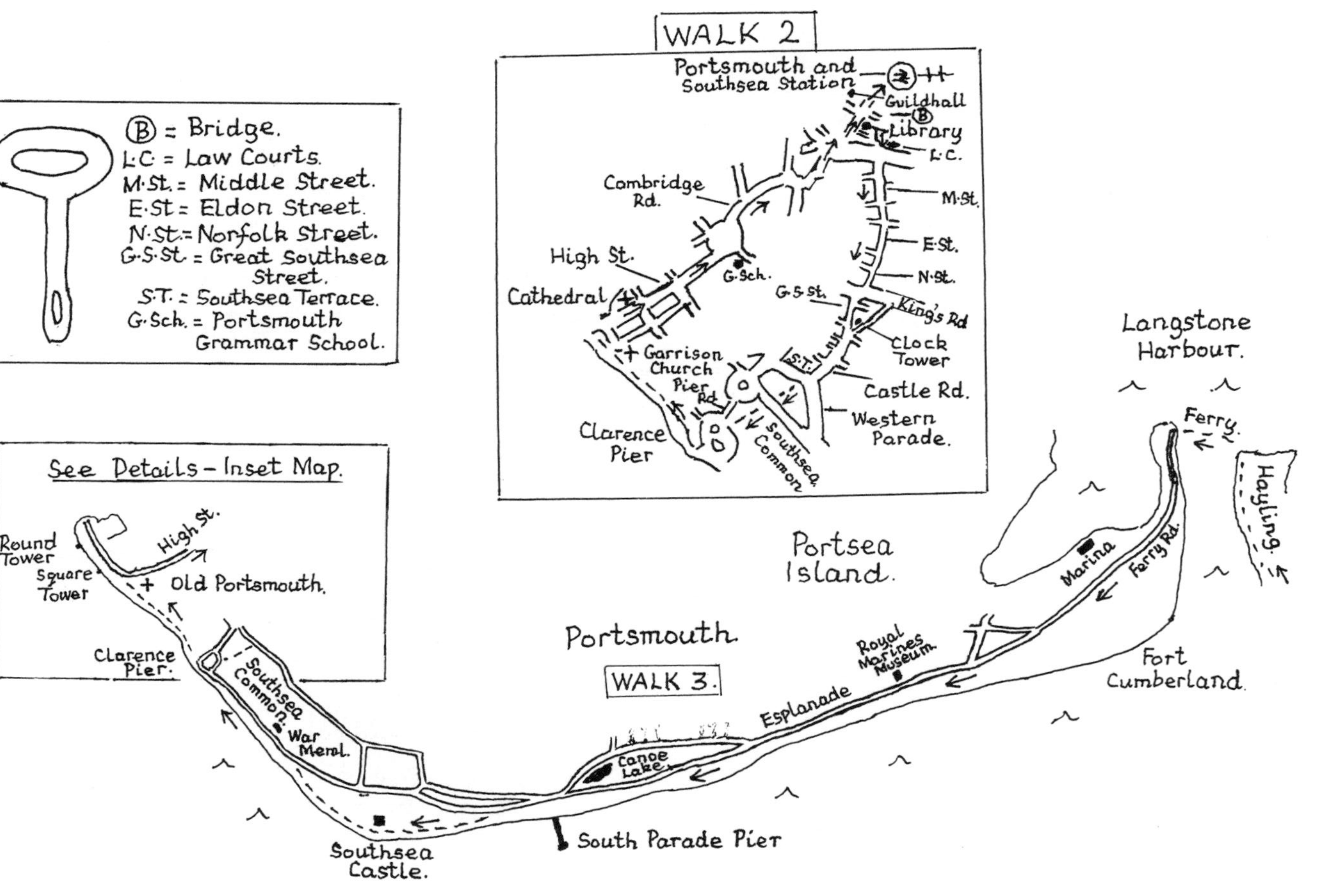

the railway line, north - south across Hayling Island from Havant. The line was one of those closed by Beeching. It has become a cycle and walking route. The wooden railway bridge over Langstone Harbour was dismantled in 1965, so walkers to Havant have to use the busy road bridge. Langstone Bridge carries many commuters and holiday traffic.

Gunner Point (Walk 3) to quote the tourist leaflet, 'is a freely accessible area and has one of the best developed sand dune systems of the Hampshire coast, although the dunes suffer badly from erosion. The plant life is dominated by introduced tree lupins but you can also find yellow-horned poppy, sea kale and sea bindweed. Green winged orchids flower in April and May'.

The Churches

Hayling has long been a 'holy island'. A late Iron Age Celtic shrine, central in north Hayling, was converted into a stone temple when the Romans came in 43 A.D. In 8th century the Saxons built a hamlet there. In south Hayling there stood a later Saxon church of All Saints. After flooding of much of the island, it came to lie under the sea. This elusive church has never been found. After the Norman Conquest, the church and tithes of Hayling Island passed from the monks of Winchester to the Abbey of Jumièges. A prior and monks came from Jumièges to assert their claim.

Hayling Island

St Peter`s, North Hayling, built in 1150, is the oldest surviving church on this island. The nave with three bays and rounded pillars is of that period; the carvings of the capitals have the stamp of the Abbey of Jumièges. The lancet windows of the north aisle are original; the matching windows of the south aisle are restored. The old roof timbers have carvings in the middle of the tie beams. Two carvings of heraldic beasts, a Yale and a Griffin can be seen in the centre of the beam as you look towards the chancel. The lovely chancel and north chapel were added in 13th century. The chapel now contains a fine Barlaston organ, a gift from Staffordshire (1998). The many plain glass lancet windows of the chancel have fresh flowers today to give them colour. The east wall, despite several buttresses, leans outwards. The bell turret, housing three of the oldest bells in the country, is above the east end of the nave. This unusual arrangement has left space at the west end for a delightful new structure, a curved spacious meeting room with modern facilities, known as 'the Arc'. This church is in good hands today!

St Mary The Virgin, Hayling Island began to be built in 1253 and has kept its original shape. Older than the church itself is the font of 870, a relic from the lost Saxon church. It was probably the base of a Saxon cross and has been inverted and hollowed to form a font. There is a second 13th century font, a central drum and 4 shafts support the bowl. Earlier in the 13th century, monks from the Benedictine Abbey of Jumièges had arrived on Hayling to claim the tithes from this island. They chose the highest point of the island for their Priory Church. The large chancel was the province of the monks. They built a beautiful Early English east window, similar in style to that of Bosham. A double piscina in the chancel enabled the priest to wash his hands in a separate basin from that for the holy vessels. The tomb of a prior or a benefactor in the centre of the chancel is mid 13th century. The tower stands above the crossings where there are four equally wide arches of Caen stone. There are human heads on the Corbels. Finely carved capitals and corbels are probably inspired by Jumièges. There are no transepts. Instead the north chapel and the lady chapel are a continuation of the nave aisles. The spire, also 13th century, has a timber frame of notched lap joints, a rare example of Norman carpentry. The monks did not neglect the people of Hayling and built a fine nave with three wide bays. The arcades of Caen stone match those of the tower. The slender pillars are of Purbeck stone. The great west window in Perpendicular style retains the shape of the original frame. There are several 13th century carvings of animal and human heads on the walls and pillars of the nave.

The Cathedral Church of St Thomas of Canterbury, Portsmouth began in 1180 when a rich merchant John de Gisors had the canons of Southwick Priory build a chapel here. It became the Parish Church in 1320. The choir and transepts survive from that early church. The arcades of the choir each has two pointed arches inside a larger rounded one as in Boxgrove Priory. The nave and tower were rebuilt in 17th century, after damage in the Civil War. The tower of 1691 was used as a naval watch tower. In 1693, the people of Portsmouth met in 'Domus Dei', now Garrison Church, (see below), to plan the rebuilding of the Parish Church. The distinctive cupola was added in 1703. The church became a cathedral and was enlarged at the west end with the addition of a new nave with twin towers. Inside, you can enjoy a tour through the contrasting parts of this spacious building and there is much of interest. Outside, the creamy stone throughout makes all parts blend into one handsome whole.

Royal Garrison Church, Portsmouth was founded in 1212 as one of the religious houses of the Bishop of Winchester, Peter de Rupibus. He joined the Crusades in 1227. A monastery hospital was formed, dedicated to St Nicholas with a chapel to St John the Baptist. Monks and nuns took care of the Crusaders as well as the sick and aged of the neighbourhood. The present chancel was the original 'Domus Dei' chapel. The stone work, including the frame of the east window has remained unchanged. The aisles of the nave were used as the hospital with beds fitted between the pillars. In 14th century a chantry was added to the east end of the south aisle. The existing piscina bears evidence of this. After the Dissolution, the buildings were neglected and used as a store house for arms. The church was rescued from decay when a Governor`s House was built nearby in 16th century. The Church became a Royal Chapel, visited by a succession of monarchs. In 1662 King Charles 11 married Catherine de Braganta of Portugal in Portsmouth. Samuel Pepys, among others attended events at the church. In 1794 Queen Charlotte and six Royal children came to celebrate the victory of Admiral Howe. In 1799 the Royal Garrison Volunteers paraded to Church. There were many parade services, attracting the crowds. In 1826 Government House was demolished and the Church once again fell into decay. As usual, the Victorians came to the rescue. The fabric was restored and the nave extended. In 1941 a severe air raid on Portsmouth destroyed the roof of the nave and the windows were blasted. The nave remains open to the sky as a memorial to the service men who fell in World Wars. The replacement glass in the chancel is all 20th century. In 1995 roofs were added to the north and south aisles.

The church is open until 4 p.m., Monday to Saturday, April to October.

John Pound Chapel is half way along the High Street, Old Portsmouth. It has a blue plaque to John Pound, a poor crippled cobbler (1766 – 1839). He opened his home to the starving children of Portsmouth and gave them food and clothes. He also gave them an elementary education so that they could earn a living. He is buried in the little chapel garden next to a tiny cottage.

The Walks

Part 1, Hayling Island (Six mile circular walk). *Look for the double arrows ➤➤ on the map.*

***Note 1:** This walk includes some roads at the start. After 9 a.m. there should be fewer cars. The return walk is over fields or beside the harbour on a rail track 'Hayling Billy', converted for pedestrians, cyclists and horses.*

***Note 2:** The short stretch along the coastal inlet on the east side of Hayling is usually passable but avoid it at very high tides.*

****From St Peter`s Church,** head south along St Peter`s Road. Pass a row of poplars on the right and Gutner Lane on the left. In 1 kilometre you come to Upper Tye Farm on the right. Turn left here into Woodgaston Lane. Meadow Farm, a plant nursery is advertised at the entrance to the lane.

Follow this narrow lane, passing the nursery on the left. (Tea and coffee are on tap from a machine). Continue to a T-junction at the end. Turn left here then right, after Victoria Cottage, into an alley leading to the coastal inlet with views to Chichester Harbour. Turn right

There is a grassy path up above the water. Pass large houses on the right. Their gardens come right down to your path. Soon after the last house, you reach a patch of waste land, with the appearance of an abandoned boat yard. Pass two sheds on your left.

On the nearest corner of the second shed there is an arrow for the footpath. Follow its direction beside the narrow channel and towards a caravan site. A hedge on the left separates you from caravans as you head to Copse Lane.

Turn left onto Copse Lane and walk for 200 metres to a fork in the road. Fork left intoYew Tree Lane and pass the entrance to the caravan site then a black and white cottage on the left and a pub on the right. You emerge to the main Havant Road, A3023 and turn left. There are pavements on both sides of the road. Pick your moment to cross to the other side.

In ¼ mile you pass the Maypole Pub on your right. Turn right immediately and go into the pub garden to find a footpath on the left. The footpath runs parallel to the main road, heading south across fields for 1 kilometre. Just over half way, you go through a rough field border and keep on course in the next field, following the hedge on your right.

You come out at the main road again. On your right is a junction. Cross with care to Church Road. Again there are pavements and in 500 metres you reach St Mary`s Church.

I recommend the first path through the churchyard for this circular walk.
*Take the second path through the churchyard for the Long Walk, See below**

**From St Mary`s Church** head northwest on the recommended footpath. It is a well worn path across the open field towards another caravan site. Pass this on your left and then join the twitten into Higworth Lane. Once again you reach A3023 and cross with care to Bright`s Lane opposite.

Bright`s Lane leads to West Lane and you now have to seek out 'Hayling Billy'. At West Lane turn left then take the first road to the right, Saltmarsh Lane. Take the first right again and walk along to the end of Denhill Close. Here is a path through rough grass and scrub. It veers left and soon joins the elevated railway track, 'Hayling Billy'. Turn right, heading north.

Langstone

You can now enjoy 1½ miles of traffic free straightforward walking. The water of Langstone Harbour is on your left, marine birds visit the muddy shore, bluebells, violets and primroses grow under the patches of woodland. The occasional bench offers an ideal picnic site.

All too soon, you have to leave 'Hayling Billy'. You have been getting gradually closer to the main road and when you reach a car park on a nature reserve, turn right to the A3023 again. Victoria Road is opposite. On your right there are traffic lights to enable you to cross.

Head east along Victoria Road. At the end you come to a footpath and turn right. A concrete track leads to an electric sub station. Pass this on your right then continue a little way into a field. Almost immediately turn left into an enclosed footpath and then open fields to maintain an easterly course.

St Peter`s Church can be seen a mile ahead to your right. You soon join a wide, firm farm track that leads all the way to the church, after a bend to the left. Take the gate on the left into the churchyard. **End of Part 1.**

Part 2. Portsmouth and Southsea Station to Old Portsmouth to visit Garrison Church, Portsmouth Cathedral and a memorial to a cobbler

A short stroll through Southsea to the sea front and the old fortified town of Portsmouth, then returning along the High Street on the route taken by many of the nation`s monarchs.

From Portsmouth and Southsea Station turn left to go under the railway bridge, cross the road, go through the archway of the modern glass building and immediately you are in the lively open space of Guildhall Square. The grand Victorian building, the Guildhall presides on your right.

Beach at Gunner Point

Veer left to mount some steps to the Library. Pass this on your right and note some pedestrian signs, one pointing to the Law Courts. This is our way over a wide pedestrian bridge to Crown House on the left and Courts of Justice on the right. Go straight on to the main road, Winston Churchill Ave.

On your right there is a pedestrian crossing with traffic lights. Cross to Middle Street opposite and pass a large white building, part of the University on the left. Middle Street becomes Eldon Street and despite the Recession, has flourishing pubs. Pass the 'Eldon Arms', 'Kitch n d`Or' and 'King Street Tavern'. Eldon Street leads into Norfolk Street and already the 19th century houses have an expectant air of seaside.

We join Castle Road at a corner where a dramatic half timbered shop has a magnificent clock tower above it. Built in 1900, this used to be an antique shop. Keep on course along Castle Road to crossroads at Southsea Common.

Take the wide path opposite, crossing Southsea Common diagonally right, over Duisburg Way and towards Clarence Pier. Turn right and walk along the promenade. You have entered the medieval fortified town of Portsmouth. Garrison Church is on your right and the Cathedral tower can be seen ahead.

To return to Portsmouth and Southsea Station, see instructions below at the end of the long walk***

Part 3. Havant to Hayling Island Ferry:

Havant Station to Langstone and St Peter`s Church North Hayling

From Havant Station turn left and go through the car park following a central cycle track. At the end of the car park, go through double gates and cross the road with a level crossing on the left. The cycle track continues through matching gates opposite.

The tarmac track heads south under a canopy of trees. In ¼ mile go through an underpass to a car park serving Havant Museum and Theatre up on the right. (Refreshments are served here). Keep on along the cycle track continuing its tree-lined way to another underpass, this time below A27.

On the south side of A27 keep going a little way on the cycle track looking for a nearby footpath on the left. Turn left and cross a small footbridge over the stream to the welcome sight of fields. The enclosed path leads to a track. Turn right passing scattered houses including Wade Court with its imitation church tower on the right. In ¼ mile you reach Langstone Harbour.

Turn right and walk on the harbour path, also part of Wayfarer`s Walk. Pass a pond, a converted mill and Langstone High Street with its assortment of old and new houses. Two very popular pubs overlook the harbour.

Warning: *Do not attempt to cross the harbour on the 'way', marked by two posts on the left. It is an old Roman way through the mud to Hayling. In medieval times it was the only access to the island and is known as the 'Wadeway'. It is shown as a path on Ordnance Survey but it is no longer passable even at low tide.* Now the only way is the busy Langstone Bridge!

After the second pub, you come up to Langstone Bridge and turn left. At least pavements are provided but you might have to share them with cyclists.

After crossing Langstone Bridge, turn immediately left into Northney Road. It is signed to North Hayling and St Peter`s Church. The harbour is on your left. Avoid the first path to the right. Pass a small rough layby, then turn right to cross the road to a footpath along a tarmac farm lane.

Look out for a path on the left. You have to cross to the other side of the hedge here and walk on the edge of a field to T-junction. Turn left on a rough track that becomes a tarmac access road to the occasional houses here. You rejoin Northney Road at a pond and turn right. Walk on the grass verge for 50 metres then turn right again.

Here the path heads south, hugging the thick hedge on the left. At the end of the hedge turn left. You have a view across the field to St Peter`s Church. Walk along the edge of the field, heading west. Turn right at the corner and pass gardens on the left as you make your way to the church.

*From St Peter`s to St Mary`s, Hayling see Part 1 above***

***St Mary`s Hayling to Ferry Point**

Pass the church porch on your right and take the footpath in the left hand corner of the churchyard. Head southwest across a flat wide open field. Avoid a caravan park and veer left towards a lone hedge.

Turn right and follow the hedge towards housing. You come to the main road, A3023. Turn right and cross to Newtown Lane opposite. The lane soon curves left, heading south, down to Station Road and shops in West Town.

Turn right away from the shops. In 100 metres turn left into a short alley leading to a park and playing fields. Keep on course along a tree-lined path to Bacon Lane. Cross the lane to Stamford Ave. This leads to a T-junction with the road known as 'Sea Front'. It becomes 'Ferry Lane' further west.

To reach the shore, turn right then almost immediately left beside a large block of flats. Cross the grassy common land to the sea. Turn right and walk beside the beach on your left. You are on Sinah Common and follow the track to pass a café, a putting green and a large white club house beyond.

In about ½ mile, after some holiday huts, you come to a high wire fence that surrounds the golf links.

For the road route, turn right then left to walk along Ferry Lane for nearly 1 mile to Ferry Point.

I prefer to take the longer and rougher coast path. Turn left at the high wire fence. There is a path beside the fence on the right. At first you walk on pebbles then grass or with the option of sand at low tide. (beware incoming tides!). You have a view ahead of Spinnaker Tower, Portsmouth. Once the path rounds Gunner Point, it heads northwest beside the channel dividing Portsmouth from Hayling. You pass sand dunes and finally come to the hard track in the car park. Pass the pub and cross to the ferry point. Take the ferry

From the landing stage on Portsea Island, the route is straightforward. Follow Ferry Road past cafés, the Marina and blocks of flats. In ½ mile, fork left into Melville Road. At the end turn left, pass toilets then follow the Esplanade for 3 miles from Eastney to Old Portsmouth.

On the way you pass historic maritime buildings. At the quieter eastern end you pass Eastney Fort and the Royal Marines Museum. After South Parade Pier you come to Southsea Castle and then the War Memorial on Southsea Common. After Clarence Pier and the fair ground, you pass King`s Bastion, once the old town of Portsmouth. You are now in sight of Garrison Church and the Cathedral tower beyond.

See **Part 2** above for the start of the shortest walk. It continues below:
*****From Portsmouth Cathedral to Portsmouth and Southsea Railway Station,** head northeast along the High Street, away from the sea. Pass John Pound`s Chapel on the left. At the end of the road you come to a roundabout and Portsmouth Grammar School is on the right hand corner.

Cross to Cambridge Road opposite and keep on course. At the end of the road you pass Blackwells bookshop on the corner on the right. Go round this corner and cross to Hampshire Terrace opposite. Café Parisien is on the left.

At the next major junction cross to a road known as Guildhall Walk where the famous and lively New Theatre Royal is to be found. Pass this on your left. The next landmark is the Guildhall, a grand Victorian building in classical style. Cross the Guildhall Square to go through the arch in a modern dark glass building then under the railway bridge to the nearby Portsmouth and Southsea Station on the right. **End of Walks 2 and 3.**

Isle of Wight Ferry

Walk 5: Southwick to Boarhunt

Sheltered by Portsdown Hill, little villages have survived the intense urban development to the south and the close intrusion of naval establishments so we are able to walk through almost quiet countryside.

Starting Point: Back Lane, Southwick. **GR**624087 **Map:** OS Explorer 119
Terrain: Fairly flat but rough in places and some muddy sections in winter
Distance: 5 Miles **Note:** Southwick has two pubs.
Local Information: William Wykeham, founder of Winchester College (see the Introduction) was born in Southwick. His parents, John and Sybil Long were poor. Kind friends sent their son to Winchester for his education. At their death he buried his parents in Southwick Priory.

Churches

Southwick Priory was formed when monks moved from Portchester Castle to Southwick in mid- 12th century (See Walk 25). This Augustinian house suffered the fate of other monasteries under Henry V111`s Dissolution. It was dismantled. In 1539 John Whyte acquired the buildings and converted them into a small mansion. He took away much of the rest of the Priory to rebuild the church. In 1548 his wife died in the mansion. The house burnt down in 1750. Today, only scant ruins of the Priory are left on the site.

Southwick Priory

St James Without the Priory Gate, the Peculiar of Southwick existed before the Priory. In 1566 John Whyte rebuilt the church and incorporated some pieces from the Priory he had demolished, including the octagonal pillars of the north aisle. Ornate capitals give an idea of the size and style of the Priory. The medieval south wall has moulded stonework from the Priory. An impressive tomb stands in the north chapel. It was probably brought to the church when John Whyte`s wife died and the canopy added in 1566. On top are brasses of the couple and their children. The Tudor type windows of the north aisle contain fragments of glass from the Priory.

Southwick to Boarhunt

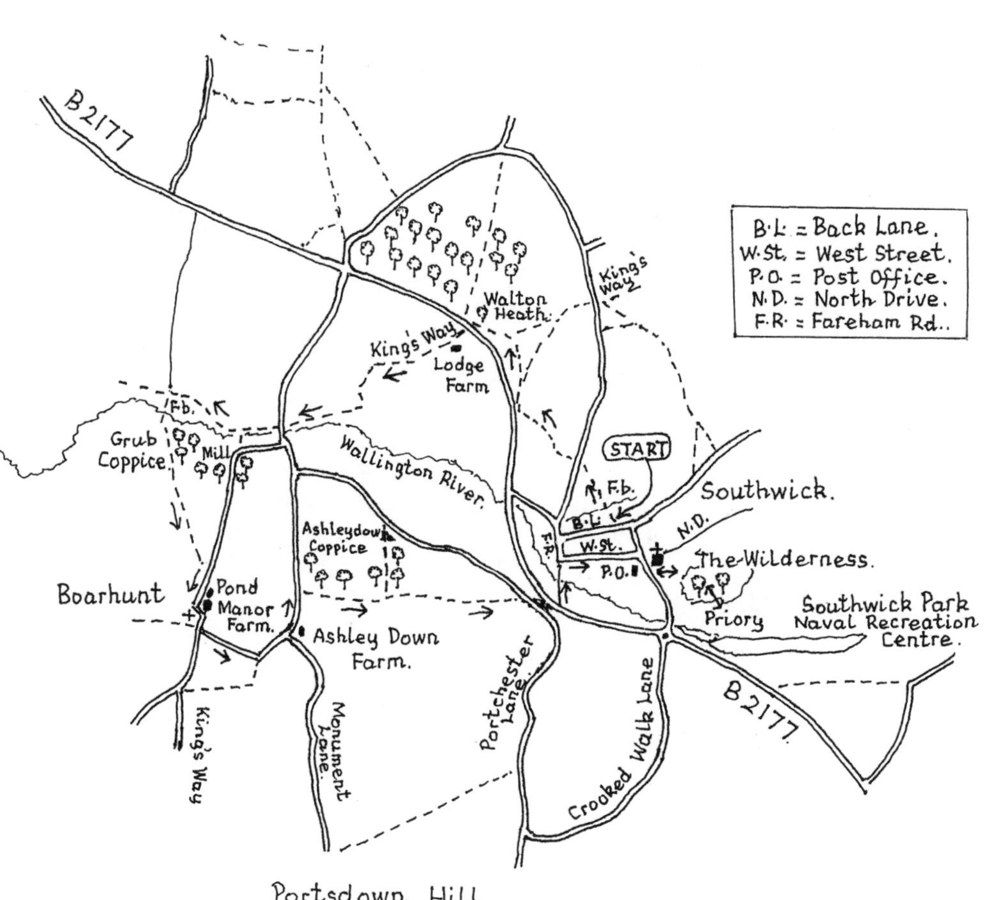

Southwick

The east window has been re-set. It is 15th century Perpendicular. The chancel is splendid with two 17th century upholstered boxed pews and several monuments to the Thistlethwaite family who, I am told, still own the village. The 18th century reredos has a central painting of fat cherubs and doves floating in the sky. The artist was Italian. The gallery, supported on four posts, has fine 17th century panelling. In 1981 new bells were installed in the tower. The church presents a pleasing whole partly thanks to the light blue coved ceilings of nave and chancel. **Boarhunt, St Nicholas** is one of the earliest Christian churches. It has an elevated position overlooking pastoral and woodland country. The Manor Farm is across the road. The church retains its original shape and many Saxon features, including the large font. Outside, on the east gable a thin pilaster strip is a Saxon feature. The small blocked Saxon window has some carving at the top. Most of the other windows are 13th century lancets. The tall plain chancel arch, 7 feet wide, is Saxon. Arches on either side are later.

The Walk

Back Lane, as the name suggests, is a quiet road, a turning off the High Street. There are some thatched cottages at the east end, near the bend in the main road. From the main road walk along Back Lane for 100 metres.

Turn right into a footpath and head northwest passing a brick house on the left. Cross the little Wallington River on a footbridge. Keep on course along the well worn path over a small flat field. Pass a spinney on the left with some tall Christmas trees. In 300 metres you reach Common Lane.

Cross to the footpath opposite, ignoring the sign pointing up the lane. Continue northwest over a wide open field towards woodland. You have a view of the slope of Portsdown Hill on your left. You pass two lone trees before reaching the fringe of uncultivated land at the edge of the field. Here marsh orchids flower in May and June. A low two-plank wooden footbridge at one point may be useful in wet weather.

Enter the woodland and turn right on the wide dirt track. You are walking roughly parallel to the B2177 for 350 metres. The trees screen the road. In 150 metres the woodland falls away and you have a view over Walton Heath on the right. Two paths join us from the right; the second one is King`s Way. Your track, now King`s Way, continues on gravel then tarmac to more woodland. As the tarmac surface widens, turn left to B2177.

Cross with care to Lodge Farm opposite. Go into the farmyard as far as an arrow on the left. Turn right here and go through a barrier then a gate. *This section was cleared of slurry on my last visit. There is usually a farmer at hand if you have a problem here. On the first occasion he directed me on a diversion south to avoid the slurry. On the second he opened the barrier.*

Once you have passed through the farm gate, the path is straightforward heading southwest along the edge of a field with a wire fence on the left. In 350 metres at a thick hedge, cross a stream to the next field where a rounded hillock faces you.

Either go over the hillock in a southwesterly direction *or follow the edge of the field (our farmer`s diversion came through the hedge on the left). At the end turn right and follow the river on the left.* At the furthest left hand corner of this field, you come out onto a public road.

Cross to the footpath opposite, still King`s Way and still following the river on the left. For 150 metres as far as a stile on the left, you may have to battle through an overgrown path. *If this is too difficult follow the roads shown on the map.* After this stile you come to a small well-manicured field.

Boarhunt

Avoid going down to the footbridge to Boarhunt Mill. Instead, turn right and follow the hedge on the right. This is a narrow field bounded by the river and woodland, Grub Coppice on the left. At the far right hand corner of the field turn into the next field and STOP!

Immediately on your left there is a footpath leading behind the narrow field you have just crossed. In 75 metres you come to a footbridge over the river, overhung with trees.

Cross the bridge to wide open farmland. Turn left and hug the wood, the other side of Grub Coppice, on the left. You are still on King`s Way heading southeast. The path changes to rough tarmac then joins Boarhunt Road.

Turn right and walk on the verge. Pass a pond with magnificent water lilies in season then the thatched barns and buildings of Manor Farm all on the left. The road now narrows at a bend before climbing up to Boarhunt Church on the right. Climb up the grassy slope then steps up to the church.

From Boarhunt Church cross the road diagonally right and uphill to the lane opposite. You leave King`s Way here. This is a pleasant elevated walk with views over the countryside. The lane bends and comes to a T-junction. A signpost indicates Portchester to the right. Ashley Down Farm is opposite.

Boarhunt

Turn left and head north for 250 metres. You come to the edge of woodland and turn right. Follow the enclosed path in a dip beside Ashleydown Coppice, now on your left. At the end of the coppice keep straight on across a sequestered field, following the boundary on the right.

You enter another strip of woodland. Go through and veer left to a lonely house in the wood. Pass it on your right and follow the sign to an enclosed muddy path. You then leave the woodland for an open field. Keep heading east with the hedge on your left. Cross a farm track then keep on course through the middle of a flat field to trees at the far side. Here the path drops down to a tarmac road.

Turn right on this quiet lane. In 50 metres the lane veers to the right. You turn left to the main road B2177. Cross to the track opposite leading to Fareham Road on the edge of Southwick. Turn right at West Street (you can see the church at the end). **At Southwick Church** turn left for Back Lane.

To visit the site of the Priory, *face the church and turn right, pass the Post Office, then turn left into a short road. Go through car parks to North Drive. An enclosed footpath ahead leads through woodland, known as 'the Wilderness' to the remains of the Priory. Retrace your steps to the church and continue along the main road to the bend and Back Lane on the left.*

5 Walks
Near Petersfield

Empshott

Walk 6: Petersfield to Buriton

The Causeway, an old road above marshes and swamps once linked two Norman churches. We follow footpaths, quiet lanes and the long distance path, Hangers Way to visit these churches.

Starting Point: Petersfield Railway Station **GR**744236
Map: OS Explorer 133 **Terrain:** Undulating, some mud in winter especially along Hangers Way. **Distance:** 6 Miles
Local Information: 1. The Manor House, next to Buriton Church was the home of 18th century historian, Edward Gibbon who wrote 'The Decline and Fall of the Roman Empire'. He loved the quiet of Buriton and acquired his own library while still a boy. He is buried in the churchyard.
2. John Goodyer, an even earlier resident (1592 – 1664) was one of the earliest botanists. The arms of the Goodyer family are in a church window.
3. **Petersfield** was founded in 12th century by William FitzRobert, Earl of Gloucester. Its position at cross routes, success in sheep rearing, leather and cloth manufacture brought prosperity. Three annual fairs were held here. Petersfield is still an attractive market town.

The Churches

St Peter`s Church, Petersfield has undergone many changes since its humble roots in the early 12th century as a chapel of ease to Buriton. There were no lords of the manor or knights here and so no early memorials. It remained a chapel for 700 years until 1886 when it became the Parish Church of Petersfield. It was once a cruciform church, probably with a central tower. In the middle of the 12th century it acquired a west tower. The lower part of this tower is Norman and the upper part was added in 15th century. Inside, the Norman chancel arch may have been the east wall of the central tower. Not content with the main round arch with intricate Norman carvings, there are three similarly ornate windows above and a final window at the top. If you stand under the chancel arch and look through the nave to the west end you can see the line of the first, lower roof. The nave was enlarged in the late 12th century when north and south aisles were added. The capitals of their pillars differ, suggesting a time gap in their building. In 1731 the transepts were incorporated into the aisles. In 1873 Sir Arthur Blomfield made some dramatic changes to the church. Most of the chancel was rebuilt. The Gothic east windows of the chancel and the north aisle were removed. They were replaced with small round headed windows. The 15th century font was discarded, to be rescued from the churchyard in 1946. In 1999 another major upheaval brought the church into the 21st century. Fine quality materials and skilled

Petersfield to Buriton

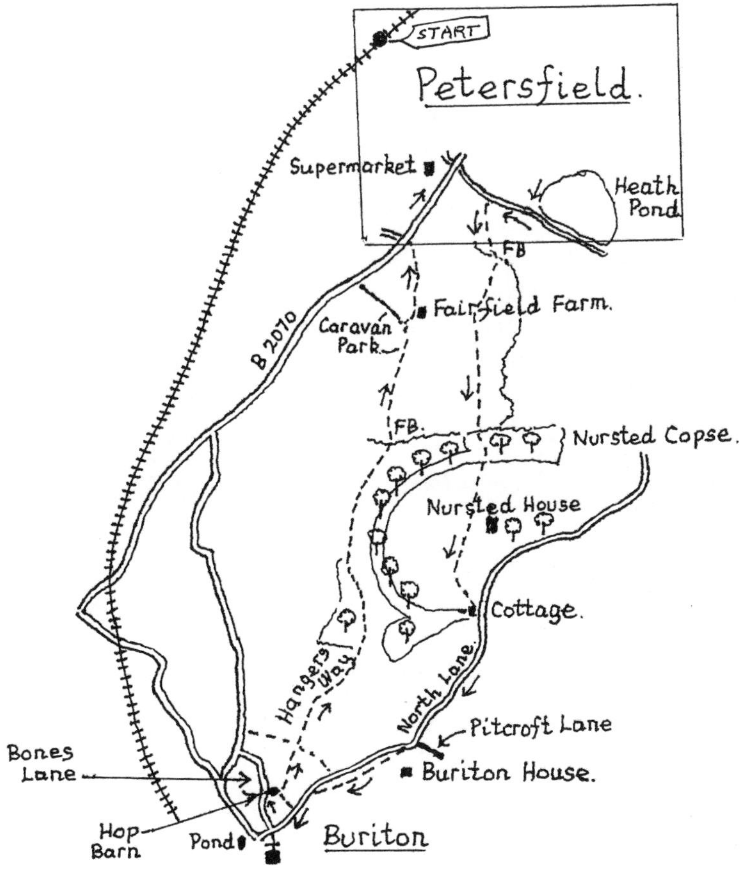

START
Petersfield.
Supermarket
Heath Pond
FB
Fairfield Farm.
Caravan Park
B 2070
FB.
Nursted Copse.
Nursted House
Cottage.
Hangers Way
North Lane
Pitcroft Lane
Buriton House.
Bones Lane
Hop Barn
Pond
Buriton

START
N
Petersfield
P
P
High St.
The Square
Heath Rd.
The Avenue
B2070
Heath Pond
Sussex Rd.

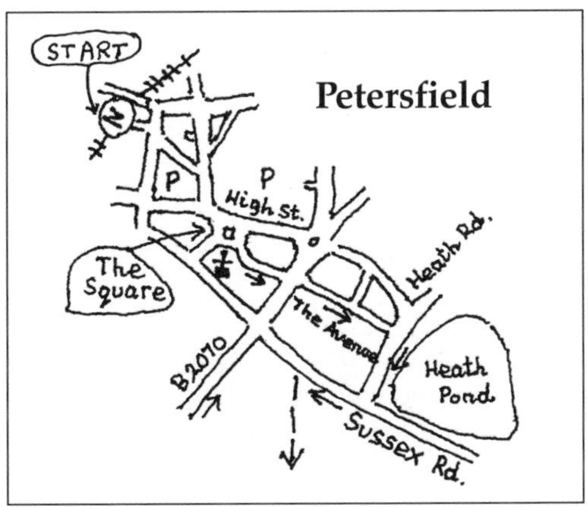

Petersfield

workmanship bear witness to this new restoration. Portland stone was fitted on the floors. Fine glass and wood were used to screen the west end providing separate rooms for meetings, a Lady Chapel and a service room. We were fortunate to visit the church when teas were being served to visitors to an art exhibition.

The Parish Church of St. Mary, Buriton was the centre of the Manor of Mapledurham. Queen Matilda, wife of William the Conqueror owned this manor; the old manor house is near the church. The church included Sheet and Petersfield in its parish. It is a large Norman Church with a fine wide chancel of Caen stone. Unusually the chancel has a wooden arch. The nave is Transition Norman with rounded pillars and moulded capitals. The south aisle was rebuilt around 1300 and the north aisle in 1764. The 80 foot tower was burnt in a thunder storm in 1712 and re-built in 1715 but only to 48 feet 6 inches. The prosperity brought to Buriton by the wool trade in 13th century is apparent in this fine church building. There is a memorial window to the early botanist, John Goodyer (1592 – 1664)

The Walk

From Petersfield Station make your way to the High Street then the Square where you will find the Tourist Information Centre and the Parish Church. From the Square, face the church and turn left, heading for the Museum.

Turn left into St Peter`s Road. This leads for 150 metres to B2070. It used to be the main trunk road until the advent of the A3. It is now a pleasant, wide thoroughfare. Cross to the Avenue opposite and walk straight through to the lake, Heath Pond.

Turn right on the elevated walkway and enjoy the view to the pond on your left. At the T-junction with B2146, turn right and walk beside 'Sussex Road' overlooked by houses. In 150 metres turn left at a footpath sign.

The footpath leads south into open meadows. Three paths confront you. Take the one in the middle, slightly to the left. It crosses two footbridges over streams. You come to another larger meadow and head south on the path that is just discernable. Pass the end of a row of trees on the left.

Go down to a stream on the field boundary. A footbridge and stile take you into the next sloping meadow dominated by two shapely trees. Pass these on your right and look down to the stream on your left. Beyond the stream is a golf course. Ahead is a wooded hill. Make for the right hand corner of the meadow for access to another small field at the base of the hill.

Cut across the left corner of this small field to enter Nursted Copse to a wide clear path. You have a short climb through woodland. The path is steeper as you approach the top.

You emerge to a wide field and views across to Butser Hill, topped with a mast. Straight ahead the path leads to the hedges around the secluded grounds of Nursted House. Shaded by rhododendrons, snowdrops flower in February. Keep on course heading south with a beech hedge on your left. At the end of the hedge veer left across a field towards cottages. The way down to the road is just to the left of these.

Buriton

Turn right onto the tarmac road towards Buriton. Pass the cottages on your right. In ½ mile at a bend in the road, you pass Pitcroft Lane on the left then the gates of Buriton House.

Look out for some steps on the left leading up through trees to a footpath. Climb the steps to an enclosed path that leads past the grounds of Buriton House on the left and then the backs of village houses before descending to the road again. Turn left, pass **Bones Lane** on the right and immediately you reach Buriton Church and the village pond.

From Buriton Church return to Bones Lane, passing the Manor House on the way. Turn into Bones Lane following Hangers Way. Walk up the lane past occasional houses for 100 metres. At a three story building, Hop Loft, turn right and go through a yard to the far corner.

A path to the left leads to a hanger. Despite the sewage works below, here is a delightful little valley beckoning you to walk on a natural platform above and beside it. Stay on the hanger and in ½ mile you reach a coppice. Pass a small barn at the entrance to the coppice. Make the short descent through the trees where bluebells and wild garlic grow in spring. You come down to a cross valley. Pass a pond on the left and re-enter the edge of the wood. At the end of the wood you come to downland and keep on course.

Veer slightly down to the right to cross a little stream. You then have to follow the damp footpath by the stream on your right with an open field on the left.

In 350 metres you escape the stream to come to a short hedge lined track. It leads to a field with mobile homes lining two sides. Cross diagonally left to a marker and go through to the access road.

Cross this towards the clearly marked Office. Before you reach the brick walls of Fairfield Farm, turn left into a leafy corner and go through trees to a sad suburban field. Follow the hedge on your right and you come to the B2070. Cross with care.

Turn right to walk along the pavement past houses on the edge of Petersfield. In ¼ mile you can turn left towards Tescos supermarket. You catch a glimpse of St Peter`s Church ahead. Follow the pedestrian way in the direction of the church. Pass the museum on the right and you come to the church on the left. Return to Petersfield Station.

Walk 7: Steep to Hawkley and Empshott

This is a long walk, divided into two sections, to be less strenuous. We walk along 'hangers' or steep, wooded slopes to discover three fine churches.

Local Information: If you have never been to the Hangers before, you are in for a treat. Here is rich woodland on chalk hills with dramatically steep slopes and lovely hidden valleys. **William Cobbett** (Walk 24) described them in his *Rural Rides:*
'...out we came, all in a moment, at the very edge of the hanger! And never, in all my life, was I so surprised and so delighted...Those who had dwelt on the dirt and dangers of this route had said not a word about beauties, the matchless beauties of the scenery'.
Today we have a sign posted route. Look out for the logo, a tree on an arrow for **Hangers Way,** a 21 mile walk from Alton to Queen Elizabeth Country Park near Petersfield. 'Hangra' is Old English for a wooded slope.

Starting Point 1: Church Road, Steep **GR**746254
Starting Point 2: The Village Green, Hawkley **GR**746292
Map: OS Explorer 133 **Terrain:** Hilly and muddy in places
Distances: 11 Miles, the whole walk. This can be divided into two parts:
Steep to Hawkley 7 tough Miles Hawkley to Empshott 5½ easy Miles
Warning: Pick a fine day for your walk in this area as some slopes are long and steep and some valleys become very wet and muddy in places.

The Churches

All Saints` Church, Steep has a Victorian appearance from the front. The strikingly ornate spire and the lychgate were added late in 19th century. It is an agreable surprise to enter the gloomy interior and experience a world that existed 900 years ago. The church is even older. The round pillars and arcades show the extent of the earlier Norman church. In 1180 the south aisle was added; its thick walls holding two small shapely windows. Early in 13th century a large chancel was built, again with small handsome windows. The east window of the north aisle and the main west window of the nave are 13th century with Victorian glass. The north door is Perpendicular, as are the roof timbers of the nave. The timbers of the north porch may have come from the original Norman roof. The font is 14th century with a carved wood cover (1979) by George Taylor. Crafts people from nearby Bedales School have produced several church fittings. Laurence Whistler has engraved the plain windows in the south aisle (1978) in memory of Edward Thomas. This poet lived nearby and loved the countryside here but died at Arras in 1917.
St Peter and St Paul, Hawkley is idyllically set on the village green on the site of an earlier chapel. The plain font may have come from this chapel. It is made of Purbeck marble. It has a square bowl on a round shaft and dates from the 12th

Steep to Hawkley - Hawkley to Empshott

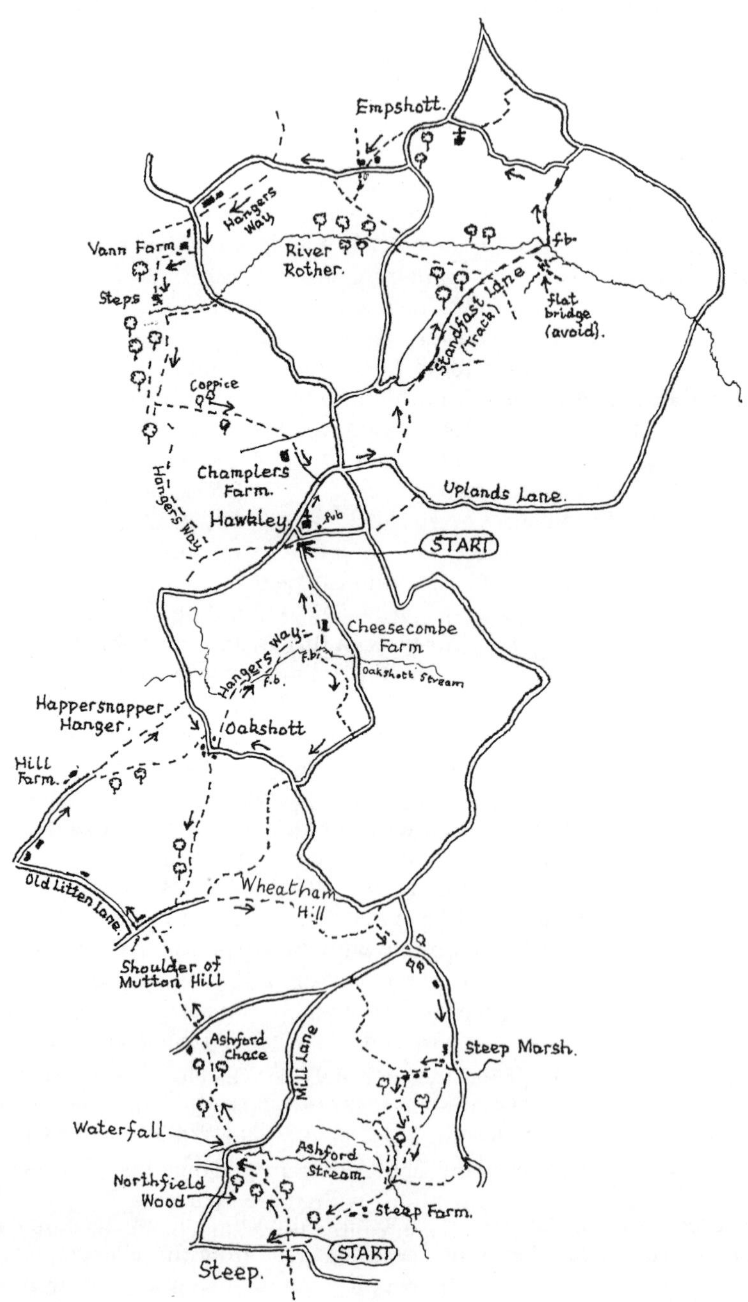

Steep

century. The rest is Victorian. Samuel S. Teulon designed this church in the 1860s in a delightful variety of styles. It has a Rhenish spire similar to that of Sompting (see West Sussex Church Walks). The main body of the church is Norman in style and has round headed windows symmetrically placed. The capitals of the pillars of north and south arcades are finely carved in Romanesque style. The Millenium window high in the west end was engraved by Simon Whistler. It shows a cockerel and the crossed key and sword, emblems of St Peter and St Paul.

Empshott Church of the Holy Rood was built between 1187 and 1220 and may have replaced a Saxon chapel. In 1181 Pope Alexander 111 mentioned a chapel at Ymbesieta in the possession of Southwick Priory (SeeWalk 5). Until the Dissolution, it was dedicated to St Lawrence. Robert Aske, who held the Manor of Empshott, was opposed to the Dissolution and was executed for his pains in 1537. We can admire much of the original church, including the pointed arches of the arcades, the chancel and the fine west arch and the assortment of lancet windows. Southwick Priory may have been responsible for the fine capitals and the wealth of dog tooth carving throughout. The arcades and windows are all different and individual. The arcades appear to lean outwards. The church was neglected after it left the care of Southwick Priory. It had to be repaired in 1620, resulting in very narrow arcades. The hewn oak benches date from the 15th century. The Victorians have enhanced the beauty of this church, repairing dangerous chancel walls and replacing the Jacobean east window with three charming lancets. They also replaced the insecure tower with an inspired turret, much of it glass, the design of Mr Pusey. This work, together with re-roofing, was completed in 1868 at the expense of Mr Scott of Rotherfield Park.

Steep

Hawkley

The Walk

Part 1

From the lychgate, Steep cross Church Road to the footpath opposite. You have joined Hangers Way. Veer slightly to the left across a small field to enter Northfield Wood. Go gently downhill on the clearly defined path.

When you emerge from the wood, you have a good view across to nearby Oakhurst Farm on a slope and a real hill at the back, Ashford Hanger.

Turn left and follow the edge of the wood on the left for 200 metres. You come to Mill Lane at a junction. Turn right and walk down the lane to a bend. A waterfall cascades in the corner.

Just to the right of this waterfall is a narrow footpath up to a T-junction (not shown on Ordnance Survey map). Turn left. Little Langleys Nature Reserve with ponds is on your right. You pass another pond fed by Ashford Stream below on your left.

Follow the Hangers Way as it turns right then left above Lutcombe Bottom. You join a driveway and continue on it to a byway. *Hangers Way goes off to the left here past a large house.* You turn right then immediately left for the approach to Ashford Hanger.

Start climbing the 'Shoulder of Mutton' hill. Take the clear way between trees on this hanger where steps are cut into the ground to help you. Near the top there is a memorial stone to Edward Thomas the poet (1878- 1917). He died at Arras in the

First World War. Above the memorial there is a welcome seat and an opportunity to recover whilst admiring the view to Queen Elizabeth Forest and the Downs.

At the top of the hill the ground flattens and you continue through trees to a T-junction with a mud track, Old Litton Lane. Turn left and walk along the lane for about 100 metres until you come to a branch in the track. Turn right into a continuation of Old Litton Lane.

This elevated track leads gently downhill for ½ mile to a tile-hung house on the corner at a junction. Turn sharp right and walk northeast on a tarmac lane for ¼ mile. Pass some farm buildings then continue on a dirt track. Now realise you are high up on Happersnapper Hanger, a lonely wooded slope.

Avoid the path on the right and go downhill on the main track under the trees. At the bottom pass an old orchard and go through the field to the tarmac road.

Turn right onto the road to Oakshott. Pass a turning on the right to Oakshott Hanger. In the tiny hamlet of Oakshott, near a converted barn, Hangers Way crosses the road.

Turn left into Hangers Way and head northeast for 1 mile to Hawkley. In this valley, walkers have tended to stay up on a natural ledge. In ¼ mile you have to leave this ledge and turn left along the little path down to Oakshott Stream. There are two footbridges to cross here. Then pass Cheesecombe Farm on the right and continue to the village of Hawkley at a T-junction. The pub is to the right. Turn left for the church.

See below 'Part 2' to double the length of your walk and include Empshott.

Hawkley to Steep Return to Hangers Way and retrace your steps on the track as far as Cheesecombe Farm, now down on your left.

At a path junction turn left away from Hangers Way and go down to Oakshott Stream where a good long footbridge takes you to the bank on the other side.

Climb the bank to the nearby field and turn left so that you walk parallel to the stream. You are climbing above the stream which is at the bottom of a precipice. Follow the path as it curves right then bends sharp left. You slip down through the hedge to rejoin the track from Cheesecombe Farm.

Turn right and walk along the enclosed track for ¼ mile to a tarmac road. Turn right on the road and avoid a nearby bridleway opposite. *This bridleway does lead up to Old Litton Lane but is distorted with slippery ruts.* Instead, continue along the tarmac road for ¼ mile to rejoin Hangers Way in Oakshott. (The familiar path of outward walk to the north is on your right).

Turn left and start climbing up a track to houses. At the end of the track turn left into a field where the path is well worn. It bends to the right and climbs into a sloping meadow. *Turn round for a view back over a widespread canopy of trees where Hawkley Church tower nestles.* Pass a fold in the hill on your left and continue climbing through beech woodland. The path bends left on its uphill course until it finally reaches Old Litton Lane at the top.

The shortest way back to Steep – about 2 kilometres – is to retrace you steps back down Shoulder of Mutton Hill and across Ashford Stream.

The alternative route – about 2 miles - is described here. Turn left and walk for 1 mile along Old Litton Lane avoiding turnings to left and right. Near the end of the lane, after a descent, there is a footpath on the right. Turn right and go down a sloping field to a road junction.

Turn right then immediately left into a shady lane that leads downhill and then flattens. In ½ mile you reach Steep Marsh. Pass an oast house then a narrow tarmac road to an industrial estate. After the next house, turn right.

Now the footpath follows a track that veers to the right, passing two houses and rejoins the industrial road. Turn left and pass workshops, now deserted. Then enter the territory of Steep Marsh Farm. Here loom huge windowless sheds.

After the second monstrous shed you come to a junction of paths and turn left. You have to go behind the shed before you can escape down a short steep slope into low lying woodland, known as 'the Moors'. You are heading southwards. In a clearing in the wood, pass a cottage where a few privileged hens are free range. Continue through the wood under some sweet chestnut trees. Cross a disintegrating bridge over a stream. In ¼ mile you come to another junction of paths.

Avoid the narrow path up on the left. Turn right away from a 'PRIVATE' farmgate. Cross Ashford Stream on a good bridge and climb up to Steep Farm, residential buildings around a courtyard.

The path takes you around the edge of Steep Farm and you have fine views to wooded slopes. Continue on the path to the southwest to enter another wood. Climb through the trees to Church Road, Steep. The Church is opposite on your right.

Empshott

Part 2

Hawkley to Empshott and back. From Hawkley village green, pass the church lychgate on your right. Continue along the village lane past well-spaced houses, among them the parsonage. The lane heads northeast for ¼ mile. **Note** a no through lane on the left for the return walk. Soon after that you come to staggered crossroads.

Cross diagonally right to Upland Lane. After 300 metres along this lane, turn left into a footpath over a dull, flat field. Continue northeast beside a broken hedge on your right. Through gaps in the hedge you are soon delighted to catch glimpses of a short precipice down to an idyllic valley.

In ¼ mile you arrive at the right hand corner of your field and descend on a ladder of roots to draw closer to the valley. You have dropped into the tarmac of Standfast Lane. Turn right and pass a house on the left.

Keep heading northeast on the lane as it becomes an enclosed track on the edge of woodland on the left. When it emerges to open fields, you will find that a higher footpath comes from the wood above and crosses to a stream down on the right.

You keep on course between two waterways, the stream on the right and the little River Rother with its ribbon of trees on the left. When you reach the northeast end of the field, do not be tempted onto the flat bridge on the right. Instead, make for the gate at the furthest tip where another bridge crosses the River Rother.

Here, you find you are still on your track, Standfast Lane as it climbs up through trees to a tarmac road at the top. Turn left and keep on climbing for ½ mile to Empshott Church.

Pass the church on your left and you soon come to a road T-junction. Turn left down the steep hill. In 150 metres, a footpath on the right takes you up through trees and across a field to a fine old house at Empshott Green. It has a driveway to the road.

Turn right and head westwards past other handsome cottages with a view to the Hangers. Avoid all footpaths until in 400 metres you come to the flat valley where Hangers Way crosses the road.

Turn left and follow Hangers Way southwestwards across two flat fields in the valley. In the second field you hug the hedge on the right and, just after passing a brick house, reach the road again.

Turn left. Avoid the path opposite up a steep slope. Instead walk along the lane heading south for 100 metres. Just past a pond and rockery, turn right into a field with the hangers ahead. Enter the next field and go to the far left corner. Here some steps lead down to a stream and more steps lead out of the gully on the other side. You are still on Hangers Way.

You have a woodland path due south along the lower edge of the hangers. Wood anemones, violets and primroses are to be seen here in the spring.

In ½ mile, turn left away from the hangers and Hangers Way. Head east across flat fields with a view to Hawkley Church to the right. Go through a coppice, not shown on Ordnance Survey map. As you emerge from trees, you come to open fields, divided by a hedge. Turn right to the other side of the hedge and cross diagonally left towards Champlers Farm. Cross a farm track to the path opposite. This leads through horse paddocks to the houses of Champlers Farm. Here you join the noted no through lane back to Hawkley. Turn right for Hawkley.

See above 'Hawkley to Steep' to complete the long walk.

Walk 8: Selborne to Hartley Mauditt

From the much loved village of Selborne, wander through meadows, made famous by Gilbert White, the naturalist. Venture through remote woodland to visit a deserted village. Two very different Norman churches reflect the state of these contrasting villages.

Starting Point: Selborne Village Car Park **GR**743336
Map: OS Explorer 133 **Distance:** 7 Miles **Terrain:** Undulating, one short, steep descent to Hangers Way and muddy patches in remote woodland
Local Information: The Reverend Gilbert White (1720-1793) made his home village famous with his book 'The Natural History of Selborne'. He was one of the first naturalists. He loved the countryside and wildlife here. His house, the Wakes with the Oates Museum is open 11 to 5.
Tuesday to Sunday + Bank Holiday Mondays 1st January to 23rd December Phone 01420 511275.
The National Trust now looks after 267 acres of countryside around Selborne. Much of our walk is on **Hangers Way** (see the end of this book) and passes through some of the National Trust land, including Short Lythe and Long Lythe. 'Hlith' in old English means a slope.
Knights Templar were a body of fighting monks. More details can be found in the Introduction to 'Mid Sussex Church Walks'.

The Churches

St Mary`s Church, Selborne is a Norman church on a Saxon site. It stands on the route taken by Gilbert White to study wildlife in the meadows. It was also the church where his grandfather preached. Gilbert himself was a curate here. The existing building began in 1180. The limestone font may be older. The walls of the tower are 4 feet thick. The round pillars of the nave are of that period. Carvings of wings are at the base of the pillars on the north side whilst the south side is plain. The pointed arches of the arcades are Transition-Norman. The south aisle was widened in 13th century. A Chantry Chapel was included at the behest of Ela Longspee, Countess of Warwick who had given an endowment to the monks of Selborne Priory (see below). The north aisle has remained narrow. The north transept was added around 1300, possibly as a chantry to Adam de Gurdon, a knight who lived at Temple Manor in the reign of Henry 111. He was a big man, as were the bones unearthed by the north wall. In 13th century Knights Templar held this manor in the southeast of the parish. The Norman chancel has undergone some changes. The chancel arch and the east wall were rebuilt in 1856. William White, great nephew of the naturalist is responsible for the east window of three

Selborne to Worldham and Hartley

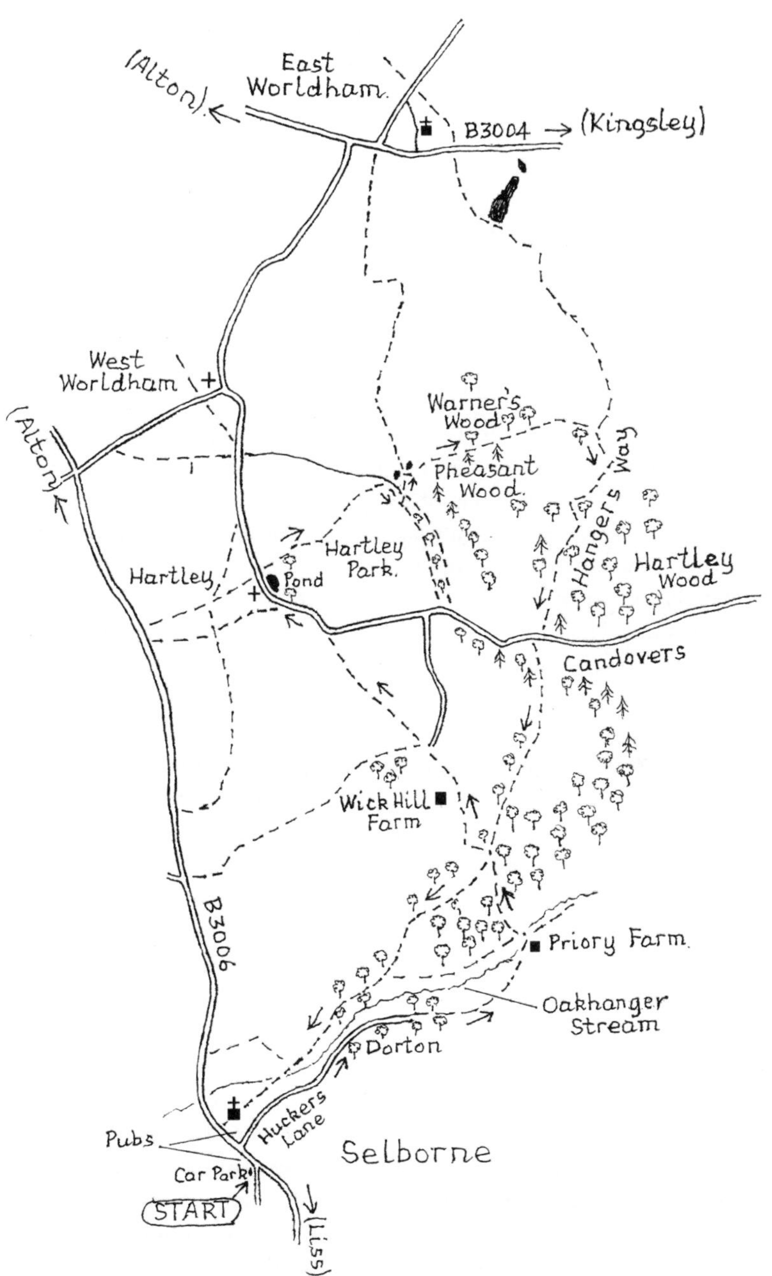

lancets. William also designed Lyndhurst Church (Walk 33). The altar rails come from St Juliot`s Church near Boscastle (see 'Cornwall, Walks to Churches').

Selborne Priory, east of the church was an Augustinian house, founded in1233. It provided a vicar for the church and took care of the parish. The Prior received the tithes. In 1486 the Bishop of Winchester had the Priory closed as it had fallen into disrepute. We pass Priory Farm early on in our walk. The remains of the Priory have been excavated here.

St Leonard`s Church, Hartley Mauditt is remote and isolated in contrast to Selborne. It overlooks Hartley Pond and no longer has the company of its medieval village. William de Mauditt probably built the church 1100 to 1125. The little Norman church still has some original features, including the simple horseshoe chancel arch and round headed windows, one near the pulpit and one to the left of the south door. We have to thank a later de Mauditt for the south door. Dating around 1190, it has a pointed arch of the Transition Norman style. The de Mauditts became Earls of Warwick and held the manor until 1267. Since then, the manor has passed through many hands. The Earl of Lancaster acquired the manor in 14th century. The east window of 1350 was replaced with an exact replica in 1972. The glass is Victorian. The stone base of the bell turret is 14th century with some modern restoration outside. A later member of the Lancaster family must have introduced the 15th century font with its Lancastrian rose. From 1614 to 1790, the Royalist family of Stuarts held the manor. Nicholas Steward fought for King Charles 11 in exile. The king rewarded him and in 1660 he became Sir Nicholas Steward. On the right of the chancel there is a stone memorial to Sir Simeon Stuart, the 7th and last of the Stuarts to be buried here. In 1790 the manor was sold and passed eventually to Lord Stalwell. He had the manor house pulled down, reputedly to spite his wife who preferred living here rather than joining him in his busy life in London. Villagers left the area when there was no employment at the Manor. Their cottages near the pond have also gone. Today friends of the church come to place flowers in spring and summer. No winter services are held.

The Walk

From Selborne Village Car Park go to the High Street and turn left. Pass a pub and the post office on the left. Cross over just before another pub on the right and enter Huckers Lane.

You have stepped into another century, a shady lane above the Oakhanger Stream. Here birds sing from cottages that seem to have grown out of the ground. After a long, lone rickety cottage, 'Dorton' on the left, the lane becomes a track through the wooded slope. Sweet celandines, woodruff, violets, primroses and a few bluebells grow in spring. Gaps in the trees offer views down cowslip banks to the stream on the left and, at one point, a vista into another valley on the right.

You leave the woodland track for an open meadow and cross towards Priory

Shelborne

Farm where you pick up the farm track. It bends to the left past a pond and crosses a bridge over the stream – an ideal setting for a priory. You have come 1 mile from Selborne, in the footsteps of monks.

Follow the path up through Coombe Wood. In ½ mile **at a path corner,** you meet Hangers Way.

Turn left into a meadow. *Later you will return to Selborne over this meadow.* For the moment, turn sharp right and climb the slope hugging woodland on your right.

At the top turn right again and enter an enclosed track that becomes a sunken way. It brings you up to Wick Hill Farm, a clutch of buildings including a double oasthouse.

Pass the farm on your left and continue along its access lane to a junction. Go straight across the road to an open footpath over an elevated field. Cross diagonally left to a marker at the corner of the gardens of Wick Hill Cottages on the left. Continue northwest for ½ mile across the wide field on a clearly defined footpath. On the way, you soon have the company of a hedge on the left and when you reach a gap, you change to have the hedge on your right (neither hedge is shown on Ordnance Survey Map).

Hartley Church with a backdrop of trees comes into view as you approach the tarmac lane. Turn left for the church and pond.

After visiting Hartley Mauditt Church, continue past the pond on your right to a nearby footpath sign. Turn right on the marked path to a woodland screen.

Emerge from the trees to an open field. Avoid the track to the right.

Keep straight on beside a thick hedge hiding a stream on the left. Pass a new tree plantation on the right. Continue to the far left corner of the field and turn right. Now you have a wooded hanger on your left. In 75 metres turn left and make the steep descent of the hanger. There are rough steps to help. In 50 metres you come down to a track at the bottom.

A lane is on the left. Go to the lane and turn right. Pass one or two houses, 'New Buildings' on the left. The lane becomes a track down through Pheasant Wood for 1 kilometre on an easterly course. Despite the steady descent, the path was not too muddy in May time. On the way you have a glimpse of a lush meadow beyond the trees on the left. Avoid a woodland track on the right.

When you least expect it, you come to an insignificant little post down on your right. You have re-joined Hangers Way. Turn sharp right and head south, still in woodland.

In 250 metres Hangers Way leads to a meadow and cuts across the right hand corner. Re-enter the wood to follow a straight path through conifers. At the end of the straight path you come to a major cross track. Turn left on this wide, hard farm track. After a pond on the right, turn right and climb gently up through Hartley Wood in a southwesterly direction.

In just over 1 kilometre after rejoining Hangers Way, you reach the tarmac road at Candovers. Turn right, passing a large barn converted to a home, then turn left on a lane signed 'Estate Office'. Pass more houses and keep on course southwards. Here is a pleasant flat track at the lower edge of Wick Hill Hanger with view across the countryside on the left. In ½ mile enter Wick Wood and climb to the familiar **path corner.** On the left is the path that brought you here.

Once again cross into the field but this time go straight on southwest along Hangers Way. In ½ mile you join a path by three lakes. Turn right into National Trust land. You are on the other side of Oakhanger Stream. Go through Long Lythe, then Short Lythe, pass the north side of 'Dorton' then climb up the Church Meadow to St Mary`s Church. You are back in Selborne. Cross the small green, 'the Plestor' down to the High Street and turn left. The Oates Museum and tearooms (see above) are on the right.

Walk 9: East Worldham to Binsted

A peaceful walk through spacious arable fields to ancient village churches that have developed along very different lines.

Starting Point: East Worldham Church **GR751382 Map:** OS Explorer 144
(Limited parking on a Sunday. You may have to find a space in Wyck Lane)
Terrain: Gently undulating, 1 short steep climb **Distance:** 6 Miles

The Churches

St Mary the Virgin, East Worldham stands on a hill at Roman crossroads. There was probably a Saxon church here. The stone outline of a Norman apse can be seen on the east wall. The present church consists of just nave and chancel under one fine roof. The church is early 13th century with lancet windows throughout. The Arnott window, depicting St Luke is in a lancet to the west of the entrance. It is a bold design by Nils Burwitz in modern glass. The church doors are Early English. The 19th century porch covers one of these doors. Cross marks at the side were probably made by Christian pilgrims. A recess in the south wall contains the effigy of a 14th century lady. She was found under the floor in 1865 and is now a picture of contentment in her resting place. The Chaucer family had links with the village. This gave rise to the theory that she is Phillippa, wife of Geoffrey Chaucer. In 1865 the 17th century bellcote was raised to a new height when a small wooden tower was fitted to the roof.

East Worldham

East Worldham to Binsted

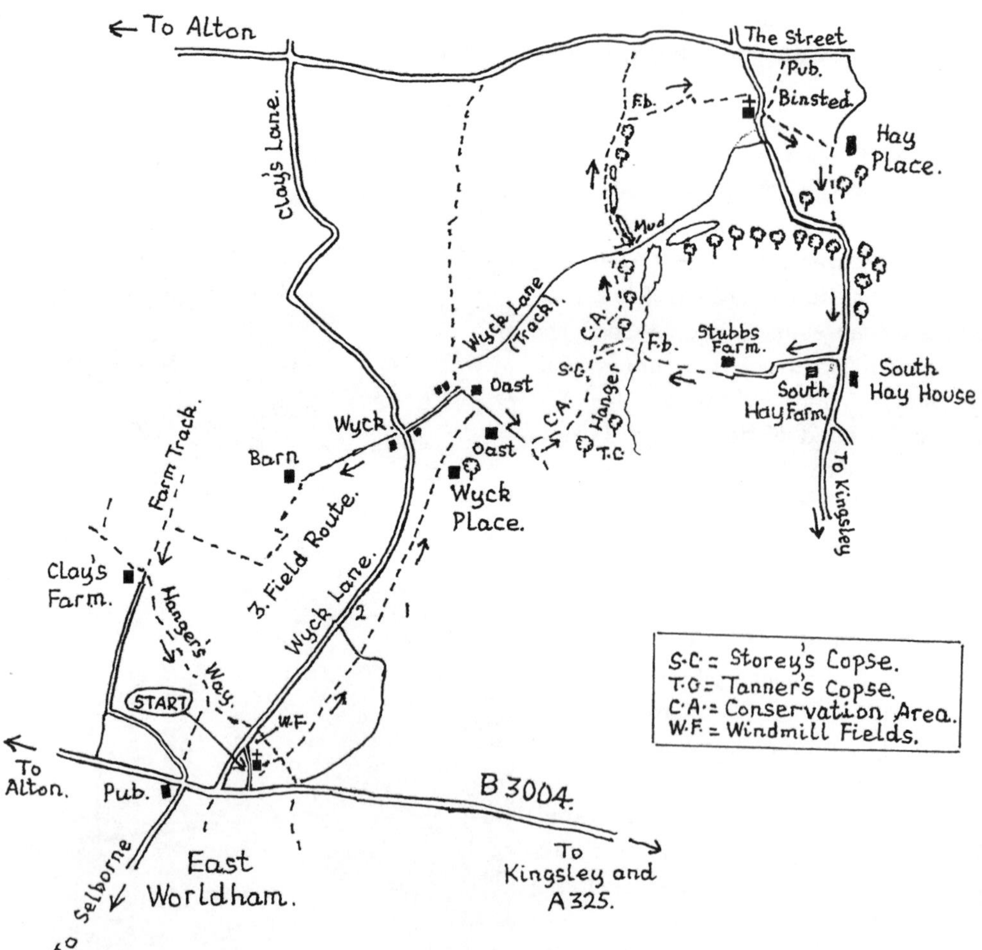

The Church of the Holy Cross, Binsted has been much enlarged over the centuries, resulting in a handsome exterior with ancient square tower and more recent spire. It stands in lovely extensive grounds with views across the Hampshire fields. Picturesque old cottages overlook the churchyard. Inside, the early 12th century church has round columns. The chancel also has round late Norman arches. In the nave the arches are slightly pointed. Soon after it was built, the church was enlarged (1180 – 1195). North and south aisles with small lancet windows were added to the nave. North and south chapels were also added, making the building in the shape of a cross. The north chapel was again enlarged in 1331 at the behest of Richard de la Bere, owner of Westcote. As a result, the cross is no longer symmetrical. This Westcote chapel is now behind the organ where you can see the tomb of a crusader in a recess in the north wall. In 13th century the chancel was extended 15 feet to the east. Early English side windows were fitted to the chancel. The Victorians have made their own changes to this church. In 1863 they replaced the chancel arch with a taller pointed one. They re-built the south wall of the nave and the north wall of the Westcote chapel. Theirs is the alabaster font and stained glass, apart from a window near the font. This has 16th century glass with the arms of local families. Field Marshall Viscount Montgomery worshipped in this church; his banner is near the tower and his grave is near the footpath on the north corner of the churchyard. We pass it on our walk.

The Walk

Go to the footpath behind the chancel of East Worldham Church. Cross the stile and walk past newly planted trees on the edge of gardens of large modern detached houses.

In 75 metres you come to crossways. Go across the long distance trail, Hangers Way to the footpath opposite. Head northeast on a well defined elevated path over fields for over 1 mile. *Through trees on the right you catch glimpses of the Surrey Hills and ahead the spire of Binsted Church.*

In 600 metres you cross a track (leading to a barn on the right and a fine view beyond). In another kilometre you reach a copse then the lawns of Wyck Place on the right. Go straight on over the driveway and avenue. (Wyck village, including an oasthouse can be seen on the left).

Turn right at the tarmac lane and go down past cottages and Bumbles Farm until you reach a fork in the ways. Fork left and pass one or two further cottages. At the end you enter a Conservation Area. Turn left immediately.

Follow the hedge on your left and you soon find the path leads down the slope to the edge of woodland. You are heading north for ½ mile above a wooded hanger 'Storey`s Copse' on your right. ***Note** a footpath on the right into the hanger.*

On your return walk you come up from the hanger here.

In ½ mile you go down steps on the right into the wood to arrive at a junction with the Wyck Lane. Continue downhill on this track through trees for 50 metres only. Turn left at the first opportunity to escape to the fields.

The enclosed track, Wyck Lane, described as a traffic free cycle route, should be the nearest way to Binsted. But between the lakes there is a slough of muddy water where cyclists have lost their shoes and bicycle pumps.

Your escape route heads north at the lower edge of fields on the left and next to ponds on the right. The ponds are diminishing in size and become no more than sludge beds. In ¼ mile you enter woodland and look out for a finger post on the right.

Turn right here and go down into the wood, cross a footbridge over a stream that feeds the lakes. Climb up through the trees to a sloping field where the path climbs eastwards to Binsted Church.

Binsted

From Binsted Church cross the road to the parking space opposite. There is a footpath sign on the right. *The path straight on leads to the village pub.*

To return to East Worldham, take the branch to the right. This path passes behind the village hall and through horse paddocks to an open field. Keep to the hedge on the right and walk towards the buildings of Hay Place.

Turn right here and walk beside the driveway down on the left. You are heading south and keep on course across a field to a wooded boundary. Here is a stile into a mini hanger. Slide down the short steep slope into a little meadow below. Head towards a stream that runs along the valley. Just before the stream turn right and go through trees to the tarmac lane.

Turn left and continue along the narrow lane for 500 metres. When you reach a cluster of houses at South Hay, turn right into the tarmac farm road.

Climb eastwards to pass South Hay Farm on the left. The road is now high in the fields and you can look across to Binsted Church on the right. Follow the road as it bends right to Stubbs Farm in a sheltered hollow.

Go past barns towards the main farmhouse and turn left at the first cottage, the Granary. Go behind the cottage where a narrow path sinks gradually down beside a field on the left and a fringe of trees on the right.

At the bottom you are level with the lakes of the outward walk. Follow the path across this spongy ground harbouring fronds of mares tails to find a welcome concrete bridge across the feeder stream.

The next hurdle is the low hanger, dark with trees, looming ahead. Do not despair! Look to the left! Steps have been cut into the side of this hanger. It is a short climb up to the familiar path of the Conservation Area.

Turn left and retrace your steps up to the cottages and Bumbles Farm. When you reach the footpath on the left to Wyck Place, **you have a choice:**

Return along this footpath that brought you here.

Road route: continue to the hamlet of Wyck where the road bends left and leads to a **junction.** Turn left here and walk down Wyck Lane.

Find an alternative **field route**, adding 1 mile to the distance.

For the field route, continue to the **junction** in Wyck and cross to the enclosed track opposite. It heads southeast for 500 metres and leads to a barn. Turn left here and follow the hedge on the left for 350 metres.

Just after crossing a Roman road, the path bends left towards Wyck Lane. You leave the main path here and turn sharp right to continue southwest for another 150 metres. Now turn right to follow the hedge on your left (O.S. map shows the hedge on your right). At the end of the hedge veer right to a farm lane. *You now have views along the lane as it delves through farmland on the right and ahead to a wooded hill.*

Turn left to walk along the farm lane for 250 metres to the dominant building of Clay`s Farm. You join Hanger`s Way here. Turn left and follow this long distance footpath through the garden of Clay`s Farm and behind the gardens of other cottages. You may see the bell tower of East Worldham Church on the left. Hanger`s Way bears left and takes you steadily southeast across flat fields for ½ mile to East Worldham

At Wyck Lane turn right then left into a path through houses called Windmill Fields. It opens into a lane and leads to the church.

Walk 10: Farringdon to Chawton

Here is the landscape that Jane Austen knew towards the end of her life. She worshipped at Chawton, but Farringdon is the church she would have recognised today

Starting Point: Farringdon Church (you may have to find a parking place in the village if there is a service). **GR**713354 **Map:** OS Explorer 133
Terrain: Mainly flat, some along a disused railway line, some over fields.
Distance: 6 ½ Miles (5 ½ Miles if you decide to return the way you came).
Local Information: Chawton House was home of the Knight family for 400 years. Jane Austen`s brother, Edward (1767 – 1852) was adopted by Thomas and Catherine Knight, who had no children of their own. He inherited the estate with Elizabethan manor house in 1784. He set about replacing the formal gardens with naturalistic landscape. In more recent times (1993), an American lady, Sandy Lerner has saved the house from decay. She has also brought a large collection of books by women writers, mainly 1600 – 1830. Added to this is The Knight collection of books, familiar to Jane Austen. They are on loan to the library. For details of **Chawton House Library**, phone 01420 541010.

In 1809 Edward provided his mother and sisters, Jane and Cassandra with a home in the village, now known as **'Jane Austen`s House'**. Jane wrote her last novels here. She was frequently at Chawton House. She had friends in Chawton and Farringdon.

In Farringdon 'Massey`s Folly' is the large red brick building opposite the church. The Rector, T.H. Massey, with the help of a carpenter cum bricklayer, spent 30 years in building it – for a school? It is now in need of repair.

The Churches

Farringdon, The Church of All Saints has a long history, much of it lost in the mists of time. It may stand on a pagan holy site. The yew tree west of the church is thousands of years old. Godwin the Priest held the village of 'Ferendon' before the Conquest. Whatever the religious predecessors, the present church has a neat 13th century tower with narrow lancets at the lower stage and an upper stage rebuilt in 14th century. Wall paintings of circa 1340 are hidden from view in the tower. The present nave ceiling conceals them. The nave, sensitively restored in 1999, retains its simple beauty. The 12th century north aisle has three plain wide arches. The west bay is the widest and highest. It may have replaced a chapel in the northwest corner. The font also dates from the 12th century. Two fine late 14th century windows on either side of the south entrance have plain glass. The brick porch has the date 1634. Woodpeckers have wrought damage to the spire this century. The wooden tiles have been removed to allow a metal lining, then replaced.

Farringdon to Chawton

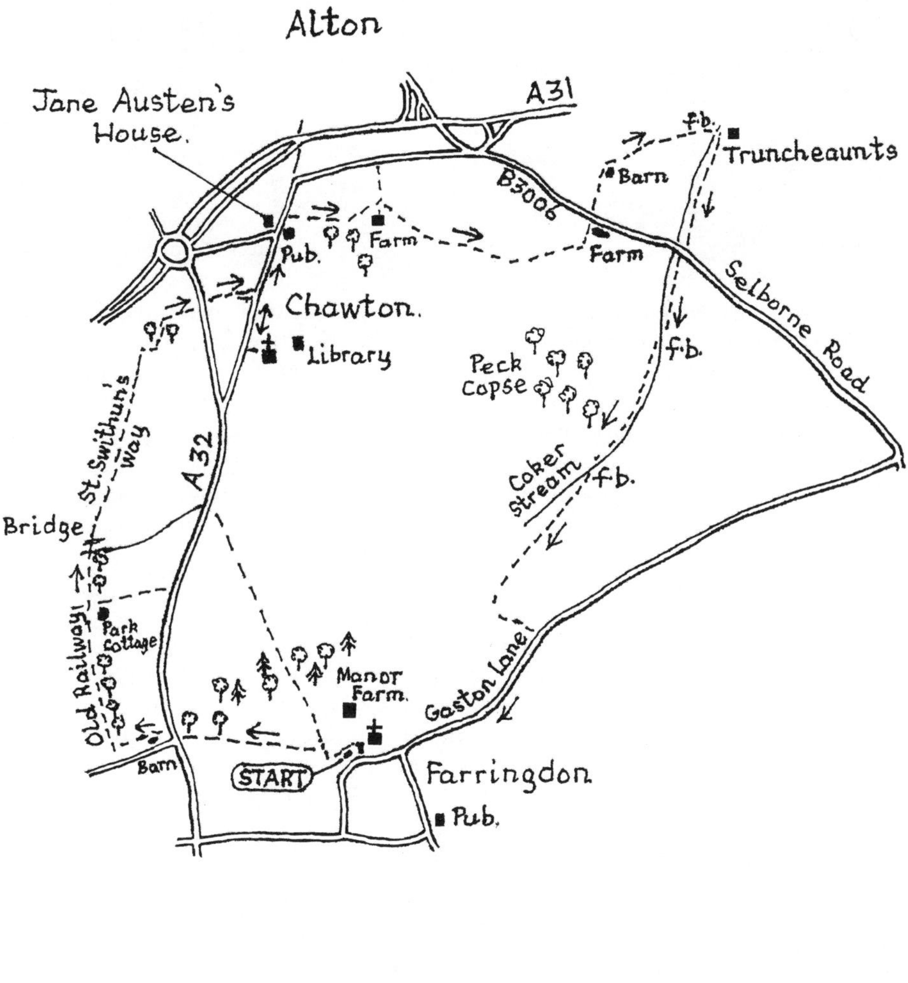

Farringdon

Chawton, St Nicholas Church is on the pilgrim route from Winchester to Canterbury. (We walk a short distance on St Swithun`s way). William the Conqueror gave the village of 'Cheltone' to Hugh de Port, a pious man who became a monk. A church, probably built here between 1225 and 1250, is first mentioned in a list of churches in the Winchester Diocese in 1270. In 1578 the Knight family acquired the manor and passed it on to the Bishop of Winchester in 1953. In 1838 Edward Knight and his son Charles overhauled the church and, in so doing, spoilt the chancel screen and destroyed the wall paintings. Restoration continued until 1871 until the nave was destroyed by fire. The new church 'designed by Sir Arthur Blomfield has many beautiful things: a screen crowned by rood figures a reredos finely painted, attractive altar rails, and nine delightful candelabra bought with the earnings of the village carving class. Rescued from the old church are a 15th century bell, a tablet of John Hinton who had been rector 58 years when he died in 1802, a rather pompous monument to Sir Richard Knight who lived in the manor house in the 17th century...' – Arthur Mee (see Bibliography at the end).

The Walk

From Farringdon Church take the wide track, fringed with lawn, up to Manor Farm. Turn left and take another track behind houses on the left. It heads west on an elevated course. Avoid forking right and keep straight on gently downhill. You have a good view over the hedge on the left to sloping fields and scattered woodland.

At the bottom cross the A32 to a footpath just to the right of a road. The path curves right to pass a barn on the left. Then follow trees on the left up to the disused railway. You have joined St Swithun`s Way.

Turn right to head north on the firm surface of the tree-lined track. You have an easy straight way for over 1 mile. In ½ mile you pass crosspaths Shortly afterwards, you pass a farm road on the right then go under an old bridge over the railway.

Your rail track veers imperceptibly to the right. You emerge from the trees and continue past fields. You are now on an elevated footpath heading towards the roundabout at the junction of the A32 and A31.

Fortunately, you avoid the roundabout. Turn right then left through trees then right again and walk down to the A32.

Cross the A32 with care to the footpath opposite. Climb a stile to enter an enclosed path. Another stile releases you to a residential road, Ferney Close leading to the Arcadian world of Jane Austen in the village of Chawton.

Turn right at the T-junction and you soon come to Chawton House and Church.

After your visit here, retrace your steps to pass Ferney Close on your left and recreation grounds on your right. At a road junction you will see Jane Austen`s red brick house on the corner on the left. The pub is opposite.

Note: *if you are short of time or unwilling to brave a plethora of stiles ahead, I suggest that you go back to Ferney Close and return to Farringdon by the way you came along the disused railway line.*

To return over fields from Chawton to Farringdon, continue past Jane Austen`s House on the left and the pub on your right. This is the old Winchester Road with individual houses familiar to the Austen family. You are heading north towards Alton. In 50 metres turn right into a narrow path between hedges.

Fortunately you soon emerge to the countryside, but <u>not</u> the Arcadia of Jane Austen territory! After a short climb, avoid the woodland walk on the right. Keep straight on then veer left across a small field with an assortment of animals, passing the untidy enclosures on the right where noisy geese guard a duck pond. You are making a detour of Eastfield Farm on your right.

Chawton

Cross the access track to the footpath opposite. Go through the squeeze stile and veer right and southeast across field corners with more stiles. At the fourth field you come to a farm gate with no footpath sign. Go through the gate then follow the hedge on the left. Make for Whitehouse Farm in sight ahead.

Here you are again restricted to a track that bends sharp left to the B3006.

Cross this busy road with care to the footpath opposite. Once over the stile, you will find two tracks leading into a desolate landscape. Follow the one on the right for nearly ½ a mile. First it leads to an industrial building. Go through the yard, so that the building is on your right. When you can go no further, turn right then immediately left to continue in the empty field.

The path follows the field boundary on your left and curves imperceptibly to the right. Keep going and you should see a finger post ahead and a house on a hillock beyond. First, cross a footbridge to a T-junction and turn right.

Chawton House Library

You are heading back south on an old tarmac track following a tall hedge on your right. In ¼ mile you are again at B3006.

Cross this busy road diagonally right. The footpath is hidden in the hedge. Look under the overhead wires! Once safely in the field, you follow Caker Stream on your right. In ¼ mile at the field boundary, turn right to cross a low grassy footbridge over the stream. Turn immediately left and keep on course. The stream is now on your left. You are walking through large flat fields of sheep. Follow a tall hedge on the right with Peck Copse beyond. The hedge curves to the right. Look out for another footbridge over the stream on the left. Cross again, turn right to keep on course on the other side.

You soon come to another long hedge on the left to guide you for over ½ mile to the way out of this long field. You come to a farm gate into an enclosed track. Enter the track, turn sharp left at a T-junction and you reach a quiet lane.

This is Gaston Lane. Turn right and walk along the lane for under ½ mile to Farringdon. (At a bend in the lane you can spy the church spire among trees).

5 Walks
in the Meon Valley

'A delightful corner of Hampshire, it lies with its interesting old cottages in the rich meadows of a winding valley, the chalky hills about it crowned with lovely trees. On these downs, 400 feet above the sea, the little River Meon rises, passing to a belt of woodland, the western end of the Forest of Bere, on to Wickham, and then on through six miles of orchards and farms to the Solent.' - Arthur Mee on East Meon. (See Bibliography at the end of this book).

River Meon

Walk 11: Titchfield Abbey to Titchfield with an optional walk in the Meon Valley to the estuary at Titchfield Haven in the Solent

The Abbey, village and Church have retained their ancient character despite nearby conurbations. The walk can be extended to include a riverside Nature Reserve, a haven from South Coast urban sprawl.

Starting Point: Abbey Nursery on Mill Lane **GR**542065
Map: OS Explorer 119 **Distance:** 1 Mile + 6 Miles to include the Haven
Terrain: Flat. A pedestrian crossing over the A27. The riverside walk is rural and may be muddy in places.
Local Information: 1. Titchfield has medieval and Georgian buildings around the central square. The town was a flourishing port at the head of the estuary until 1611. The third Earl of Southampton made himself very unpopular when he built a wall across the mouth of the Meon and had the land drained for farming.
2. Titchfield Canal In an attempt to maintain their port, the people built a canal, one of the oldest in England. It was small and not of much use to them then but has become a valuable asset to walkers and nature lovers today. Over the centuries it has developed into a limpid stream flowing gently southwards between miles of meadowland on one side and farmland on the other. In places oak and ash trees shade the water. Willows and rushes also benefit. Approaching the Solent, a branch of the canal veers left to join the Meon and walkers are left with a rather lazy stream.
3. Titchfield Haven National Nature Reserve open Wednesday to Sunday has bird watching hides. Entrance £3.60. Tearoom and shop free. Open Wednesday to Sunday and Bank Holidays. Phone 01329 662145.
3. The River Meon flows through the Nature Reserve and enters the sea at Hill Head Harbour.

The Churches

Titchfield Abbey was founded in 1232 by Peter des Roches, Bishop of Winchester. The Premonstratensian monks wore white habits. After the Dissolution, the place was given to Thomas Wriothesley who built himself a mansion. Place House became the home of the Earls of Southampton. The third Earl of Southampton was a patron of Shakespeare who may have written some of his plays whilst staying here.
The Parish Church of St Peter, Titchfield is likely to have been founded by St Wilfrid in Saxon times. The Saxon porch, with its course of used Roman tiles, is one of the oldest in England. It was extended upwards in the late 12th century to form a tower. The shingled broach spire was added in 15th century. The weight of tower and spire on the Saxon porch has caused problems over the ages. The Victorians did the most thorough

Titchfield Abbey to Titchfield and an optional extension to the Solent

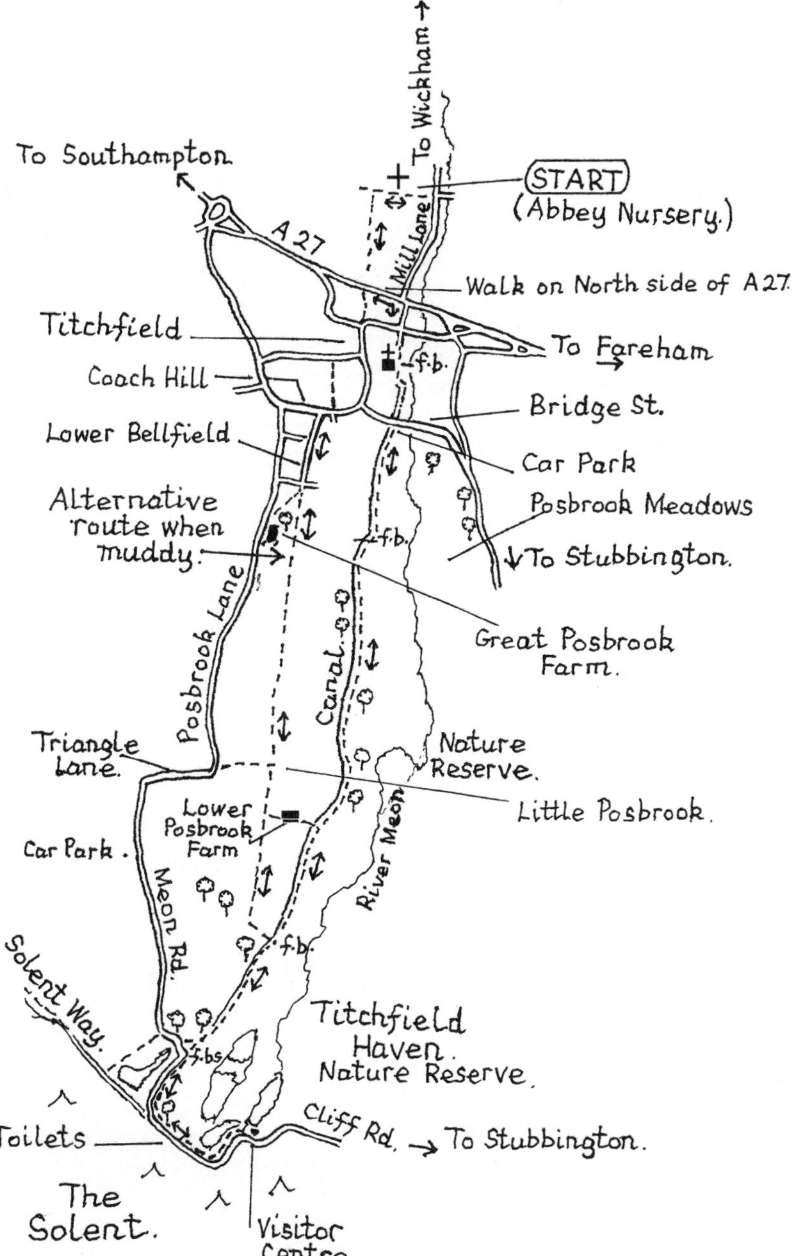

Titchfield Abbey

repairs and fitted an iron tie around the tower at a height of 12 feet 6 inches. The clock was added in 1887. Normans entered the porch, 4 or 5 centuries after it was first built, and created a fine entrance arch with carving in zigzag, leaf and other shapes, all in pristine condition still. The nave, tall and slender, maintains the proportions of the Saxon church. An early round-headed window, high in the west end was unblocked in 1982. The monks from the Abbey left their mark on the church. They are probably responsible for the building of the spacious north aisle in 15th century in Perpendicular style and the grand windows. At the same time, or slightly later the chancel was widened and reduced in height. The Victorians remade the chancel east window as it was inferior to those in the north aisle. Unfortunately in 1867 they rebuilt the Norman south aisle. The south chapel, added in 14th century, has become a mausoleum to the Wriothesley family who acquired the Abbey at the Dissolution. (See Titchfield Abbey above). They have a huge chest tomb with several alabaster effigies. More poignant is the monument on the south wall of 1615 to the little girl, Mary, daughter of the third Earl.

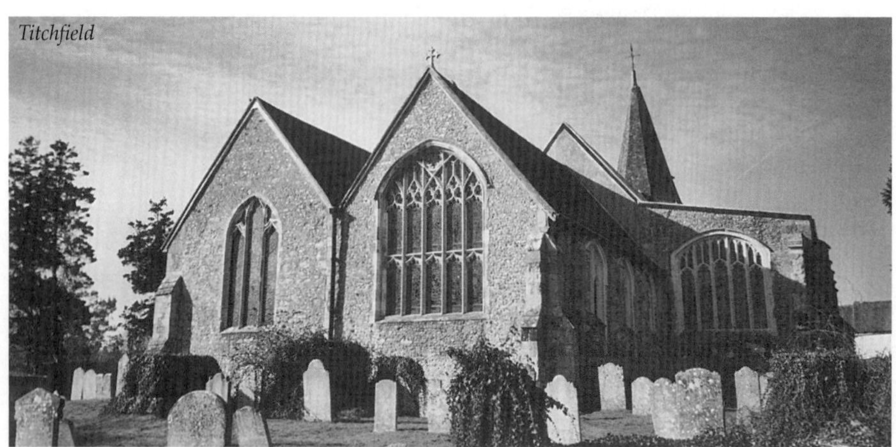
Titchfield

Titchfield

The Walk

To visit the Abbey from the car park, walk to Mill Lane, turn left and the entrance is nearby on the left. Return to Abbey Nursery for the main walk.

A track leads between the Abbey Nursery and the car park. Walk up this track for 250 metres. The Abbey is on your right. Ignore a path on the right. Shortly after this, turn left into a path heading south.

When you reach the A27, it would be unwise to cross to the path opposite. Instead turn left and go down on the pavement to traffic lights. Cross here to a quiet road on the edge of Titchfield, Mill Street.

Walk to the end of the street then turn left and immediately right into Church Path. This leads directly to the spacious, grassy churchyard.

For the short walk: *leave the churchyard at the main entrance by the tower, walk along the short lane to the High Street. After browsing in the village, retrace your steps to Abbey Nursery.*

For the full walk: go through the churchyard to the southeast corner where you will find a bridge over the old canal that runs alongside the River Meon. You are on the Meon Valley Trail for 2½ miles to the Solent.

Turn right and walk beside the canal for ¼ mile as far as Bridge Street.

If you are finding the ground too wet, you can escape here, turn right and walk along Coach Hill on the southern side of the village as far as Lower Bellfield. Turn left here and keep going until you reach a footpath and open country. This path leads south for 1½ miles to eventually rejoin the canal walk by crossing a ***bridge*** *on the left.*

Continue south on the canal walk with views across the nature reserve on the left. Soon after the **bridge** a branch of water veers left towards the river. The path now follows a slow moving canal. As it approaches Meon Road, the path divides. Fork left on an enclosed path beside and below the road.

When you reach the sea, turn left. There are public toilets opposite. Walk along the irregular promenade. You can enjoy views across the Solent to the Isle of Wight. In ¼ mile you reach the sailing club at Hill Head Harbour and the Visitor Centre at the entrance to the Nature Reserve and refreshments.

To return to Titchfield, retrace your steps along the canal.

Walk 12: Exton - Meonstoke - Corhampton
with a possible extension up to Old Winchester Hill

Three contrasting churches confront each other over the River Meon. Saint Wilfrid brought Christianity to this region in 7th century.

Starting Point: Exton Church, roadside parking in the village **GR**614211
Or An informal car park outside Exton, just west of A32 **GR**618213
Map: OS Explorer 119 **Terrain:** Flat, apart from the optional extension
Distances: 3½ Miles
Add another 3½ Miles if you extend the walk to Old Winchester Hill
Local Information: The South Downs Way follows an ancient route at this point, linking two Iron Age forts: Beacon Hill to the west and Old Winchester Hill, in the parish of Meonstoke, to the east.
The River Meon was wide and navigable in the Middle Ages. The Old Meon Valley Road was built then.

The Churches

Exton, St Peter and St Paul stands on the site of one of the earliest settlements in the Meon Valley. In Domesday (1086), the name 'Essessetun' means 'East Saxon Town'. Exton was on the eastern edge of Wessex. The Saxon church would have been wooden. The present flint building replaced it in the 12th or 13th century. It is a simple church consisting of nave and chancel with a solid bell turret. It has been much restored. The lancet windows are quite big. At the east end they are filled with delicate leaf colours; apricot, brown and orange. The design is by Charles Spooner (1898). He also drew the 'Tree of Life' stencil behind the altar.

Exton

Exton to Meonstoke and Corhampton with extension up to Old Winchester Hill

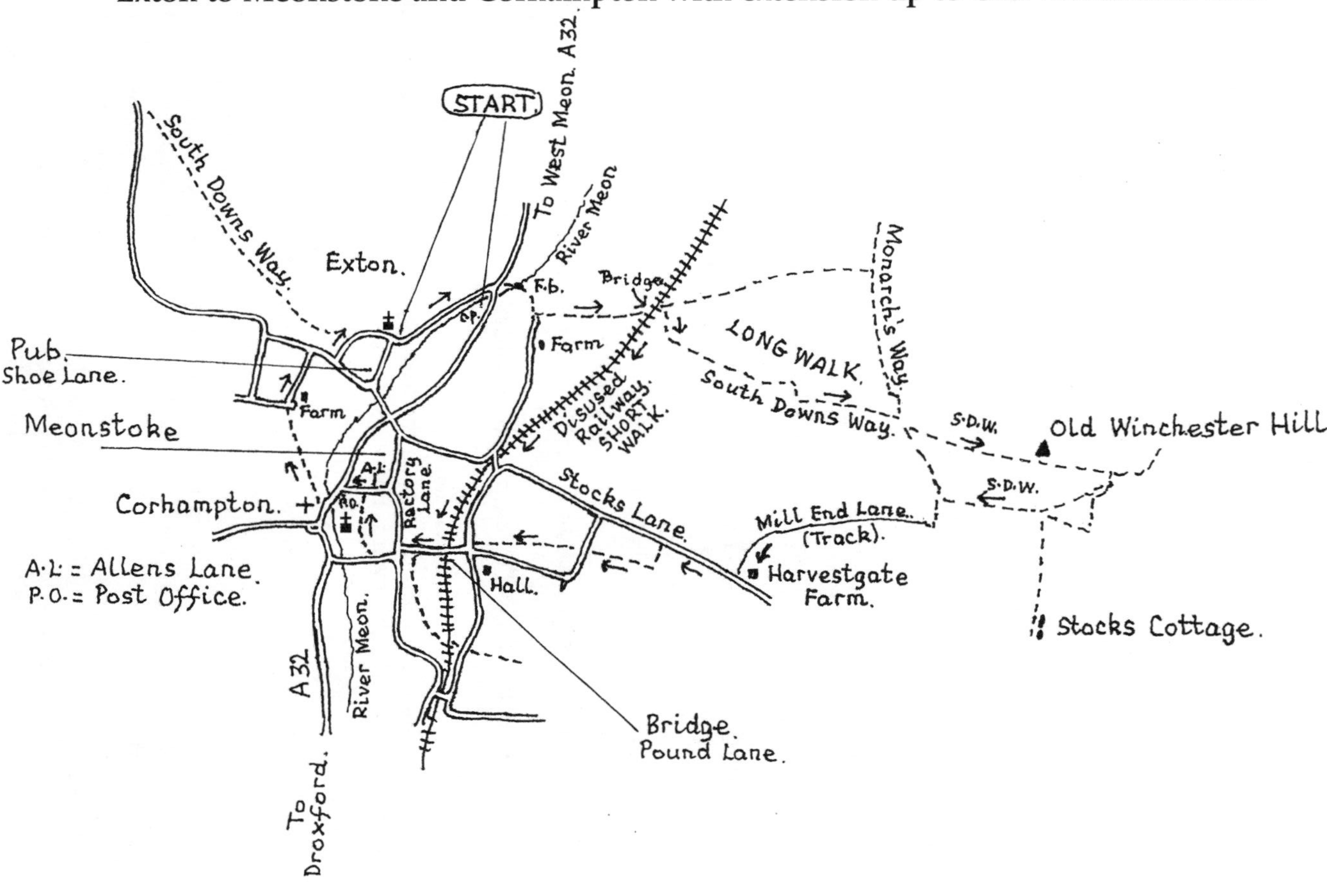

St Andrew`s Church, Meonstoke is on the other side of the River Meon in a slightly elevated position so that it has escaped flooding. The village was important in 'Meonwara', the province of the Jutes. How did Wilfrid cross the river when he came on his pilgrimage? It was wider then and the enemy tribes did not build a bridge. There would have been an earlier wooden church in 'Menestocke', mentioned in Domesday. The present church was started in 1230 in Early English style. Since that time, the only major changes have been made in 15th century. The tower was rebuilt then of flint and rubble. The roof over the chancel is also 15th century. At that time the aisles had separate roofs. In 18th century they were removed and the new roof was built over all. The nave, now higher, seemed to dwarf the tower. The distinctive open cap was added to the tower in 1900. Henry V1 visited Meonstoke in mid 15th century. The village folk must have felt they could cock a snook at their rivals across the river.

Corhampton Church has no dedication. Wilfrid converted the people of Cornhamptone to Christianity. The church stands in a circular, possibly Pagan enclosure. It is a small Saxon church, built of stone in 1013 to replace a wooden structure. Fortunately it has escaped restoration. Saxon features include two blocked doorways, the chancel arch, the 'long and short' stones at the corners and the pilaster strips that recall the upright wooden beams of the earlier church. There is also a Saxon sundial with 8 'tides' next to the porch. Only the brick east wall is out of keeping. Inside the church, there are 12th century wall paintings: the expulsion from Eden on the chancel arch and events in the life of St Swithun on the chancel walls.

The Walk

The South Downs Way passes in front of Exton Church. With your back to the church, turn left and walk along Church Lane. Pass Shoe Lane on the right. Your lane curves to the left heading away from the village. The River Meon flows beside this lane. Just before the A32 you will find the car park mentioned above.

Cross the main road diagonally left to a footpath, still the South Downs Way. You now enjoy going over a wide bend of the River Meon on a footbridge. The path then curves to the right towards Shavards Farm.

Avoid the track to the farm. Turn left following South Downs Way into a narrow path on the line of a hedge. It heads eastwards above the bed of a dry stream on the right. In 500 metres climb up steps to the disused railway line. For the Short Walk look below*.

For the long walk up to Old Winchester Hill, *turn left on the railway line then immediately right. Descend to follow the bed of the stream again. In 50 metres you reach a finger post at a junction. Avoid the footpath to the left and fork right for South Downs Way. It takes a southeasterly course along the edge of wide sloping fields with occasional bends. You are climbing gently beside a hedge on your right. Old Winchester Hill is in view. In nearly 1 mile the track joins Monarch`s Way for the final climb.*

(If you do not fancy the climb to the top, take an early opportunity to turn right into a field, an alternative route of South Downs Way. When SDW turns left, you cut across to ***Mill End Lane,*** *see below).*

Meonstoke

Corhampton

To reach the top of Old Winchester Hill, *continue climbing on the enclosed path through woodland then downland. At the top you pass tumuli and the ancient arena of the Iron Age hill fort. The views are extensive in all directions. Keep on course through the middle.*

To descend the hill: *when you reach the far end of the fort, you pass a seat with a view to the north. Go through the nearby wide gate and you soon find a finger post. Turn right into South Downs Way. There are vines growing on this side of the hill. The path takes you back on yourself for 50 metres then plunges down to the left for 125 metres.*

Near the base of the hill, you leave the enclosed area and turn right on a grassy platform with views over farmland to the left. In ¼ mile turn left, leaving South Downs Way. (Walkers who took the easy route join here). In 125 metres at a field corner, turn right into a track, ***Mill End Lane.***

In ½ mile Mill End Lane leads to the byway, Stock`s Lane. Turn right and walk for ¼ mile to a footpath on the left. This heads south across a wide field then takes a sharp turn right to a lane. Cross the lane to the footpath opposite and skirt behind some houses to reach the far left corner of the field

*You have now reached Meonstoke, cross the bridge over the disused railway and continue on the Short Walk below**.*

***For the short walk** turn right on this elevated railway track, going over the stream bed. In 1 Kilometre you reach Stock`s Lane. No bridge over this lane survives. You have to descend to the lane and cross to the path diagonally left opposite. Climb up to the track and keep on course for another 400 metres. The track is now in a cutting with banks on either side. You reach the bridge carrying Pound Lane over the railway line. Leave the line here climbing steps on the right up to the lane.

Turn right towards the village of Meonstoke.

** ***The long walk joins here.*** Pass new bungalows and continue to a T-junction. Rectory Lane is on the right.

Turn left to a junction in the centre of the village. Turn immediately right into Bucks Head Hill. Stop just short of the pub and turn right into a narrow lane. Meonstoke Church is ahead.

Just before Meonstoke Church, find a footpath through the churchyard. It heads north past spacious gardens on the right and leads to Allens Lane.

Turn left and walk to the village stores and post office. It is on the corner with the A32. Cross this main road again diagonally left to Corhampton Church. Pass a private access road on the right. You have to walk past the church to find the path up to it.

From Corhampton Church, return to the access road and turn left. Follow the path past the north wall of the church then turn right into a short cul de sac. Pass an ancient brick and timber house on the left.

Climb the stile next to the farm gate. Here is an enclosed path at the edge of a field. The River Meon flows past the far edge. The path curves to the right, passes Exton Farm and leads to Allens Farm Lane.

Keep straight on along the lane to a T-junction. Turn right to the village of Exton and left into Church Lane. Exton Church is on the left. Then Shoe Lane on the right leads to the pub. Or the informal car park is straight on.

River Meon, Exton

Walk 13: Soberton - River Meon - Droxford

A riverside walk between churches, then a gentle climb to open downland

Starting Point: The road in front of Soberton Church, Station Road
Map: OS Explorer 119 **GR**611167 **Terrain:** Mainly flat, one slope
Distance: 3 Miles

The Churches

St Peter's, Soberton was built as a chapel of ease to the mother church of Meonstoke. The east window is Decorated with reticulated tracery. The glass is Victorian. The 15th century tower was added to a Norman church. The tower is Perpendicular with carvings of animals and heads at the top. Below them is a carving of a skull, two heads, a key and a purse. They remind us that servants managed to collect £70 in Hampshire, a building fund for the tower. The main body of the church was renovated in the 16th century. As a result, the area of the church best preserved in its antiquity is the south transept, built in 12th century. It is named after a Bishop who fled from Oliver Cromwell to Soberton, 'the Curle Chapel'. His memorial is in the corner. On the walls are faded murals dating from 1330. They have been interpreted as the Virgin Mary and Child, St Anne, St Katherine of Antioch and St Barbara.
Droxford, St Mary and All Saints Church is situated near the River Meon in a Saxon village. It was called 'Drocenesford' in a charter of 826. A Saxon cemetery has been found in beech woods above the village. Inside the present medieval walls of the church is a Norman building, the most noticeable feature being the chancel arch. The pillars of the nave, the east and west ends form the boundary of that 12th century Norman church. The north and south doors of that church were removed and added to the larger building in 13th and 14th centuries. The north aisle was added in the late 12th century and the south aisle in the 14th century. We enter the church through a Norman door. There are four medieval sundials; two in the south porch and two outside on the south wall. The east window has fine 15th century masonry; the Victorian glass in it was damaged by a bomb blast in the Second World War and has been replaced. The tower is late 16th century. Dormer windows in the steep roof are 19th century. New stained glass depicting Noah's Ark is in a window in the south wall. It is a beautiful work of art by Vanessa Cutler. Parishioners raised the money for this window to celebrate the Millenium.

The Walk

From Soberton Church go back a little way towards the road. Take the footpath on your left. It passes between the church and a green and leads to a narrow lane, Cutts Arch.

Turn left into the lane, joining the Wayfarers Walk. The lane bends right, then left and crosses the bridge over the disused railway line.

Turn right into a meadow above the River Meon. Wayfarers Walk heads northwards for 1 mile. The river is to your left and the railway line on your right. You go through a small grove of trees then veer gently left over more meadows. You can see Droxford Church ahead. Follow a hedge beside the river then turn left at a field corner.

Soberton to Droxford

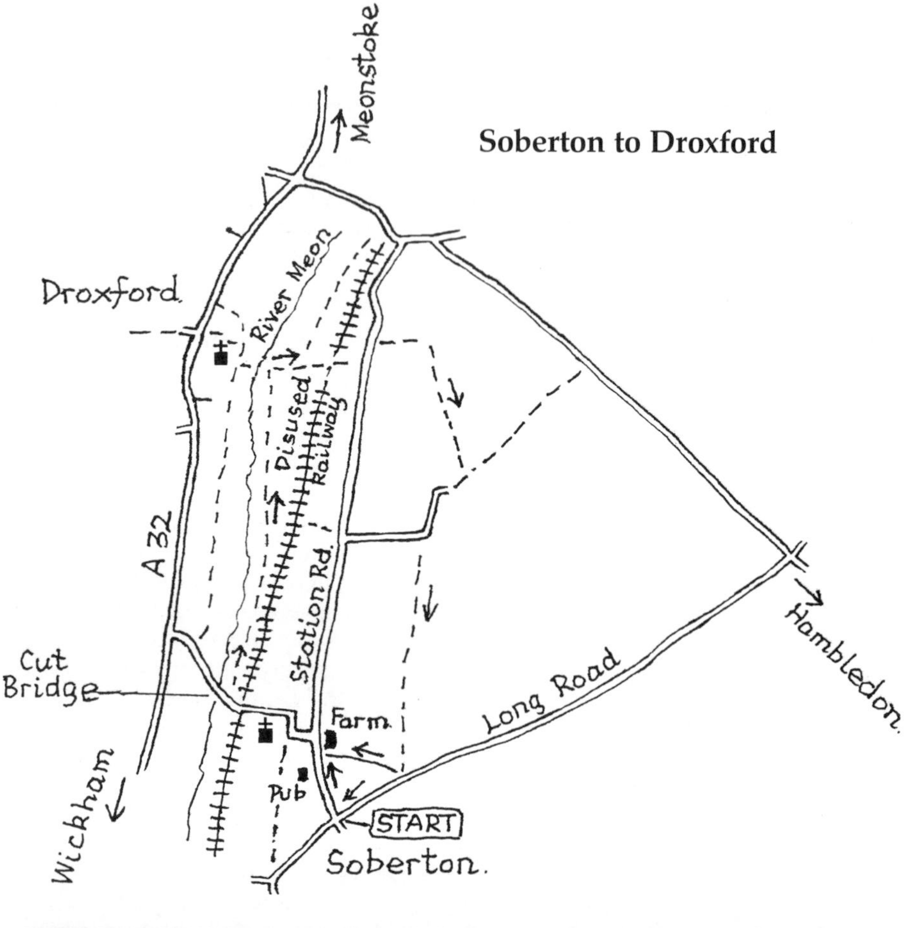

Meonstoke
Droxford
River Meon
Disused Railway
A 32
Station Rd.
Cut Bridge
Farm
Pub
START
Soberton.
Long Road
Hambledon.
Wickham

Soberton

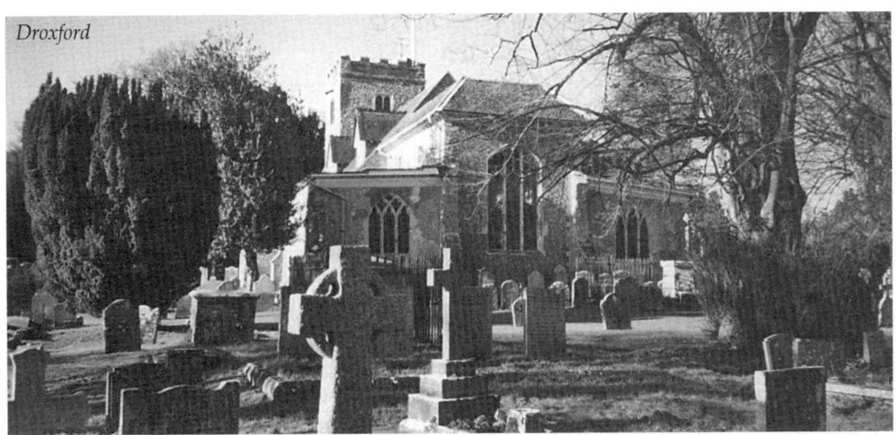
Droxford

Cross two footbridges. Wayfarers Walk takes you over the river and right up to Droxford Church. *If you wish to see the village where there are two pubs, keep straight on through the churchyard to the A32.*

From Droxford Church retrace your steps over the footbridges. Instead of turning right along the path that brought you here, keep straight on following the hedge on your right up the gentle hill. After a stile, avoid the path to the left and keep on course. Your path has a tight squeeze through hedges up to the disused railway line. Cross the bridge over the line and keep heading east.

You soon come to a lane lined with houses, Station Road. Cross the road diagonally left to another path that hugs the fence on the right then turns sharp right.

You have reached Little Common where there are no fences. You are heading southeast on a clear path over gently rolling open countryside.

All too soon you come to a T-junction. Turn right to join Crookhorn Lane. In ¼ mile leave the lane which bends to the right. Climb a stile into a field and keep heading south only veering slightly left to avoid enclosed fields. Pass these on your right. Ahead the trees on Soberton Down stand out against the sky.

In ½ mile you come down to Long Road. The track on your right leads straight to the church, past a muddy farm. *If you wish to keep your boots clean, turn right in Long Road and right again at the crossroads.*

The pub is next to the church.

Soberton

Walk 14: Warnford to Hinton Ampner and Kilmeston

Climb out of the Meon Valley and make for the Hampshire hills and woods towards the source of the River Itchen and Hinton Ampner tearooms.

Starting Point: Warnford Village, beside the watercress beds, Lippen Lane. **GR**624233
Map: OS Explorer 132
Terrain: Some slopes, some lanes some open fields **Distance:** 9 Miles
Local Information: 1. The A32 was built by prisoners of the Napoleonic Wars in 18th century. Before then, Warnford village was near the church. It is now ½ mile away. The Meon Valley Road ran close to the church. It would be a benefit to walkers visiting this church if the old road could be used as a footpath.
The ruins of a rare 13th century hall, built by the St John family, lie just past the chancel of Warnford Church.
Hinton Ampner House was burnt in a fire in 1960. The dining room Adam ceiling has been rescued. The gardens are the main attraction.

The Churches

The Church of Our Lady, Warnford is surrounded by private parkland. St Wilfrid may have made this place his base in 682 when he came to convert the heathens of the Meon Valley. There is a Saxon sundial above the south porch with the inscription: "Brethren, bless in your prayers the founders young and old of this temple; Wulfric founded it; good Adam restored it". Adam de Port held the manor 1171-1213. Little remains of the Saxon church that stood here in 8th and 9th centuries. It is contained within the existing Norman church and had an apsidal east end. The nave walls are 6 feet outside the Saxon walls. The nave and chancel are all one in this barn-like building. The continuity of the Early English windows on either side give it its character. The solid Norman tower of around 1130 was built of Quarr stone from the Isle of Wight. The big round bell openings are unusual. This modest country church contains two grand alabaster monuments in the chancel to members of the Neale family. They are early 17th century.
All Saints Church, Hinton Ampner stands in the grounds of the Manor House. It retains the proportions of the Saxon church that once stood here. The nave still has some Saxon remains. The 'long and short' stone work in the northeast and two pilaster strips north and south on the outside walls. The church was rebuilt in 13th century. The chancel has some details of that period. There is a sedilla and double piscina, also the priest`s door on the south side. In the floor of the chancel a memorial stone lies surrounded by some medieval tiles. The pulpit is Jacobean. The nave was rebuilt in1880. Lord Sherborne was seeking monuments. In 1970 the sealed entrance to the vault containing monuments was found. Two modern stained glass windows, the work of Patrick Reyntiens illuminate the east end:
"The Lord went before them by day in a pillar of cloud to lead them along the way, and by night in a pillar of fire to give them light that they might travel by day and by night" – Exodus, Chapter 13.

Warnford to Hinton Ampner and Kilmeston

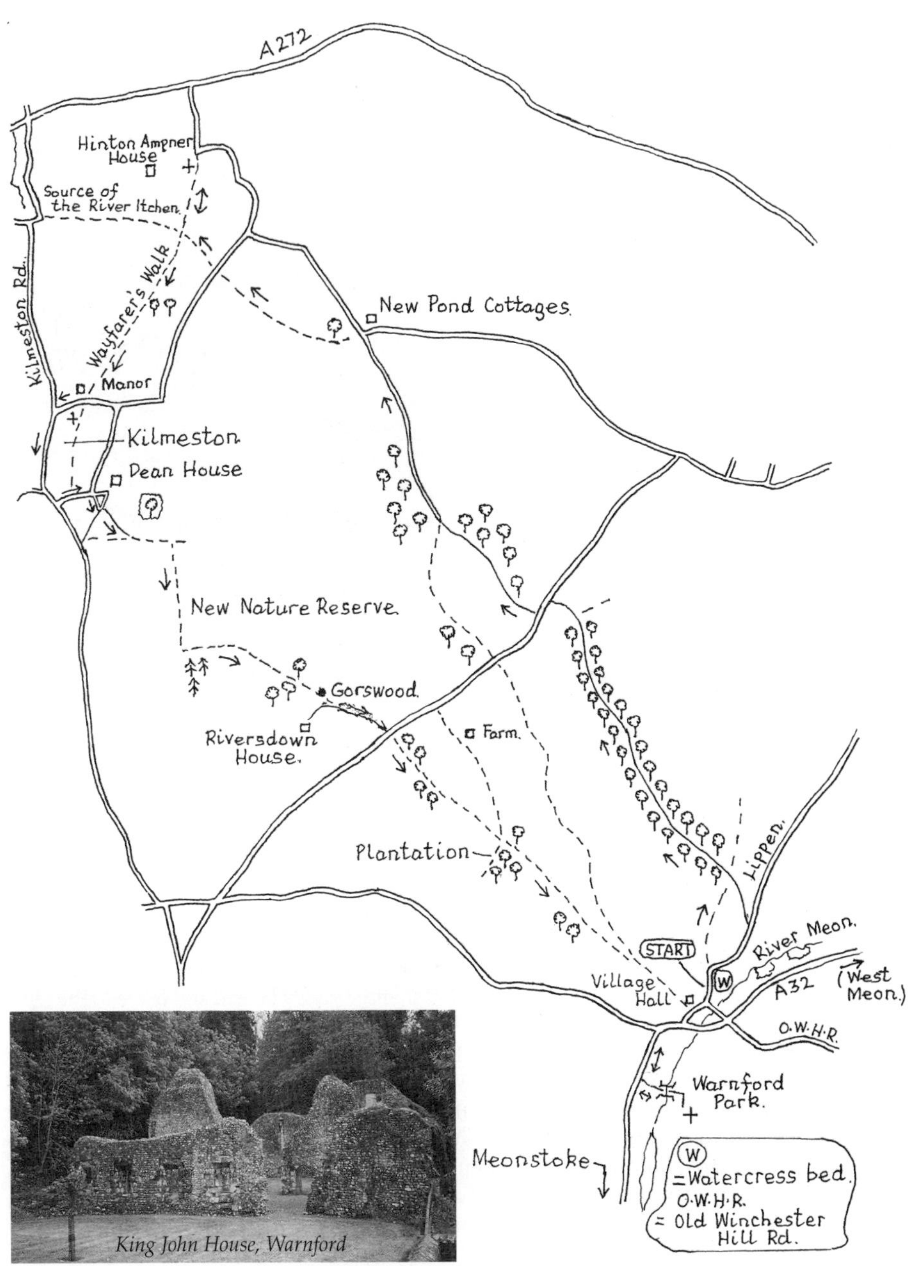

King John House, Warnford

The Walk

Detour to visit Warnford Church, either walk or drive ¼ mile south on the A32. There is a gated entrance on the left, set in from the main road. Cars are not allowed beyond the entrance.

Main Walk From the watercress beds continue north along Lippen Lane. In 50 metres the lane bends to the right. Turn left here into a short residential cul de sac. At the end of the cul de sac, turn right into a footpath across an open field below a hill.

In 450 metres the path crosses a line of trees. Turn left here and walk on the earth track with trees on either side. This is Bosenhill Lane and leads northwest uphill for over 1 mile. Trees obscure the view but give protection from wind and sun. It is a steady climb with occasional deep ruts. In spring you find bluebells, stitchwort and many curved stems with hanging white flowers, 'Jacob`s Ladders'.

Hinton Ampner

Do not turn until you come out at the top of the track. Avoid the green lane to the right. You turn left on the muddy track to the nearby tarmac road. Turn left on this elevated road. In 50 metres turn right into another tree-lined track with no apparent footpath sign. Resume your course northwest. The trees are less dense here. In ¼ mile a path joins from the left. You continue on your track which now becomes a tarmac lane through the rolling Hampshire countryside.

In 1 mile you reach New Pond Cottages on the right. Turn left into a byway, hugging the edge of a wood on the right. In 1 kilometre, cross a road to parkland with scattered trees and flocks of sheep.

In 200 metres Wayfarers Walk crosses your path. Turn right here on the enclosed path beside the garden of Hinton Ampner. In ¼ mile turn left for the church. National Trust tearooms, shop and entrance to the gardens are beyond the church.

From Hinton Ampner, return to the Wayfarers Walk and retrace your steps to the cross paths. Go straight on across the sweep of open parkland, heading southwest for 1 kilometre. First you reach a wooded corner. Turn round to look back at Hinton Ampner House. Cross the next field diagonally right to walk through a shallow valley before you come to the road on the edge of Kilmeston.

Turn right on the tarmac road and pass **Kilmeston** Manor on your right and the little church on your left. Continue along the village road to a T-junction with Kilmeston Road. Turn left heading due south past houses to the village green.

Veer left on the road to Warnford. Then immediately turn sharp left into the lane towards Dean House. In 250 metres turn right into a signed footpath passing in front of a cottage. The path crosses a track and takes a narrow enclosed way southeast. In another 250 metres pass a gap in the trees and veer left into a grassy lane between two hedges.

The lane opens to a field and there is a small copse to your left Follow the hedge on your right until you are level with the end of the copse. On your right there is an insignificant footpath sign and a narrow gap in the hedge.

Turn right and head south on a well defined path across a flat field. Keep on course in the next field. Ramblers are confined to a straitjacket between a tall metal fence and an encroaching hedge on the right.

In ¼ mile you have to turn left and pass a thick dark evergreen copse on your right. There are extensive views through the metal fence on your left. Once past the copse you can also peer through the fence on your right. *This fence is to protect a new nature reserve from the 'menace' of ramblers!*

You escape the straitjacket to enter woodland and emerge to a small golf course. Keep to the left hand side of the golf course – *there is nothing to protect ramblers from stray balls!*

Turn left when you reach the lane, the access road to both Riversdown House and the golf course. Pass a house called Gorsewood and continue down the lane under a light covering of trees.

At a T-junction, cross the road to a footpath in the field opposite. Walk beside trees on the left. In 100 metres go through to the other side of the hedge on the left. Resume your southeasterly course on a straight, clearly defined path for ½ mile. At the far corner of the field you enter woodland.

Avoid first the path to the left and then the track to the right. Instead take the narrow path, marked 'Footpath Only', and go through a young tree plantation.

You come out onto an elevated field. **Stop!** There is no footpath sign. Look across to the hedge on your right. It ends in 200 metres with a tree. The footpath cuts across the field corner to the end of the hedge. Make for the tree at the end of the hedge.

Turn right here and follow a track heading southeast, steadily downhill with wonderful views over the Meon Valley. Old Winchester Hill is ahead. In 500 metres pass Pinks Hill Wood on the right. Continue down to new plantations and veer left. Another path joins from the left. The track finally comes down through a farmyard and ends at the Warnford Village Hall on the left.

Turn left for the watercress beds.

Kilmeston

Walk 15: Oxenbourne Down near Butser Hill, South Downs Way, East Meon with an optional extension to Clanfield

From the height of the South Downs Way, we look down slopes to the spire and gradually approach the magnificent Norman church in a lovely village.

Starting Point: Cross ways at the top of Hogs Lodge Lane on the approach to Butser Hill. **GR**706191 **Maps:** OS Explorer 120/119 **Terrain:** Quite hilly
Distances: Short walk (To East Meon and omitting Clanfield): 7 Miles
Long walk (To East Meon and including Clanfield):10 Miles

The Churches

All Saints Church, East Meon is the grandest church in the Meon Valley. It is a fine Norman building, close to a rounded hill and overlooking a Saxon village. After the Conquest, the Normans replaced a humble Saxon structure with this cruciform church in flint and stone. Bishops of Winchester were lords of the manor who would oversee the building work from 1080 to 1150. The Court House across the road was the summer palace of the bishops. The Norman west door with round arch and carvings in leaf and zigzag was probably part of the early building. The magnificent tower with three richly carved bell openings on each side came later in that time span. It is similar in style to the tower of Winchester Cathedral. The lead-covered broach spire was added in 13th century. At the same time the Lady Chapel and the south aisle were built in Early English style. Their arches are pointed in contrast to the round Norman arches. Their larger windows admit more light into the church. The Norman south door was moved to this larger church. Architect Sir Ninian Comper refurbished the chancel and the Lady Chapel in 20th century. His influence can be seen in the east window, the altar and the screen between the chancel and the chapel. Two outstanding treasures in this church are: a rare, beautifully carved 12th century Tournai font and the 21th century Millenium Embroidery, a beautiful tribute to the artistic and craft skills of today`s parishioners. For more details, see the church history, a separate leaflet on the font and another leaflet on the embroidery.
Clanfield Church, St James is situated in an ancient manor, belonging to Earl Godwin, King Harold`s Father. The Normans seized all the land after the Battle of Hastings. Roger Montgomery took a leading part. After the Conquest he was rewarded with this manor. The present church is on the site of the old building. Usually the Victorians restored old crumbling churches. In Clanfield in 1878 they pulled down the old and built a new church. R. J. Jones designed a compact nave and chancel in 13th century style. Inside, the walls are faced with red and yellow brick, giving a warm effect. Outside the walls are flint and the two medieval bells are on display in the belfry. Improvements to the church in 2009 include a beautifully crafted vestry screen.

Oxenbourne Down near Butser Hill to East Meon and Clanfield

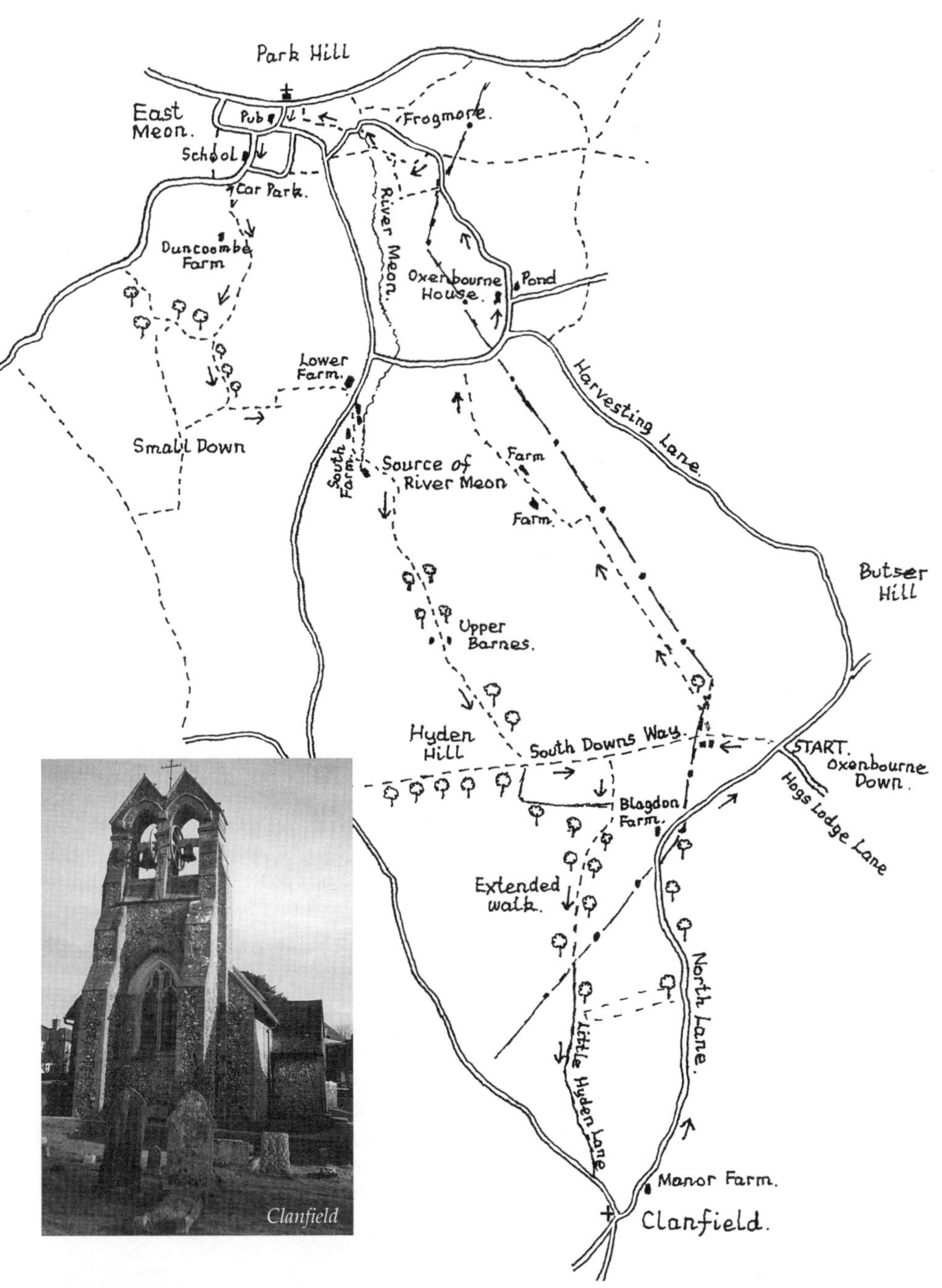

Clanfield

The Walk

Make sure your vehicle does not block any field entrance and set off along the straight track westwards on the South Downs Way. In ¼ mile, pass a tall hedge on the left with only monkey trees betraying a property there.

Immediately after a barn on the left, turn right into an enclosed bridleway. On your descent northwest, look down over fields and trees in dips to the church of East Meon in the distance. Beyond the wood on your right, a line pylons takes a parallel route.

In one mile the bridleway bends left than right to form a firmer track and resume its course northwest, passing farm buildings. It is not so steep now.

In one kilometre you come to a T-junction. Turn right and walk along the byway to pass the pylons and go under the power line. The lane curves left to cottages at a road junction.

Turn left and head due north towards Frogmore. Avoid a turning to the right. Keep straight on along the lane past Oxenbourne House on the left. It overlooks a delightful pond where snowdrops cover the banks in February.

Continue along the lane for ½ mile. Avoid the first path on the left. Just round the corner another path on the left leads into a small flat field. Follow the trampled path to the corner and ignore the finger post in the hedge. East Meon Church forms a better guide. Follow a short enclosed path to the right, it passes the River Meon and a thatched cottage on the left. Do not enter the garden. Instead, keep on course down to the village lane.

Turn left on the lane and pass the front of the thatched cottage. Go over the river on the road bridge, then cross it again on a footbridge. You have another glimpse of the church.

The footbridge takes you to a footpath to Eames Cottages. Turn left and pass close to this terrace. Next pass a vegetable allotment. You come to crosspaths beside venerable buildings. Turn right and walk up to the main road, passing the 14th century Court House with its high roof. East Meon Church is to the left. Cross the road with care.

From East Meon Church, follow the main path down through the lych gate. Look out for traffic and cross to Church Street opposite. Walk to the end of the street. You have a good view along the Meon of the High Street on the left. Turn away from this view towards The Old George. Pass this pub on your right. Turn right then left into Chapel Street. Pass the school on the right. The road bends to the right and there is a small car park opposite.

Turn left and go through the car park to a footpath leading to wide open fields. Head south, passing Duncoombe Farm at a little distance on the right. In one kilometre you enter woodland and veer right up to a gate. Emerge from the wood and turn immediately left to follow a thick hedge on the left.

Keep beside this hedge for ¼ mile and avoid climbing the slope on your right. You pass one metal farm gate on the left and come to a similar gate facing you on the left. This is your turning. There are no signs on the gate but if you peer down the slope, you will see a finger post below.

Go down to the finger post and follow the route eastwards across lower fields. Follow the field boundaries on the left. After the first field, turn left then right to keep on course to Lower Farm.

East Meon

Here you come to the tarmac road and cross to the footpath near a cottage opposite. Turn right to cross a small bumpy field. In the left corner you gain access to the main drive through the buildings of South Farm.

Turn left on the concrete drive and wend your way through the buildings then down past fields to a bridge over a natural water course. You have reached the source of the River Meon. The drive continues up past Spring Cottage and a boggy hollow down on the right.

Pass a horse arena on the left. The drive bends left and begins the climb uphill. Saunter up through a delightful avenue ending with Upper Barns, one on either side. Veer left across a field to an enclosed downland path. You now have a steep climb up Tegdown Hill with woodland on your left. At the top veer left to join the South Downs Way.

Turn left and walk eastwards for one mile along South Downs Way back to Hogs Lodge Lane. *In ¼ mile along the way, pass a footpath beside the hedge on the right.*

To extend the walk to Clanfield, turn right into the above footpath beside the hedge. Follow the hedge on the right. In 450 metres the path veers right into Hyden Wood and continues on its course southwards for 2 kilometres. At first the path is enclosed then open to bluebell woods on the left. At the end of the woods, avoid the path on the left and carry on your way southwards. Your path becomes an enclosed track merging with Little Hyden Lane and leading down to Clanfield. Pass a school on the left. At a T-junction, turn left to crossroads.

Clanfield Church is nearby on the right. *There are shops opposite.*

To return to the starting point, from Clanfield Church, turn left. Go back to crossroads. Cross into North Lane. It heads north for 1½ miles up to the corner with Hogs Lodge Lane. On the way you pass Manor Farm and Lowton`s Copse. Avoid paths on the left that lead back into the bluebell woods. The lane veers left at Byden Copse. It veers right at Blagdon Farm and heads northeast to the cross ways at Hogs Lodge Lane.

5 Walks
Near the River Itchen

River Itchen, St Cross

Hampshire was covered in forest in prehistoric times and the valley of the Itchen was an oasis in agriculture. The Celts improved the fields by adding chalk loam to the soil, a method known as 'marling'. The river rises near Hinton Ampner (Walk 14) and it has tributaries further north, notably the Arle which gave Alresford its name. The river was a means of transport. Immigrants came here from the continent. The Romans arrived in 43 A.D. and built a road from Winchester to Silchester. They also built a canal to channel some of the water away from the town of Winchester. This canal is known today as 'Itchen Novigation'. See Walk 16. 'Weirs Walk', between the canal and the old walled town, has a surviving piece of Roman wall near the City Mill. The nearby City Bridge was originally built in 9th century for the Bishop, St Swithun. Hundreds of mills on the Itchen provided wealth to Winchester and other centres. At Alresford another Bishop, Godfrey de Lucy built a dam across the river and dug a huge reservoir. He wanted to make the river more navigable. Now this great chalk stream draws discerning people who live in the pretty riverside villages or come here for leisure pursuits, walking and angling. The Itchen Way is a long distance footpath that follows the river to its confluence with the River Test at Southampton Water.

Walk 16: Chilcomb to Winchester

From a humble early Norman church nestling in trees under the hill, take a pilgrim route through country ways to the old capital of Wessex to find one of the finest cathedrals in the land.

Warning: nearby Chilcomb Down is an MOD firing range. There are red flags and locked gates when they are practising. To find out whether firing is planned on the day of your walk, phone the Range Warden: 01962 853663
Starting Point 1. : Chilcomb Village on the grass verge where the South Downs Way follows the village street. **GR**507285
Starting Point 2. : Winchester Train Station **GR**479299
Map: OS Explorer 132 **Terrain**: downland, riverside, town and country.
Distances: The circular walk from Chilcomb: 7 Miles
A shorter linear walk to Winchester on the South Downs Way : 5 Miles
If starting from Winchester Station, add 1Mile
Local Information:
**St Catherine`s Hill** with its rounded top, is a popular landmark near Winchester. It offers views over the city and countryside. Rings of ditch fortification are from the Iron Age. St Catherine`s Chapel on the ramparts was demolished under Henry V111 in 16th century.
Historic Buildings
St Cross Hospital was founded in 1136 by Bishop Henry of Blois to provide accommodation for 13 poor men and refreshment for 100 travellers. He might be amazed to find almshouses still here.
Winchester College was founded in 1387 by the energetic Bishop William of Wykeham so that students could go on to New College, Oxford to train to be priests. The Plague had wiped out many priests.
Wolvesey Palace was the traditional seat of Bishops, starting with Saxon Ethelwold in around 970. Henry of Blois replaced it in around 1129 and it became a great centre of ecclesiastic power in the medieval period. In 17th century Bishop George Morley built a new baroque palace using material from the old building. Most of the old palace is now a ruin.
The Great Hall and the Round Table stands near the site of the great Norman castle, the seat of government. Henry 111 rebuilt the castle and this magnificent hall (1235). It has survived when all around perished in the Civil War. Inside is a medieval version of King Arthur`s Round Table

The Churches

St Andrew's Church, Chilcomb. Despite its idyllic setting on a wooded hillside, at a distance from the busy roads around Winchester, the peace of Chilcomb is often shattered by gunfire. (See 'Warning' above). Parishioners have to plead with the MOD warden for respite during services – not always successfully! It was not always thus. Go back to 636 A.D. when the Saxon King Cynegils gave the large estate of 'Chiltecumbe' to the church. The Dean and Chapter of Winchester Cathedral have held this estate until 1900 – over 1000 years. During that time the land here has been used for agriculture The Saxon influence on the building of this church can be seen in its tall, narrow shape, in the small windows in the

Chilcomb to Winchester

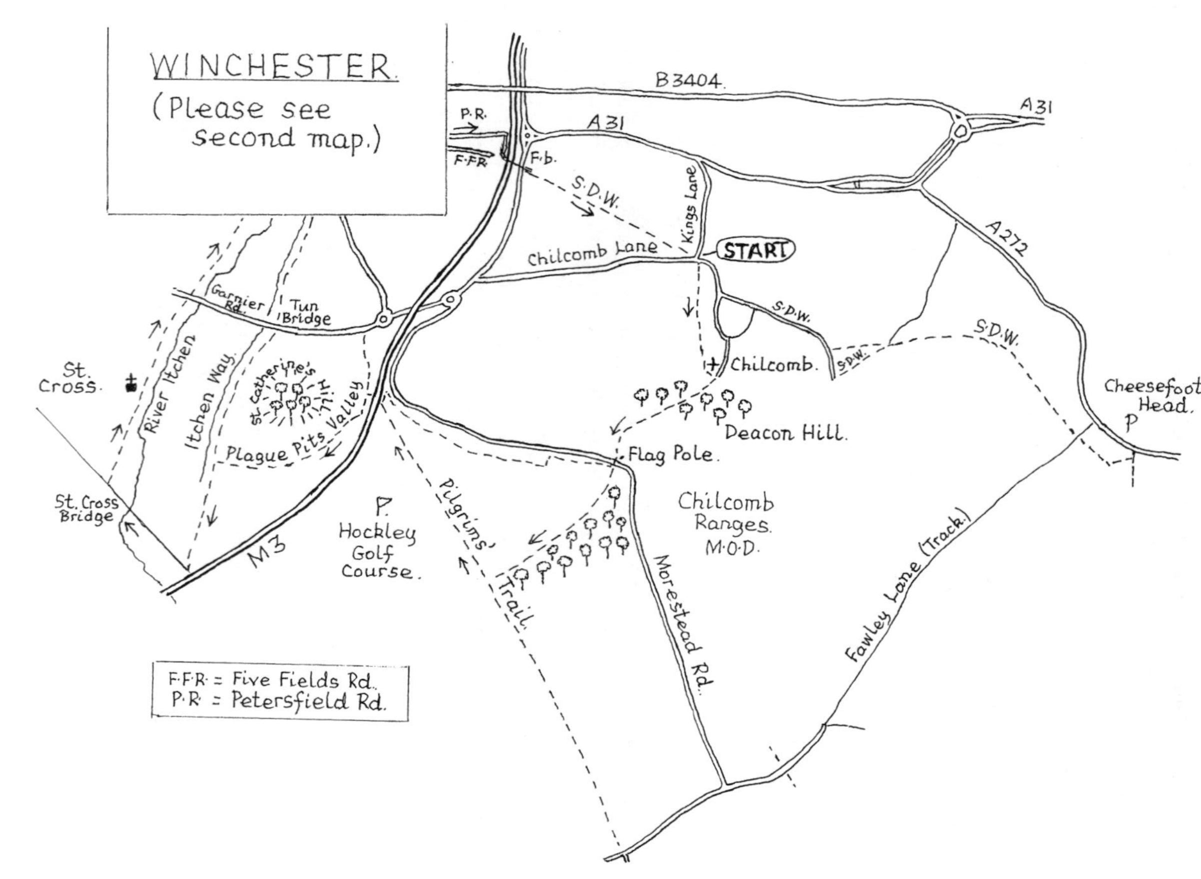

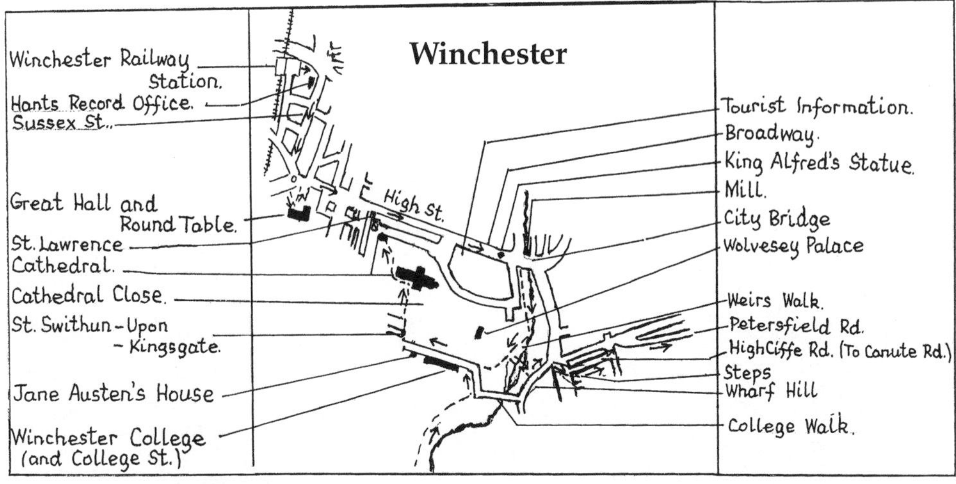

Chilcomb

eastern gable. The chancel arch is small and unsophisticated. The church is fortunate to have been overlooked by reformers and restorers so that it has changed little since 1060. Medieval tiles are laid in the floor of the chancel. Contemporary artists have made furniture in keeping with this rustic building. Notices welcome walkers.

Winchester Cathedral

You need plenty of time and some money (about £6 entrance) to enjoy the rich history of this cathedral. King Alfred (871 – 899) made Winchester his capital and his bronze statue stands in Broadway. The town already had a church, the 7th century Old Minster. This was replaced in 10th century with a New Minster. The Normans demolished the Saxon building but retained the ancient monuments. They did not waste any time. The new Bishop Walkelin began rebuilding the cathedral in 1079 in the shape of a cross. It was an expression of Norman power. The three storied north and south transepts of that sturdy building have

Winchester Cathedral

survived. The original Norman crypt can be visited in summer via steps from the north transept. In the winter it may be flooded. The modern statue in the crypt, 'Sound 11' by Anthony Gormley has been designed to stand in water. The first tower collapsed in 1107. The replacement tower is short with strong piers. Even the piers of the nave were Norman, embellished in the14th century to appear completely Perpendicular. This subsequent beautiful work of master mason, William Wynford, under Bishop William of Wykeham took from 1366 to 1404. The magnificent nave has 12 bays. The succession of piers with slender mouldings rise to the ribbed vault in harmonious splendour. The Quire, between the transepts, has some of the oldest choir stalls in England. Carvings made 1308 –1310 depict an enchanted forest with many creatures, including a musical monkey. There is a fine reredos or screen originally carved around 1420, behind the main altar. Next, heading eastwards is the Retrochoir, a square space for walking. Appropriately, it contains a fine array of medieval tiles, the earliest dating from 1230. Finally, we come to the Early English chapels at the east end. They include the Lady Chapel. The Perpendicular east window has seven lights.

This outline has omitted the many beautiful works of art and architecture inside Winchester. They really deserve the best part of a day to do them justice. One man I cannot omit is deep sea diver William Walker who saved the cathedral from collapse early in 20th century. He spent five years under the east end, digging out rotten timber from the raft of beech logs and replacing it with bags of cement concrete to make a firm foundation.

St Cross Church dates back to 1160. Simon Jenkins in 'England`s Thousand Best Churches' describes it as 'a Norman Cathedral in miniature'. He also admires its setting among water meadows. The chancel with round headed windows is the oldest part. The chancel aisles have doorways with zigzag carving. The north transept is also rich in zigzag. The nave is Transition Norman. Later vaulting of 14th century has the arms of Bishop William Wykeham on the bosses. At that time the church was thatched. Crusaders left for the Holy Land from this church.

St Swithun-Upon-Kingsgate is a tiny church above one of the two ancient city gates.

Anthony Trollope in 'The Warden' makes Harding describe it as 'a singular little Gothic building perched over a gateway, through which the Close is entered, and is approached by a flight of stone steps...'

St Lawrence in the Square is tucked away between the High Street and the City Museum. It has a pleasant 15th century interior. It is a tradition for bishops to pray here before their enthronement.

The Walk

From Winchester Railway Station: leave by the main exit (platform 2). Walk straight on down the approach road and take the first turning right. This leads along Sussex Street, past the Hampshire County Council Offices. At the roundabout turn left for the High Street *Or straight on for The Great Hall with the Round Table.* Walk down the High Street, part of it a traffic- free precinct. At the Buttercross turn right, go under the arch to St Lawrence in the Square, the City Museum and on to the Cathedral. Continue at *Walk to Chilcomb below.

From Chilcomb

Head south on the road towards Chilcomb Church. Pass a lane on your right and one or two handsome houses on your left. Avoid turning left, on the road taken by South Downs Way towards Eastbourne. Instead, fork right and pass one or two further venerable houses. You come to St Andrew`s Church at the end of the lane.

Pass the church on your right and keep straight on through the gate at the end of the lane (and the start of the Ranges). A path here skirts through trees on Deacon Hill then climbs to come out on an elevated field. Walk across this field heading for a flagpole at the far edge of the Ranges.

You reach Morestead Road. Cross to the track opposite and follow it down for 1 kilometre. At first your way is tree-lined with woodland on the left. The trees give way on the right and you pass a wide cultivated field.

At crosspaths below, the trees peter out. Turn right to follow Pilgrim`s Trail up a pleasant downland path. Pass a golf course on the left then come to a fine view over Winchester. Go down to cross the M3 on a sturdy bridge

The bridge takes you to the east side of the famous St Catherines`s Hill in an Area of Outstanding Natural Beauty. Follow the clear path leading gently down through the valley where sheep pasture, below the hill on your right.

Too soon you come out of this lovely place to Itchen Way. Here is a firm track beside the old canal, Itchen Navigation. Turn left to walk on this dank path for 500 metres, heading back towards the A3. The canal dries up but there is a disused railway line. Soon after going under a bridge you come to a gap in the line on the right. Here, unsigned, is tarmac Five Bridges Road.

Turn sharp right into this straight narrow road to the River Itchen. Pass over St Cross Bridge where you have views upstream to an island then a mill and downstream to meadows.

In another 150 metres turn right into a footpath towards St Cross Farm. Here is a stile into a muddy field. Follow the stream on your left to reach a fine, traffic free avenue and a view to St Cross Church and almshouses. Pass the church on your left then turn left to find the entrance to St Cross. **After visiting St Cross,** resume your path. The River Itchen is nearby on the right. Clarendon Way has joined your path northwest for nearly 1 mile. When you come to Garnier Road, cross diagonally right to continue beside the river on your left. Playing fields of Winchester College line the river. The College Chapel (omitted from our crowded itinerary) can be seen ahead.

You have to swing to the right to avoid the private entrance. Then turn left into College Walk leading to Wolvesey Palace and a path to the right.

Turn left into College Street. Pass Winchester College on the left then turn right and go through the medieval gateway, originally Roman. This is Kingsgate where stone steps lead up to the little chapel. Continue through the Close to Winchester Cathedral. Enter at the West End.

St Cross

From Winchester Cathedral cross the forecourt to City Museum. Head for the arch and find St Lawrence in the Square. Go through to the High St.

If you wish to see the Great Hall, turn left.

***For the Walk to Chilcomb,** turn right and walk down Winchester High St. Pass TIC, the Guildhall and Abbey Gardens on the right then the statue of King Alfred in the middle of Broadway. Keep going to Bridge Street and, opposite City Mill, now a Youth Hostel, turn right into Weirs Walk.

Here is a popular walk beside the River Itchen on the walled boundary of the Roman town. In 50 metres, a piece of Roman wall can be seen on the right. Keep to the riverside for 250 metres then turn left to cross a bridge.

You come to a grass triangle and walk up Wharf Hill, passing a pub on the right. Continue up to crossroads where there is another pub on the left. Cross the main road diagonally right to steps that lead up to a house, Sunny Mount and a road, Cathedral View. Veer left to continue along Highcliffe Road. At the end you come to Canute Road. Turn left then immediately right to pass a flint church on the right. You are now in Petersfield Road. At a fork in the road there is a South Downs Way sign.

Avoid Fivefields Lane to the right and fork left to continue along the more elevated Petersfield Road. Detached houses are perched above on the left and you have a view over the outskirts on the right. At the end, do not be tempted up a new residential road on the left. Instead turn right into a track that leads to a footbridge on the left over M3 and A31.

After crossing the motorway, avoid the cycle route. Instead, turn left on the South Downs Way Pedestrian route. Go through a kissing gate to the open field. You are now homeward bound, following the hedge on the left. You can enjoy a wide view to the right over open fields to Chilcomb Church nestling in the wooded hill. In 1 Kilometre you reach Chilcomb Lane.

Turn left for the village. Turn right for the church.

If you started at Winchester Station, *go to the beginning of this walk and continue at the heading,* 'From Chilcomb'.

If you did not check on the Ranges and you find they are closed, *you will have to head back to the South Downs Way and retrace your steps crossing the M31 and the motorway to the outskirts of Winchester. See the map.*

Walk 17: Cheriton to Tichborne

The River Itchen links two contrasting villages and churches that have developed in very different ways. We take a downland route to visit them.

Starting Point: half way up Hill Houses Lane, north of Cheriton Church
GR579286 **Map:** OS Explorer 132
Terrain: Undulating **Distance:** 5 – 6 Miles
Local Information: Tichborne is not just a pretty village. You can find more about its fascinating history in the booklet, available in the church, £3.
Tichborne House has been the seat of the Tichborne family since 1293. The present house was built in 1803. The estate is private. We pass the following on our walk: **Sevington Farm,** Manor House for the Bishop of Winchester probably dates back to Saxon time **Grange Farm**, a 17th century farmhouse. The coachman lived above the arch of the coach house. **The Old School House** was built in 1870 near the church.
Gander Down has prehistoric field boundaries and burial grounds.
The Battle of Cheriton (1644) was a decisive victory for the Parliamentarians. The battle site, east of the village is not on our route.
Advice to Ramblers: Do not be deterred by the sign, 'Restricted Byway'. You have a right of way along these tracks. The sign 'Private' is another matter. Apply to locals for permission to walk there or find an alternative route, as I reluctantly have had to do.

The Churches

The Saxon estate of 'Ticceburne' included Cheriton and Beauworth. Farmers had to pay their overlord, the Bishop of Winchester a rent of ale, bread, ox, sheep, pigs and cheese. If the Danes attacked the farm he was exempt!
Tichborne Church, St Andrew was built on a hill above the village in mid- 11th century. The chancel still has some Saxon features: a double splayed window and pilaster strips on the outside walls. In 12th century the south then the north aisle were added. The arcade arches are thick and plain. In around 1330 the Saxon east window was removed. It was replaced with a larger window with three lights and reticulated tracery. The Tichborne Chapel in the north aisle is separated with railings. It contains monuments of that family, established here since 1135. There is one alabaster monument of 1621 to Benjamin Tichborne, his wife and 7 children. For his support of King James 1, he was rewarded with titles and allowed to worship in this chapel as a Catholic. The brick tower was added in 1703. The church interior retains an air of great antiquity with few changes over the centuries. There are some Jacobean enclosed pews. Four Millenium windows in the south wall celebrate agricultural festivals: Plough, Rogation, Lammas and Harvest.

Cheriton to Tichborne

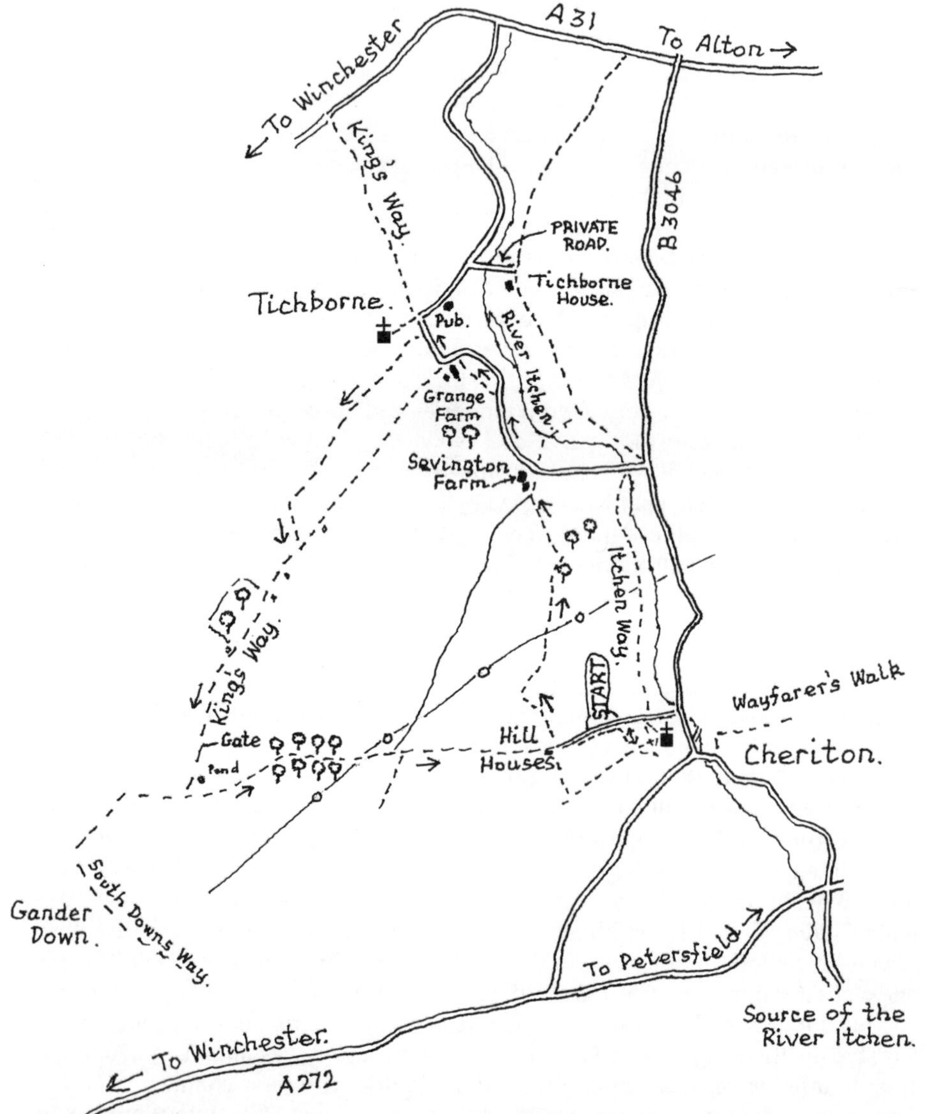

Cheriton

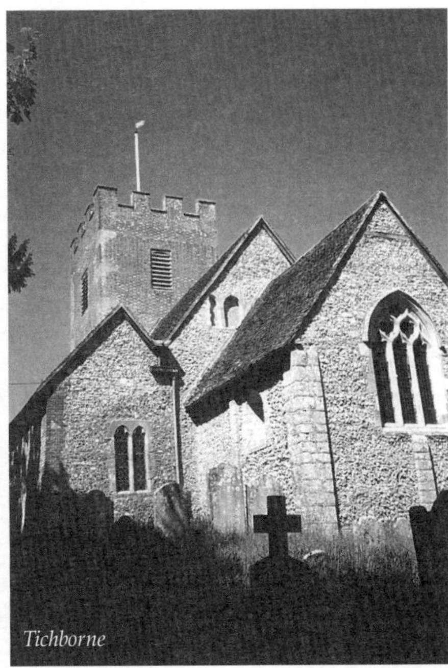

Tichborne

The Church Of St Michael And All Angels, Cheriton is also built on a little hill. The steeply sloping east end did have a crypt below. The Victorians filled in the crypt, first removing all the monuments, some of them 13th century. Henry de Blois, Bishop of Winchester (1129 – 1171) established a church here. The building has changed radically since then. In 13th century the church was enlarged. On either side of the nave, arcades of three bays and round pillars were added. The high arch to the tower is 13th century. The chancel has two lancet windows facing each other. The chancel was enlarged in 15th to 16th centuries and has an assortment of Perpendicular windows. The east window has four lights. The unmatching windows in the north and south walls may have been inserted after a major fire in 1744. The fire destroyed windows and even melted the bells. Fundamental repairs were needed. The Bishop gave replacement timber and the rector had the chancel repaired. The remaining cost of over 650 pounds was raised and the church restored in two years. Some of the 13th century porch may have come from Beauworth Church, abandoned in 1517. The heads of a bearded man and a woman in a headscarf may be from there. The curly carvings below the heads are a mystery. There is a Norman scratch dial on the right side.

The Walk

Continue on foot up Hill Houses Lane to the top. Just before you reach the houses ahead, turn sharp right.

First pass two houses then continue on the elevated tree-lined path. You enjoy fine views over the Hampshire countryside. Keep the oak and ash on your right and in ¼ mile turn right into another avenue.

A new aspect has opened over fresh fields. Head north down over the field towards a signpost on the edge of a copse. Go through this strip of trees to a track leading down to **Sevington Farm** where you join the Tichborne lane.

Avoid the path opposite, leading to the Itchen, as you need to stay on this side of the river. Instead, turn left and walk along the hedge-lined lane with glimpses of water meadows on the right.

In ¼ mile, after a wood, turn left into a path that cuts off a loop in the lane. Pass the barns of **Grange Farm** on your left and rejoin the lane at a pair of semi-detached cottages. Turn left. At a nearby bend, pass a farm track and bridleway on the left. You are now entering Tichborne village.

Take the first turning to the left; there is a sign to the church. Note the path to the left, described as a 'Restricted Byway'. Follow the road as it bends to the right to visit Tichborne Church. *If you wish to explore the village and the pub, continue past the church and take an enclosed path down to the tarmac lane. Follow the lane around bends, passing several thatched cottages. The pub is on your right. Further along the lane past the pub there is a private road to the River Itchen and a bridge over to a pottery and a walk on the other side, Itchen Way. This long distance path leads beside the river back to Cheriton. But we cannot trespass!*

Return to the 'Resticted Byway' near Tichborne Church and follow this enclosed track, heading southwest for 1 kilometre. At first there are hedges on either side, then the ground opens on the right. Keep following the hedge on the left and look out for an insignificant path. You can peer through the hedge down to a barn below.

Turn left and cross a field down to a farm track at the bottom. Avoid turning left back to Grange Farm. Instead, turn right and resume your southwesterly course for another kilometre walking along the farm track. On the way you pass three separate barns and a small wood. When you come to a gate, go through to an open field. You are approaching **Gander Down**.

Follow the arrow straight ahead and you pass a small, enclosed pond on the left. In another 50 metres turn left at a scarcely discernible T-junction with no signpost. You are going back on yourself slightly and pass the other side of the pond, still on your left.

Head for the thick hedgerow over to the northeast. (If you had turned left when you first went through the gate you would have followed the field boundary up to this hedgerow). Walk uphill beside the hedgerow on your left and you enter a delightful strip of elevated woodland where bluebells grow.

In 250 metres you leave the woodland under power cables. Veer left to head due east on a tarmac farm road through open fields. Avoid all turnings.

After ½ mile the road turns right. You go straight on along the track to approach Hill Houses from the top end. Continue on this familiar road, walking downhill for ¼ mile. A path on the right leads up a bank to a field with a view down to Cheriton Church.

Walk down to visit the church and then return to the starting point.

Walk 18: Easton to Martyr Worthy
Kings Worthy and Headbourne Worthy optional extra

This walk is based on 4 fine churches near the River Itchen. There are views of the river, footbridges over the river and subways under the motorway.

Starting Point: Church Lane, Easton (limited parking near the church, you may have to seek a space in the village if there is a service) **GR**509322
Map: OS Explorer 132 **Terrain:** Flat, riverside
Distances: 5 Miles the whole walk
3 Miles if you omit Kings Worthy and Headbourne Worthy
Local Information: The name 'Worthy' comes from the Saxon 'Wordie', meaning place or hamlet. In a Saxon charter of 868, King Ethelred granted land at Worthy to Thagn Hunsi. It is not clear which Worthy. There are two pubs in Easton and one in Kings Worthy.

The Churches

All four churches are on or close to St Swithun`s Way, a pilgrim route from Winchester to Canterbury. (See Long Distance Paths at the end of the book).

St Mary`s Church, Easton near a quiet backwater of the River Itchen, retains much of its late Norman character. The lower part of the tower and the tower arch are original. The south door has Norman shaft rings and two windows of the nave are Norman. The chancel arch also has shafted responds. The large apse at the east end is Victorian. In 1860 Woodyer made an imposing restoration of the church, including the intricate top of the tower. The Victorian rood screen replaces an earlier one of 15th century and is probably similar to the original. There is a memorial to Agatha Barlow who died in 1598. Her remarkable achievement was to produce five daughters who each married a bishop and two sons, one of whom was rector here for 48 years. The wooden panels of 1909 were the gift of John Freshfield, a minister here for 50 years.

Easton

Easton to (Kings Worthy, Headbourne Worthy), Martyr Worthy

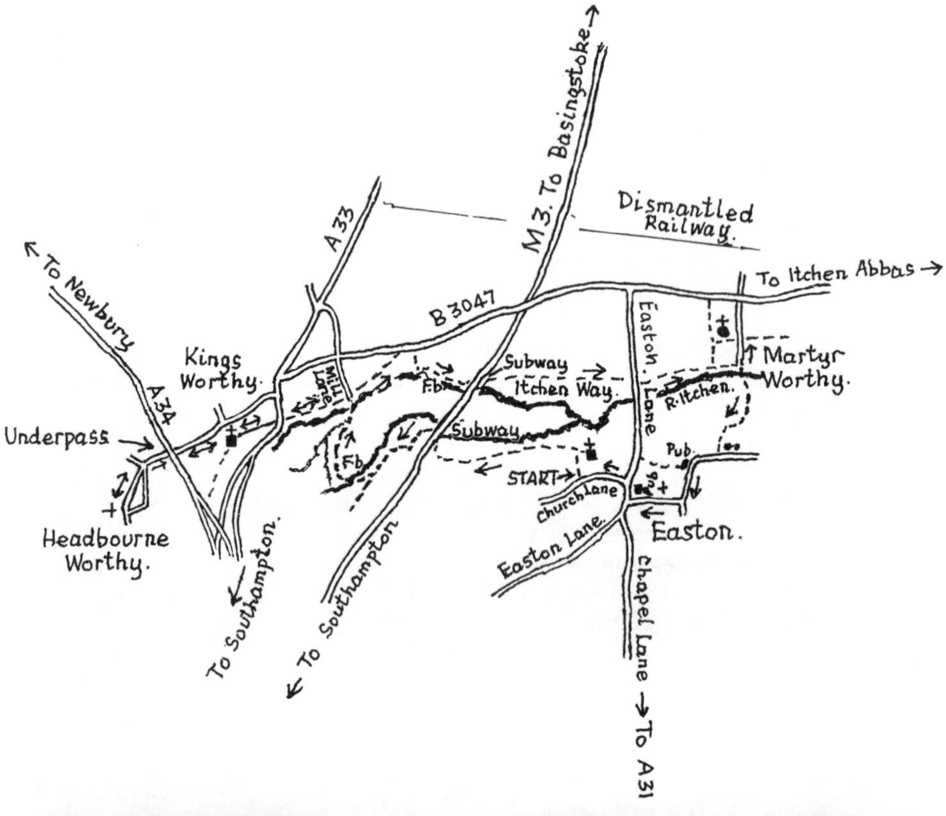

M3. To Basingstoke
Dismantled Railway.
A33
To Newbury
To Itchen Abbas
B3047
Kings Worthy.
Mill Lane
Subway
Itchen Way.
Easton Lane
Martyr Worthy.
R. Itchen.
Underpass
A34
Fb
Subway
Pub.
START
Church Lane
Headbourne Worthy.
Easton Lane.
Easton.
To Southampton.
To Southampton
Chapel Lane
To A31

River Itchen

Headbourne

Kings Worthy

Martyr Worthy

Note: You have to cross the A33 at a traffic island to reach Kings Worthy, following St Swithun`s Way and Itchen Way.
For Headbourne Worthy you walk along a pavement beside B3047

St Mary`s Church, King`s Worthy overlooking a pleasant green, has had thorough restorations in 1849 and 1864. Only the tower and the base of the font are Norman. Two Perpendicular windows in the south aisle have Victorian glass. One small round window, high in the south chapel has glass dating from 1490 and depicting St Swithun and St Birinus.

Saint Swithun`s Church, Headbourne Worthy stands above the Hyde Bourne, a tributary of the Itchen. Trees shelter the site from the nearby B3047. The church still has its Saxon shape and masonry north and west in the nave walls and west in the chancel. The limestone came from Binstead on the Isle of Wight. At the west end of the nave a Saxon arch holds a 13th century door. You can open this door into the vestry. Turn to look at three figures above the arch. They are all that is left after their destruction at the Reformation. They are part of the 11th century rood and represent Christ in the centre with Mary his Mother and St John on either side. The belfry is 13th century and holds three medieval bells. The extension of the chancel is 13th century. On the south side, also 13th century are the sedilia or seat and the piscina for washing vessels and the priest`s hands. On the north wall of the chancel you will find a brass that has been raised from the floor and framed. It is of a scholar of Winchester College who died in 1434. The scroll from his lips: 'My song shall be always of the loving kindness of the Lord'.

Saint Swithuns, Martyr Worthy stands and has stood amid farmsteads and agricultural land since it was built early in 12th century. Even before the building of this church, the land here is mentioned in 908 when Edward the Elder confirmed the grant of Worthy to the Church of Winchester. The hamlet is mentioned in Domesday. In 1251 John La Martre passed the rights to elect the clergy of the church to the Prior and Convent of St Swithuns. The Norman nave was originally the extent of the church. It has 12th century north and south doors. The north door has columns and zigzag tracery. The Norman work of the south door was revealed in 1837 when a porch was removed. In 1866 the Victorians further enhanced the church by adding an apsidal chancel. In 1871 the bell tower was built and houses three bells, one dated 1632, inscribed 'God is my Hope'. Before the gallery was removed in 1911, two dogs are known to have been smuggled there to attend service.

The Walk

As you walk from the village of Easton along Church Lane, you pass the church on your right. Almost immediately turn right into a recreation field with swings and slide. Pass these on your left as you head towards the river.

Veer left and walk on the edge of fields with a branch of the river on your right. The noise of traffic can be heard ahead. In 500 metres you turn right towards the motorway. An enclosed path takes you beside the motorway and then turns left into a subway.

You have crossed the M3 without having to dodge any cars! On the other side, the path is still enclosed and takes you through the dank shade of bushes and trees. In ¼ mile you reach habitation.

Turn right to a line of lovely old cottages perched so close to the river. This seems to be a wide meeting point of all the branches of the Itchen. Cross the long footbridge over the river and turn right to follow the path through reed beds. In another ¼ mile you pass a lovely garden on the other side of the river. Cross a footbridge and emerge opposite **Mill Lane**.

Turn right for the footpath to Martyr Worthy and continue below*.

If you decide to go to Kings Worthy, *turn left here so that the river is away to your left. You have a pleasant wide path through open woods for ¼ mile to A33. Cross with care to the traffic island then the path opposite.*

You are now in Kings Worthy. Walk through the cutting, St Mary`s Close, past the thatched Tavern`s Cottage to the Church on your left overlooking the green

From Kings Worthy Church, *cross the green diagonally left to the main road, B3047. Walk on the pavement to pass the village hall on the left and continue to a bridge. Your road goes under the A34. Keep on course at a road junction. In another 250 metres you find St Swithuns Church opposite.*

From St Swithuns Church, Headbourne Worthy, *retrace your steps to Kings Worthy, pass Tavern`s Cottage, now on your right, cross the A33 and walk back through the woods to* ***Mill Lane.***

Cross to the path diagonally left opposite. The river is on your right.

***From Mill Lane,** head northeast up the sloping field. You are walking away from the river up to the B3047 where you turn right. Immediately turn right again and resume your walk by the river.

In ¼ mile you have another subway under the M3. When you emerge, turn sharp left into an enclosed path. It swings to the right then heads eastwards in a straight line between fields for ½ mile. The river is still on your right. As you proceed, you can look across the Itchen to Easton Church.

Ahead is a lone house on Easton Lane. Cross the lane and keep on course on a path to Martyr Worthy. The church bell tower soon comes into view. Avoid the first path to the left. Your path veers left up to Church Lane. Turn left for the church.

From Martyr Worthy Church, go back down Church Lane, pass your path on the right and continue southwards for the few yards to the end of the lane – you have now seen Martyr Worthy!

Keep on course along a footpath to the river where you can linger on the long footbridge and admire the clear, fast flowing water where green strands like wavy hair flow forever.

On the south bank of the river the footpath heads southwest across the meadow to the edge of Easton. Turn right on the lane that then bends left past cottages to the pub on the right. Carry on along the through lane, past the pub. In 100 metres the lane bends right and brings you to a T-junction and another pub on the corner.

Cross diagonally right to Church Lane, Easton and the end of your walk.

Walk 19: Ovington to Itchen Stoke, Itchen Abbas and Avington

Easy strides across the Hampshire Downs take you from Paris to London to find churches inspired by those capitals. The clear waters of the Itchen rush on regardless.

Starting Point: ¼ mile west of Ovington at the entrance drive to Lovington House.
Map: OS Explorer 132 **GR**556317 **Distance:** 6 – 7 Miles
Terrain: Gently undulating but may be muddy near the river and exposed on the Downs – perhaps most suitable for a pleasant summer`s day!

The Churches

Itchen Stoke

St Mary, Itchen Stoke is an amazing church, not always meeting with the approval of past visitors. Others are delighted with it. There are plenty of discreet village churches that have grown gradually and reflect local talent. This is not one of them. It replaces an earlier riverside church. The Rev. Charles Coneybeare paid for and imposed this building on the village. It is an imposing building with high walls and very steep roofs. Outside, as you approach from the west, you look up to a large bold west window. At the sides the brown and grey stone walls present a succession of tall, slender windows. Inside, you are dazzled with the bright stained glass of the three windows in the apsidal east end. Turn around and find the west rose window is also filled with gleaming glass. The lower side walls are lined with an assortment of patterned tiles. The inspiration for this church is in Paris. Now, this English version is in the care of the Churches Conservation Trust.
St John the Baptist, Itchen Abbas. Nuns of Nunnaminster Abbey held the Saxon village here. Falkswith, wife of King Alfred established a Benedictine nunnery about the year 900. The name, 'Itchen Abbas' describes the situation near the River Itchen and the link with the Abbey. The village is described in Domesday but no church is mentioned. The Normans did build a church here. In 1839 John Puthy describes it as having two Norman doors and a clumsy porch, also a mixture of tiles in the chancel. Another witness, Jessie Corrie (1855 – 1945) in 'Records of the Corrie Family' wrote: 'It was a curiosity. There were old high pews with a whispering gallery, for if you spoke into a hole in the chancel arch, what you said could be heard in the loft'. Today`s cruciform church was founded in 1862 by William Coles. He kept strictly to the Norman style. In a century or two when it has weathered, visitors will think it is the real thing. Inside is a gallery and marble stone on the chancel floor. It has attractive stained glass windows in muted colours. In the graveyard is a stone to John Hughes, a gipsy. He was sentenced to death in 1825 for horse stealing. The rector, Robert Wright tried without success to

Ovington to Itchen Stoke, Itchen Abbas and Avington

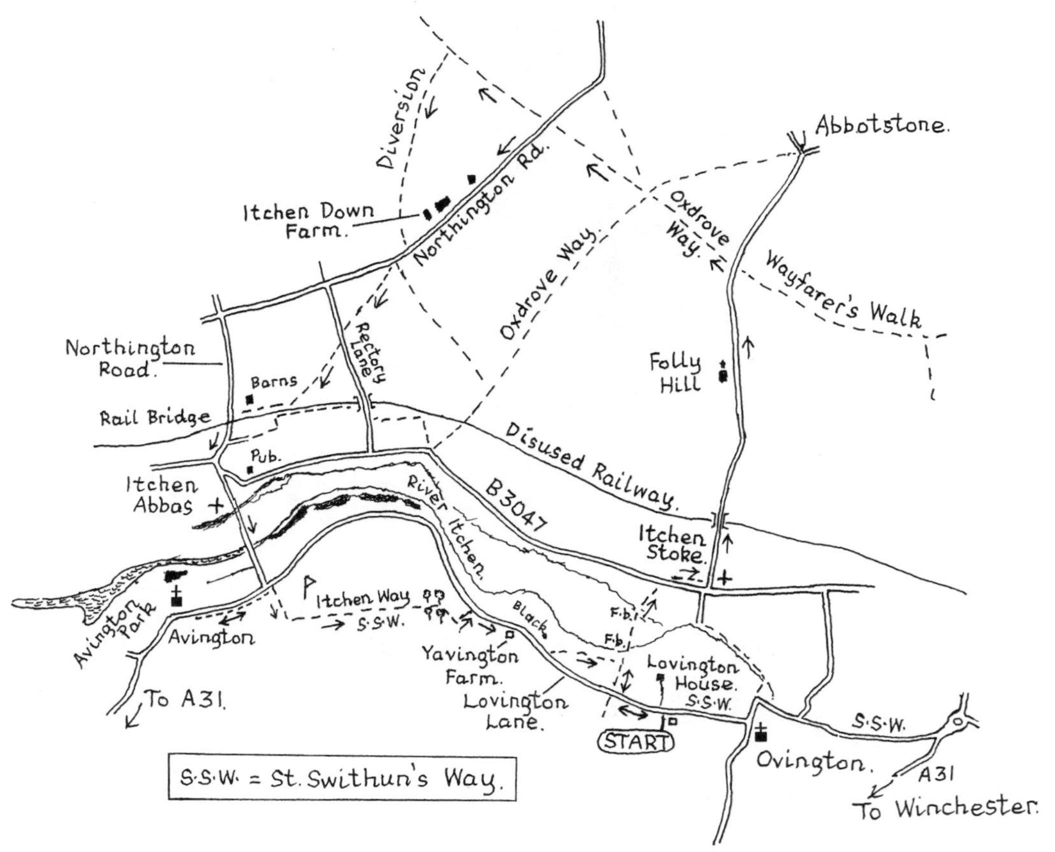

save his life. Instead, he promised to bury the poor man near his little daughter under the big yew tree.

St Mary, Avington is really an estate church and matches the big house, brick for red brick. Margaret, Marchioness of Carnarvon is responsible for the building in 1768, a rare example in the county of a complete 18th century church. It is based on a London church. A marble memorial in praise of her virtue, devotion and freedom from fanaticism is to the left in the chancel. She never saw the completed building. Another monument is to John Shelley, younger brother of the poet. This church has retained its original high box pews, its reredos and pulpit with a dove resting in the canopy. In fact, all at Avington Park recalls past centuries.

The Walk

Walk along Lovington Lane, away from Ovington. In 250 metres turn right and drop down into a footpath enclosed with bushes and trees.

In 200 metres Itchen Way joins from the left. Keep on course. Soon you cross the river on a footbridge. Linger to enjoy the fast flowing clear water.

Avington Park

Continue through a meadow on the other side. There is another stream to cross before you reach a little lane of thatched cottages in Itchen Stoke.

Turn right at the road B3047 and there are more thatches. Pass a green on the right and you come to crossroads dominated by Itchen Stoke`s new Church. Turn left here to walk up the hill.

You have a gentle climb on this straight lane between hedgerows for 1 mile. Shortly after passing a farm on the left, you come to a point where a footpath crosses the road.

Turn left to go through a metal arch into an elevated path, shaded and sheltered by thicket hedges. You have entered Oxdrove Way. A confusing number of long distance paths intertwine here.

The confusion is greatest when you reach crosspaths in ¼ mile. Avoid tracks to left and right and keep on course. Just past the bend, your track and one on your right lead to Northington Lane 500 metres away.

Turn left onto Northington Lane and walk gently down this open road with views over the Itchen Valley. *To avoid this road, follow the diversion shown on our map.*

On the road you pass the buildings of Itchen Down Farm on the right. In 1 kilometre of road walking you come to footpaths on the left. *The diversion brings you out opposite these paths.*

Avoid the first path. Take the second path beside a great tree. Cross the field diagonally left on a well defined path. Cross Rectory Lane and keep on course downhill. At the bottom you pass single storey wooden barns on the right. They are disused and

Itchen Abbas

neglected at the moment.

You emerge to Northington Road at the Itchen Abbas end.

Turn left and go under a magnificent railway bridge of great height and a fine example of Victorian engineering design – sadly redundant! Continue through residential Itchen Abbas to the main road, the B3047 again.

Turn left. A signpost on the other side of the road marks Avington Park. *If you want the pub, go just past this road and return to it later.*

Go down the lane towards Avington Park and visit Itchen Abbas Church on the way. Keep going to cross the River Itchen again. There are two bridges here. There is a waterfall under the second bridge. Continue on the lane to pass the entrance to Avington Park on the right and enjoy a view of the lovely lime avenue.

At the T-junction, the golf course is up on the left. Ignore this for the moment and turn right. In about ¼ mile you come to Avington Church.

From Avington Church retrace your steps for 50 metres. There is a footpath up on the right running parallel with the road. Follow this path back to the golf course.

At the entrance to the golf course, turn right and take the track up to the car park. Turn left and walk between the club house and the car park. Here is a straight cinder track heading east.

Itchen Way and St Swithun`s Way share this path. Cross a farm track and keep going to a little copse, the only woodland on this walk. Go through the copse then continue to a hedge.

Turn sharp left so that the hedge is on your right. You have to cross a stile on the right to make your way down a steeply sloping field to Lovington Lane. You have a pleasant view over the lane to the river beyond.

Turn right and walk along the lane for 1 kilometre to return to the starting point. On the way you pass Yavington Farm, climb a small hill and come back to the entrance to Lovington House.

If you wish to reduce the amount of road walking, turn left after ¼ mile along Lovington Lane and cross meadows diagonally left to rejoin the enclosed path at the start of the walk. Turn right into this path and retrace your steps, turning left when you reach the lane again.

Walk 20: Bighton to Alresford
(optional extension to Bishop's Sutton)

A walk along lanes for a winter`s day with a tour of one of Hampshire`s finest Georgian towns. Three or four churches are included.

Starting Point: Bighton Church **GR**610345 **Map:** OS Explorer 132
Terrain: Gentle hills, avoiding mud **Distances:** 7 Miles (can be shortened)
8 Miles (to include Bishop`s Sutton)
Local Information:
The name '**Alresford**' is from the Saxon, meaning 'the Ford where the Alder Trees grow'.
NewAlresford was formed in 1200 A.D. as a manorial town with an annual fair, granted by Bishop Godfrey de Lucy. A fire in the medieval town made way for fine new Georgian buildings
The Millennium Trail leaflet, in local shops, gives details of the various ancient buildings
Old Alresford was a separate Saxon manor, also held by the Bishops of Winchester.
Bishop Lucy had the river dammed so that Old Alresford Pond, a huge lake was formed.
Bishops may have landed at the Globe, southwest on the pond on their way to Bishop`s Sutton.
The pond is now a haven for otters and water birds.
The River Arle or Alre is a tributary of the Itchen. The clear water of the river and its streams is still the basis of the **Watercress beds** and a watercress festival is held every May.
The Watercress Line was built in 1865 to enable fresh cress to reach London by train daily.
The steam engines still run but now they transport mainly tourists through the countryside to Alton **Phone** 01962 733810 for times of trains.

The Churches

All Saints, Bighton stands at the end of a little lane at the entrance to the Manor House. In 959 King Edward granted the Manor of Bighton to the Abbot of Hyde. The church here is mentioned in Domesday. It is a delight to enter this ancient building. The font on the left has been carved from a whole piece of Purbeck stone and may be the oldest part here. The chancel is early Norman and the nave is slightly later. The nave has two bays with short round arches. The capitals on the south side have carved scallops, on the north side the carving is trumpet-like. North and south aisles end in chapels. A squint on the south side gives a view of the main altar. The lovely painted ceilings of nave and chancel are the work of Sir Ninian Comper. The chancel screen is also his. The royal arms above the tower arch are of 1709. The tower is low with weatherboarding at the top.
St Mary the Virgin, Old Alreford was deemed in need of repair in 1752. It was replaced in 1753 with the present large aisleless building. The tower was in less urgent

Bighton to Alresford (Bishop's Sutton)

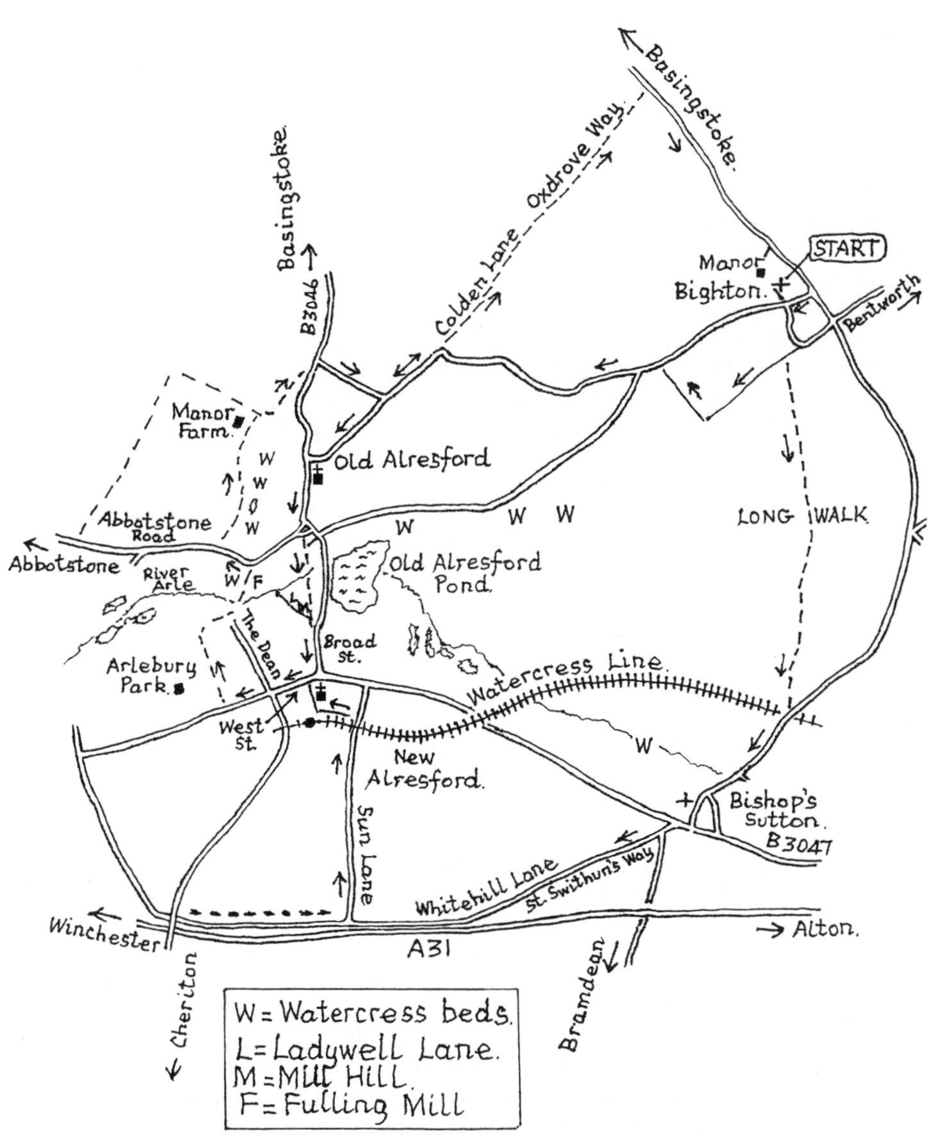

Bighton

need of repair; it was rebuilt 16 years later using bricks from a derelict house. Transepts were added in 19th century. A major restoration by the Victorians caused the church to be closed. It was re-opened in 1871 by Bishop Wilberforce. There is a strikingly large memorial on the north wall. Admiral Lord Bridges Rodney chose coloured marble and rococo style to remember his wife Jane. Another memorial to Mary Sumner, founder of the Mothers` Union is near the south transept.

St Nicholas Church, Bishop`s Sutton stands above the clear waters of a tributary of the Itchen. The Saxon name, 'Sudtunan' means 'south farm'. King Harold owned the manor here and the church was then 'All Saints'. After the Norman Conquest, Count Eustace of Boulogne held the manor. Later (1136), the manor passed to Henry de Blois, Bishop of Winchester. (See the Introduction). He established one of his palaces here and Sutton Park became his hunting ground. The Norman Church would have been built then. The village flourished in medieval times, under the auspices of succeeding bishops. The Civil War wrought much damage, incuding the destruction of a north chapel and side altars. In 1649 Sir John Evelyn bought Sutton Park, and although the manor later reverted to the bishops, the village never regained its prosperity. Two doorways opposite each other in the nave are Norman. The south doorway is more ornate with carvings of beak heads. The north or 'Devil`s' door was left open during baptisms to let out evil spirits. The window to the right of the north door is Norman. The chancel arch, originally Norman, was rebuilt in 13th century. The capitals on either side still have chevron carving. The trefoil east window is Early English. A priest`s door and a 14th century window are in the south wall. A blocked squint in the north wall would have enabled people in the north chapel to see the altar. Fortunately the Victorians did little to restore the church which is simple and plain. We can be grateful for their report: *'In one way the church is more beautiful than when it was built for 7 centuries have passed over it and the hand of time has given colour, tone and softness and endowed it with* *dignity which man cannot give although man can take away'.*

St John the Baptist, New Alresford stands in the centre of the town. The old church was destroyed by a fire in 1694. The early 14th century tower has survived. High on the west wall is a small Saxon rood or crucifix. The blocked south doorway is also early 14th century. Most of today`s church is Victorian and externally is quite handsome with lovely flint walls that meld well with the tower.

The Walk

From Bighton Church walk back to the nearby crossroads. *If you want to shorten the walk, turn right here and walk along the road for ½ mile and join the shorter walk at * below.*

For the short walk in full, cross the road to the little lane opposite, known as Malthouse Lane. At the junction of tracks at the bottom, turn right. Continue below.

***To include Bishop`s Sutton**, take the footpath up the hill opposite. It heads south for over 1 mile to Bishop`s Sutton. The path runs over wide, gently sloping fields and through hedges. First it passes Henrys Wood at a distance on the right. It goes through a gap in the cross hedge then ascends to a wide, newly planted screen of trees, in front of an existing hedge. Replacement stiles to the next field are needed. (There is a gap in the hedge on the right).*

Old Arlesford

Pass Bighton Bottom Farm on the left. Find a metal gate in the left hand field corner then turn sharp right to climb up to another hedge gap. Continue to a final hedge with two stiles. Now you have a view to Bishop`s Sutton Church.

Go through a field gate to join Bighton Lane and keep on course. Cross the bridge over the Watercress Line. Descend on a bending road to the clear running stream that feeds watercress beds. You join Church Lane.

*After visiting the church, on the right, continue along Church Lane to B3047. Cross diagonally right to Whitehill Lane and avoid Scrubbs Lane on the left. You are now on St Swithun`s Way. In 1 mile at a T-junction, you reach Wayfarer`s Walk on the edge of Alresford. Turn right and walk up the lane to Alresford town and station. Continue at ** below.*

***For the shorter walk (not including Bishop`s Sutton)** turn right at the junction in Bighton and follow the hedgelined track to the end where you may have to climb up onto the bank to avoid a puddle.

Here is a similar track at right angles. Turn right and walk up to the road. You have to squeeze beside a locked farm gate and clamber over a heap of soil to get onto the road and turn left. *(The short cut joins here)

Walk to the nearby junction and fork right into a quiet lane. Follow this lane for 1 kilometre. On the way, it bends to the right and offers fine views on the left to distant hills. Finally at a T-junction, Colden Lane joins from the right. (This will be our route for the return walk).

Turn left and walk down for ½ mile past large lone houses, Upton Park Farm, Upton House and Old Alresford House. Before you reach this 18th century mass of brick, you will have passed **Kiln Lane** on the right, part of the return walk. Just after Old Alresford House, you come to the church.

From the churchyard, you enjoy a magnificent view west over watercress beds to the Hampshire countryside. To the south, the ancient pond is hidden behind trees. *See Local Information, 'Old Alresford' above.*

From the Parish Church of Old Alresford, go to the tower and look over towards the watercress beds then veer left on a grassy path that takes you down to the road, B3046. Cross with care to the pavement opposite. Turn left down towards New Alresford. Cross the Abbotstone Road and keep on course on the other side. The path continues along beside the little river and into the lane, Mill Hill. Pass a waterfall and Town Mill, converted into flats.

You have entered Alresford`s Millennim Trail. There are roadside plaques with local information. Mill Hill leads up past Ladywell Lane to Broad Street, one of the finest in Hampshire. Saunter up past Georgian houses and shops to the T-junction with the B3057. The church is opposite. Behind the church, a path through the churchyard on the right leads to Station Road and the start of the Millennium Trail at the Railway Station**.

Those who ventured over to Bishop`s Sutton join here.

From New Alresford Church return to the junction on B3057 and turn left into West Street where there are further individual shops. Avoid all turnings until you come down to the road on the right 'the Dean'. A sign here directs you to the 'Riverside

Arlesford

Bishops Sutton

Walk', but, if you prefer to follow the Millennium Trail, keep on the main road a little further.

Veer right to Arlebury Recreation Ground and go through gates to take the path straight ahead to the river. The big house up on the left, Arlebury Park is now divided into apartments.

At the river turn right. You have a firm path beside the clear waters of the River Arle for ¼ mile with benches for walkers and nature lovers to enjoy the river. At the beautiful black and white 13th century Fulling Mill, you cross the river on the left. *(The path to the right leads to Ladywell Lane).*

The path on the other side of the river leads to Abbotstone Road. Turn left here and walk along the road for 100 metres. Cross to an access lane to cottages overlooking watercress beds. After the last cottage, continue on the footpath down on the right through fields. Keep to the right hand edge of the fields so that you can look down on the watercress beds and up to Old Alresford Church beyond.

You join a lane at Manor Farm and keep on course to a byway. Turn right and you are back on Oxdrove Way. It heads towards the B3046 then veers left at a recreation area. Keep on past cottages overlooking the green, 'the Brook'. After Churchy Hall on the left, turn right to cross the main road and enter Kiln Lane.

You are still on Oxdrove Way and have quite a steep climb up to the familiar lane at the top. Turn left and pass Upton Park Farm on your way to the junction with Colden Lane. Follow Oxdrove Way along this track for over 1 mile. There are lovely views to the left. At the end you come to stables and cottages before reaching crossroads.

Turn right and walk gently uphill along Nettlebeds Lane for under 1 mile. After the Manor on the right and the playing field on the left, turn right then immediately right again for Bighton Church.

5 Walks
Near Southampton

St Julian and walls, Sothampton

Walk 21: Southampton Parks and Old Town

Behind the shopping centres, the city of Southampton has retained its lovely gardens and below the 'Bar' fine medieval walls and churches still stand.

Starting Point: Southampton Central Station **GR**413122
Map: OL Explorer 22 **Distance:** 1½ Miles
Terrain: A gentle climb up from the station. Hard surfaces until you reach the parks. Some steps in the Old Town.
Local Information: 1. Ever since Saxon times, the northern entry to the Old Town has been through the **Bargate**. The Saxon gate was wooden. The Normans built a stone arch around 1175 and succeeding centuries have made changes to this basic Norman structure. Pevsner describes it as 'probably the finest and certainly the most complex, town gateway in Britain'.
2. Details of **guided walks** of the walls are given at
Southampton Tourist Information Centre, Civic Centre Road, SO14 7FJ.
Phone 023 8083 3333.
3.**The Civic Centre** with Guildhall and landmark clock tower (1929) by E. Berry Webber is still the only impressive modern building in Southampton.

The Churches

St Michael`s is the best medieval parish church of five that once existed in the Old Town. The others were dismantled or damaged in World War 11. The Normans built this church around 1070 when they realised here was an ideal spot for a town to trade with Normandy. Trade flourished in the Middle Ages and walls were built to protect the town. In 1160 St Denys Priory held the patronage of these churches until 1536 and the Dissolution of the Monasteries. The Normans built a cruciform church. The lower part of the tower and the semi-circular arches below are original. Chapels north and south of the chancel were added in 13th century. In 14th century the north aisle was widened to reach the extent of the transept. Similar extension of the south aisle in 15th century meant the church building is now rectangular. The walls to the transepts were removed and the tower was left standing on its 4 round arches. The impressive black marble font may have been brought from Belgium by Henry de Blois, Bishop of Winchester (1129 - 71). There are other rare Tournai fonts in Winchester, East Meon and St Mary Bourne (Walks 16,15 and 29). Two medieval eagle lecterns are highly treasured, particularly the earlier one from Holy Rood Church. In 1338 cruel Pirates from France and Genoa raided the town, even murdering those inhabitants who had taken refuge in the church, later reconsecrated. In response to this raid, Edward 111 hastened the building of the south wall. Such was the haste that some merchants` houses were incorporated in the defenses. Early in Queen Elizabeth`s reign, many uneducated clergy, including those in Southampton, lost their livings. By the end of her reign

SOUTHAMPTON
Central Station, Central Parks, Old Walls and Churches

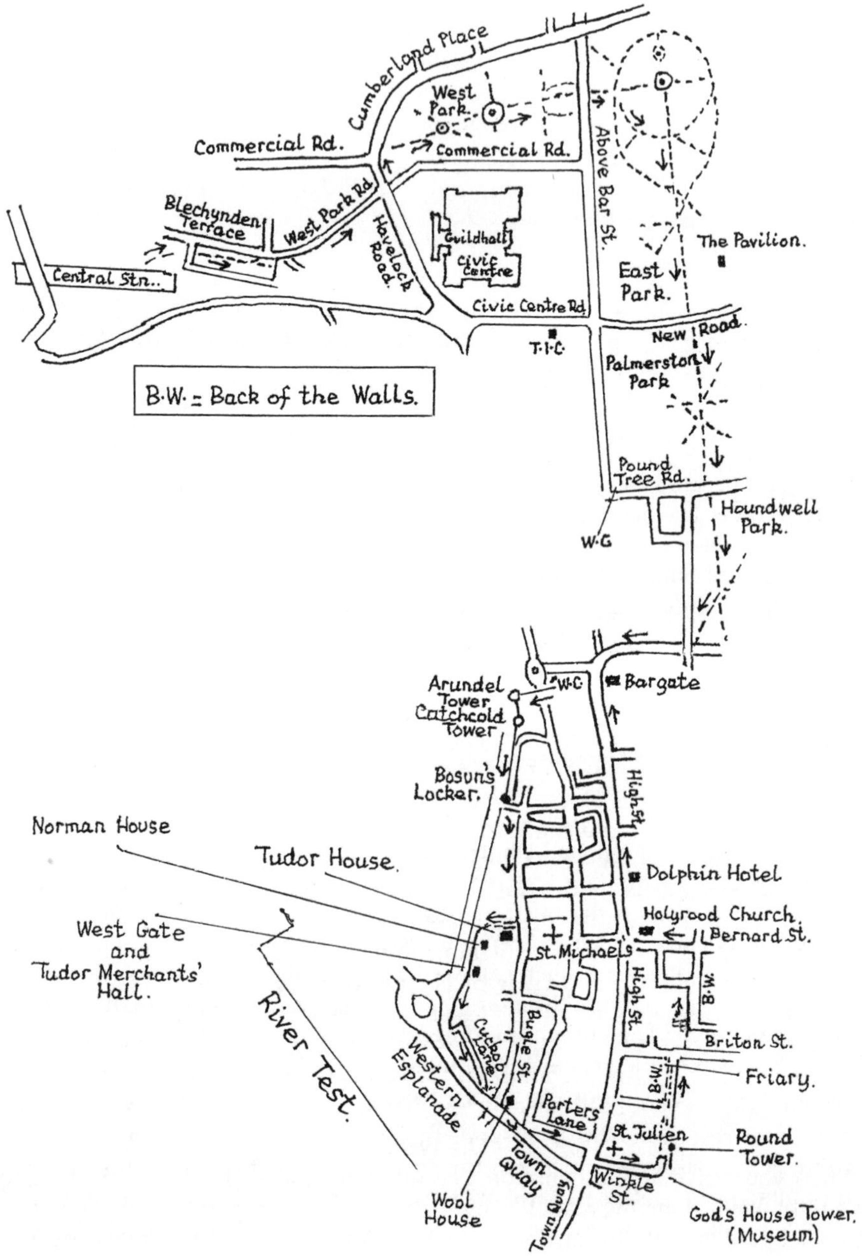

Holy Road and St Michael, Southampton

the standard of scholarship had improved. Outside, the elegant slender spire rises above the town. The first 15th century spire was reconstructed in1733 and again in 19th century when it was heightened to 165 feet to be a landmark for shipping.

Holy Rood was built in 1320. Crusaders prayed here on their way to the Holy Land, as did knights on their way to battle in Crécy and Agincourt. The church had a thorough Victorian overhaul but was blitzed in 1940. The roof and all the Victorian work were destroyed. The original chancel and tower have survived. The Perpendicular chancel windows open to the sky are poignantly beautiful. The handsome tower in three stages still has a tall window with Y tracery and the quarter jacks facing the High Street. They ring every quarter hour. Restored in 1957 as a memorial to merchant seamen, this shell of a church contains a wistful garden.

St Julian, known as the 'French Church' is not usually open to the public. In 1196 Gervase le Riche, a local merchant founded a hospice here to accommodate pilgrims from France on their way to Canterbury to the tomb of Thomas a Becket. This church was part of the hospice. St Julien was the patron saint of pilgrims. Gervase had already paid the ransom for Richard Coeur de Lion`s release from Austria. In 1567 Queen Elizabeth allowed Protestant refugees from France and Belgium to stay here and use the church. There are two almshouses in the grounds behind the church. The church building was restored in 1861 and retains little original Norman work. Inside the pointed chancel arch survives. Outside the blocked square-headed doorway is 15th century.

The Walk

When you arrive at Southampton Central Station, leave by the north exit and turn right. Walk along the road, Blechynden Terrace where you have the option of a parallel garden path for part of the way. In 250 metres fork left into West Park

Road, a gentle climb up to the park.

You have to cross Havelock Road to get into West Park on your left. The impressive Guildhall is on your right. Keep on course through the Park and you come to Above Bar Street.

Turn right for shops on this street. TIC is at Civic Centre Road on the right.

To avoid shops and enjoy the parks, cross Above Bar Street to East Park. Veer to the right and you can walk under the wisteria pergola. You head south, passing the Pavilion on the far left. You come down to New Road and cross to Palmerston Park. Your way is enhanced with swathes of grass beside the paths, flowering shrubs, trees and flower beds.

Continue south through Palmerston Park and cross Pound Tree Road to Houndwell Park. It is hard to believe that you are walking behind the shops of Above Bar. You reach the end of this green idyll at Hanover Buildings.

Turn right here for Bargate at the Precinct at the bottom of Above Bar Street. *The shoppers also arrive here if they have not been waylaid!*

Bargate is the entrance to the medieval town. Go to the right of Bargate where you will find toilets and the start of the **Walls Walk**. Steps lead up to a high footbridge across a modern road to the 13th to 14th century Arundel Tower, also known as Windwhistle Tower! You then descend to the west walls and follow them southwards, passing Catchcold Tower. The remains of the old castle are on your left and bleak modern hangars with the docks beyond, are on your right.

You pass a row of houses, named 'Forest View', as the New Forest was once visible across the water. At the inn, Bosun`s Locker turn left away from the walls.

Holy Road

St Michael

We are still in the Old Town. Jane Austin stayed from 1806 to 1809 in a house that stood on the site of the inn.

Turn right into Upper Bugle Street. This leads past Simnel Street to St Michael`s Square. **The Church of St Michael** and the Tudor House face each other across the Square. The Tudor House is now a museum.

Turn right into the walkway beside the Tudor House and come down steps to the level of the modern road, Western Esplanade. Turn left and walk beside the walls. You can in fact peer into the remains of a Norman house.

You soon reach Westgate and turn left to walk under the arch into a little square, Westgate Street. Pass the Tudor Merchant`s Hall on your right. In 1634 it was moved here from St Michael`s Square where the residents had objected to its use as a fish market. In 1970 it was restored.

Cross to the left corner of the square and continue southeast along Cuckoo Lane. You pass the Mayflower Memorial on the right and you have a view across the main road of the Docks, built on reclaimed land.

Stay on this side for the Walls Walk and cross Bugle Street. Pass Wool House on your left. In 14th century this was a wool store for Cistercian monks of Beaulieu Abbey. It continued as a store for Henry V111. It was a prison during the Napoleonic Wars. It is now a Maritime Museum.

Continue along Porters Lane and you pass the ruins of a two storeyed Norman house. At High Street cross diagonally right to enter Winkle Street. Here you will find the pale stone building of **St Julian`s Chapel**, part of a Hospice, founded in 1196 and still active today.

At the end of Winkle Street is God`s House Gate, built early in the 14th century and named after the Hospice. God's House Tower was added 100 years later. The gate and tower now house an Archaeology Museum.

Turn left at God`s House Tower and you come to the East Walls. Pass Friary Gate on the right. Friars used this gate to reach their gardens outside. On your left, I understand some ancient vaults still exist. Ahead is the site of the 13th century **Friary.** Here stands an office block, Friary House. As you walk beside it, you can see the history of the friars, depicted in tiles on the walls.

After passing Friary House on the left, you cross the road to steps opposite and come to a shabby section between storage sheds. You soon reach Bernard Street and turn left. Pass the employment bureau on the right and here is the shell of **Holy Rood Church**, a handsome and moving memorial.

Holy Rood faces St Michael`s Church across the High Street. (you have walked round nearly in a circle). Bargate is to your right.

If you wish to continue exploring the Old Town, cross the High Street and climb up to St Michael`s Church. Go through to St Michael`s Square, and turn left to walk along Bugle Street, described by Pevsner as the finest in Southampton. You may also find some ancient inns here!

To return to Southampton Station, go back to Bargate at the northern end of High Street. Retrace your steps through the parks or take the alternative route through the shops on Above Bar Street and turn left following the signs.

Walk 22: St Mary, Hound to The Royal Chapel, Victoria Country Park and Netley Abbey

This walk seeks out green places in a built-up area on Southampton Water

Starting Point: Hamble Rail Station trains to Havant and Southampton **GR**474083
Or The layby for St Mary`s Church on Hound Road, near Netley **GR**472087
Map: OL22 **Terrain:** Flat **Distance:** 4 ½ Miles
Note: Part of this walk follows Solent Way through Royal Victoria Country Park with views over Southampton Water. When you leave the park for Victoria Road in Netley, houses obscure the view to the water. This is still Solent Way. Near the end, the walk follows Hamble Rail Trail.
Local Information: When Henry V111 dissolved the Abbey, he kept the Gatehouse on the shore of the Solent and converted it to a fort to protect Southampton.
In 19th century **Netley Castle** was built on the foundations of the Tudor fort, the former Gatehouse. The Abbey ruin is behind the castle, on the other side of the road.
The Royal Victoria Military Hospital was built 1856 – 63 at the behest of Queen Victoria, after the Crimea War. Florence Nightingale criticised the dark rooms and long corridors. When the huge building was demolished in 1966, it left 200 acres of parkland with woods, lawns and beach.

The Churches

St Mary, Hound is a country church standing back from the main road into Netley. Monks who founded Hamble Priory in 1109, probably built a church here and also at Bursledon. (See Walks 23 and 24). Hound Church has retained the simple shape of nave and chancel. Throughout this long church, all is Early English including the chancel arch and lancet windows. The chancel windows contain outstandingly beautiful modern glass by Patrick Reyntiens. The east window, mainly in blue, is of Virgin and Child. At the west end four roughly hewn timbers rise from floor to roof. The font is big and square. It has a large cemetery opening into a large flat field.
To make an appointment to see inside, Phone 023 8045 2209 or 023 8045 7055

Hound

St Mary, Hound to The Royal Chapel, Victoria Country Park and Netley Abbey

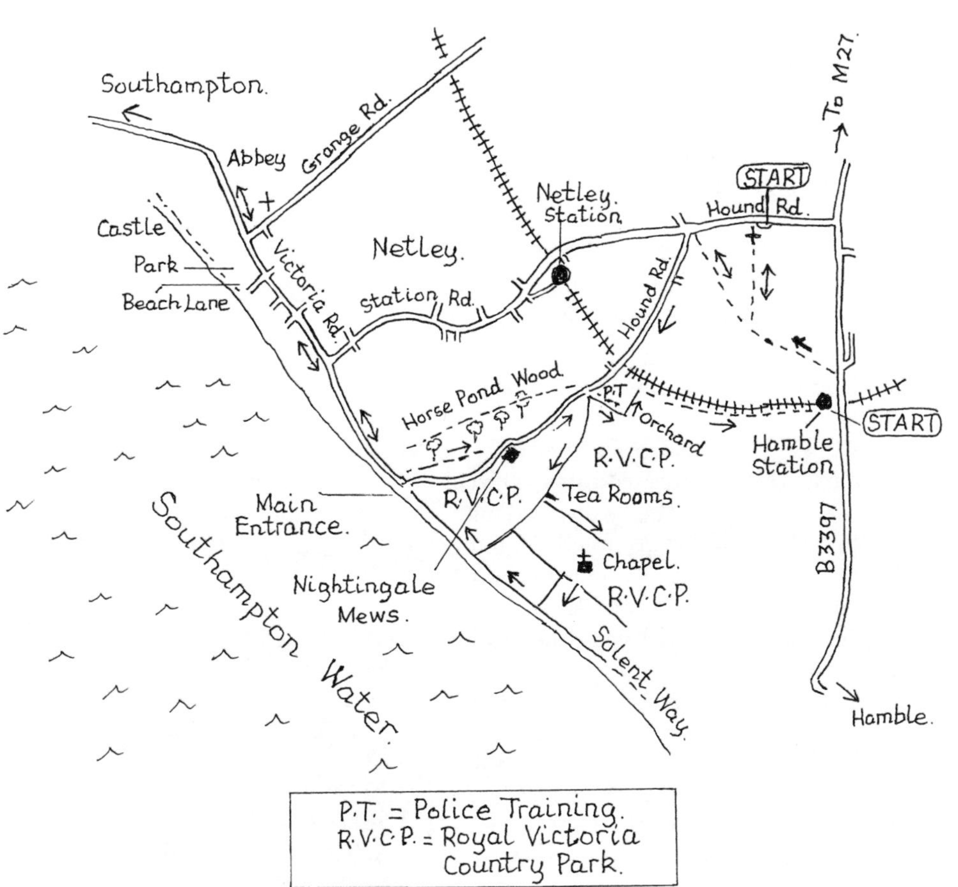

The Royal Chapel, now the Netley Chapel, was at the centre of the Royal Victoria Military Hospital, planned during the Crimea War. (See above). The chapel has survived the demolition of the hospital in 1966 and has been recently renovated for use as a visitor and heritage centre. It is a very grand and spacious building. The nave has wide galleries with cast iron pillars. The east window retains its Victorian glass promising redemption. The old organ is still in place. Otherwise, the walls now display the pictorial history of the hospital. The foyer is a shop with stairways up to the galleries and the tower, 150 feet high. This can only be viewed when there is a tour guide. Outside, the tower, topped with dome and cupola, is a distinctive landmark.

The park is open all year. For details of the Chapel phone 023 8045 5157

Edward the Confessor, Netley has overtaken Pound as the Parish Church. We walk past this Victorian Church (1886), near Netley Abbey. To make an appointment to visit it, phone the numbers given for Pound Church above.

Netley Abbey was a Cistercian house built in 1239 by monks who moved here from Beaulieu. They chose a spot near the River Itchen, where it enters Solent Water. They were fortunate to have Henry 111 as patron. The high standard of masonry is similar to that of Westminster Abbey. This handsome building has gone through many transformations. At the Reformation Sir William Paulet acquired the Abbey, never completely dismantled, and made it his private home. It became a romantic ruin enveloped in *trees*, the haunt of Horace Walpole and later Jane Austen in 18th century. The trees have been cleared and the Abbey is the scene of open-air theatre in the summer.

Netley Abbey

Arthur Mee was thrilled: 'Yet all else is dwarfed before the awe-inspiring majesty of the abbey church. No imagination is needed, as at Beaulieu, to build up this House of God. The walls are here in their magnificent proportions, 211 feet long, 58 feet wide, and 115 feet from transept to transept. The bases of four great piers mark the position of the central tower...The two great windows, east and west, are silhouetted on a background of trees...the sheer beauty of their outline is a wonder still'.

The Walk

From Hamble Station go to the north side and exit to the main road B3397 (there is a footbridge over the line). Walk beside the road for 50 metres. Turn left at a footpath sign and you are in a huge flat field. Fortunately the footpath is very slightly raised and you can follow it northwestwards towards distant houses. In about ¼ mile you cross an old field boundary and turn right. Go through a wooden gate for walkers into a paddock. Head towards a similar gate and enter the cemetery. Follow the drive to St Mary`s Church, Hound.

From St Mary`s Church, Hound follow the main drive through the cemetery (retracing your steps if you came from the station). Go through the wooden gate into a paddock and turn right. In the corner enter a nature reserve, Hound Ecology Corner, telephone 02380 466091 for details.

Take the path through the reserve to residential Hound Road and turn left. Pass houses on the left and scattered homes above the wooded valley on the right. Cross a railway bridge and you soon come to crossways at an open square. *Avoid the footpath through woodland on the right.*

Our way is ahead along the tarmac drive. This is the back entrance to the Royal Victoria Country Park. Walk past neglected police training bungalows

When you come to crossways, leave the tarmac tracks and veer left on a rough pathway. Pass 'Tall Pines Car Park' on your right. Then come down to Cedar Tea Rooms, facing south to overlook Southampton Water. *Here is an office, a cafe and Toilets at the far end of the building.*

From the Tea Rooms walk across the lawns to the large domed chapel, now the Heritage Visitor Centre.

From the Chapel entrance, walk along the straight path to Southampton Water. *This is the site of a long pier where wounded soldiers and sailors arrived in ships to be transferred to the hospital. Distance lends a charm to the many chimneys of the Oil Refinery across the water, and passing ships and sailing boats enliven the scene.* Here you pick up Solent Way, a long distance footpath. Turn right.

At the start, the path has open views on either side. Then you reach another car park and a wire mesh fence mars the view to the water. To avoid sharing the tarmac drive with cars, you can step onto the playing fields on the right. If there is a match in progress, you may have to cross to the far side of the pitch and follow the benches alongside.

Leave the Royal Victoria Country Park by the main gate. Again there is a fine view over the water. Make the most of it. You now have to walk along Victoria Road past flats, houses and shops for ½ mile. Avoid all side turnings. Soon after a little park on the left, you come to the Church of Edward the Confessor on the

Victoria Park

right. Next, the ruins of Netley Abbey are also on the right. The Abbey enjoys a natural setting among grassy slopes.

From Netley Abbey retrace your steps along Victoria Road back to the main entrance to the park.

Inside the Royal Victoria Country Park, take the rough footpath on the left. In ¼ mile, join the drive that passes the large Italianate building, originally the Officers` Mess and now private flats, called 'Nightingale Mews'. Pass this on your right.

In another 100 metres at cross ways, avoid the familiar track ahead to the back entrance. Instead, turn right onto the drive signed 'Barbecue Area'. Pass behind the police training bungalows and in a few metres you come to more signs. Turn left to follow 'Hamble Rail Trail'.

This is a straight sunken track heading north. *Here a branch railway, built in 1900, brought troops to the hospital.* In 200 metres cross a driveway and continue on the Hamble Rail Trail, now a pebble path through a rejuvenated orchard. Too soon you reach the railway line and have to turn right.

You now have a shady enclosed path beside the railway line on the left. At places along the way, walkers have broken through to the field on the right. They have to rejoin the path at a large corrugated shed in various shades of lime green. This is part of a sport or entertainment complex that you pass next. Soon after the large brick building, your path divides. Fork left for **Hamble Station**.

If you have parked at St Mary's Church, Hound, follow the instructions at the start of this walk, under the heading 'From Hamble Station'.

Walk 23: Sarisbury to Hamble-le-Rice

This is a superb and varied walk by the River Hamble. A ferry ride enables you to approach the busy yachting village by water as advocated by Pevsner

Starting Point: The little car park on the corner of the Green opposite the Church, Sarisbury or roadside parking. **GR**502087
Map: OS Explorer 119 (also shown on OL22, Outdoor Leisure).
Distance: 6 – 7 Miles **Terrain:** Mainly flat, riverside and woodland
Local Information: Hamble is a historic ship building place. Today the leisured sailing community dominates river and village. **Hamble Valley Guide** for the official map phone 0906 68 22 001 **The ferry** across the River Hamble operates all year round except on Christmas Day. It finishes at 4 p.m. in winter and 6 p.m. in summer. At the time of writing the cost for a single crossing is £1.50 adults, £1 children.
There is also a **Hamble River Bus,** phone Blue Star Boats: 023 8045 3542
Holly Hill Woodland Park, east of the river, is a 19th century estate, bought by Fareham Borough Council in 1954. There are lakes, ancient oaks and other broad leafed trees where nightingales have been heard. The park is designated a Site of Importance for Nature Conservation. For more details, phone 01329 824543.

The Churches

The Church of Sarisbury and Swanwick, St Paul overlooks the spacious Green, once part of Titchfield Common. The mainly brick church is late Victorian. It is quite big with a small buttressed tower. Despite its size, the church is cosy and welcoming. There is a gallery at the back of the nave. Wide lancet windows are seen throughout and a set of three at the east end. The chancel arch is tall, wide and plain. The Memorial Chapel on the south side has an apsed Sanctuary.
The Priory Church of St Andrew the Apostle, Hamble-le-Rice stands up behind the yachting village. Benedictine monks from the Abbey of Thiron in France built a priory and church here some time around 1120. They brought stone from Caen. Other stones have also been incorporated in the Norman tower and long narrow nave of that period. The tower has two string courses and a large west window. Several doorways, arches and windows have Norman carving. The main doorway into the nave has zigzag work. Later fishermen have left their marks here. They cut a line before they set off for sea. When they returned safely, they put a cross through this line. Windows are high in the thick walls of the nave. The remains of a rood screen can be seen in roof beams supported by pillars. The monks used the eastern end of the church and the local people worshipped in the western nave. Two Norman doors opposite each other in the north and south walls of the nave show where the monks walked across. The chancel was rebuilt around 1250. It has lighter, richer windows than those of the nave. The south chapel was added in 1880. The glass in the west window, installed in 2002 depicts St Bernard of Thiron, founder of the church. He faces St Andrew the Apostle in the east window. The frame of this window dates from 1300. The original glass of 1856 was mostly shattered in bomb blast of 1940. The new stained glass was installed in the east window in 1954. *The key is at the Rectory, see paragraph 6 below.*

Sarisbury - River Hamble - Hamble-le-Rice

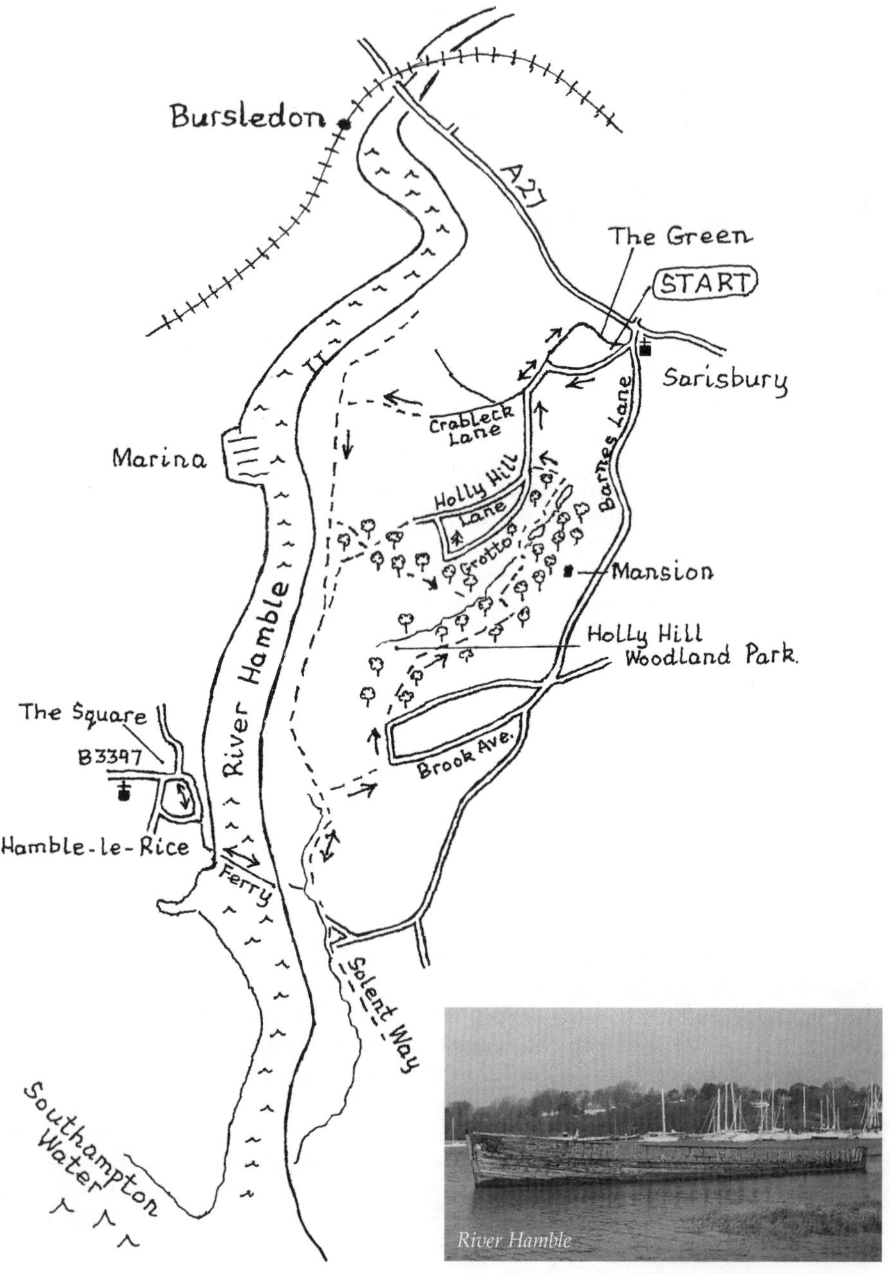

River Hamble

Sansbury

The Walk

From Sarisbury Church cross diagonally left to Holly Hill Lane, passing the little car park on the Green on the right.

Follow the lane through quiet houses for ½ mile. At a bend in the lane, note the footpath on the right for the return walk. Shortly after this bend, turn right into a private road, Crableck Lane.

In 100 metres fork left. The footpath runs alongside a track for cars to tow boats to the river. Fields on either side are the domain of horses, ponies and donkeys. In 1 kilometre you reach the River Hamble. Here is a riverside path along the east edge of the river.

Turn left and walk due south for 1½ miles on the firm stony path. *The river with its long lines of anchored sailing boats and wooded banks beyond is on your right. Watery marshes with a nature reserve are on your left. A handsome footbridge spans one channel. Your path has water on both sides. Fortunately the riverside path stays dry but some of the side paths are flooded at High Tide. As you pass the village of Hamble in view on the other side of the river, notice the square church tower at the back. Ahead, the chimney of Fawley Power Station dominates the landscape.*

You cannot miss the ferry point. A small pink brick shelter has been provided. You can hail the ferry by pressing a button at the top of the pier. In any case the pink boat plies back and forth.

At the quay in Hamble-le-Rice, veer to the right and follow the main lane uphill between pubs and eating places to the Square where buses abound. Keep to the left and pass the Co-Op and School Lane on the left. Continue along the main road, B3397 for ¼ mile. The church is behind the lychgate on the left. *Keep straight on for the Rectory, the first brick house on the left.*

After visiting Hamble Church, retrace your steps to the Quay and take the ferry back to the east side of the river.

Turn left on your familiar riverside path and return for ¼ mile as far as a path across the marsh on your right. **This is Route 1.**

If the path is flooded at high tide, you will have to continue northwards for 1 kilometre to find ***Route 2****. See below**

Assuming the first path is free, turn right here to an enclosed way up to Brook Avenue. You reach the avenue at a bend and turn left, walking past sumptuous houses that overlook the river. In ¼ mile at the next bend, the lane turns right, you go straight on to a pedestrian access into Holly Hill Woodland Park.

Keep straight on northeast along the main high path inside the wood. At a bench on the left, turn left away from the main path and pass another bench.

Go gently down to a T-junction of paths. Turn right and follow the woodland stream on your left. It leads to the lakes at a grotto and waterfall.

****Route 2:*** *The next path from the river also leads to the lakes. Follow the signpost to a wide track into woodland. Avoid the path on the left and go straight on through trees for 75 metres to a fork in the ways. Fork right up to an open grassy area overlooking the river – you can actually see Hamble Church on the other side.*

Follow the main path over this grassy space then down to the left into woodland. There is a steep valley on the right. You come to wooden steps and a slope down to the muddy valley.

Step gingerly through the mud and veer right to raised planking. Keep going for 50 metres to a T-junction with a major path. Turn left and follow the stream on the left to the lake and grotto mentioned above.

Both Routes: keep to the left and follow the lakes on your right. You come to cross paths at a picnic area. Keep going beside a narrower lake on your right. When you can go no further, turn left on an earthen path that climbs through woodland. The path soon curves left so you are above the lakes, hidden by trees. At a barrier turn right and go through to Holly Hill Lane.

Turn right and pass Crableck Lane, now on your left. At the next corner, cross to the noted footpath. It is an enclosed alley leading to the Green. Turn right for the church and the little car park.

Hamble

Walk 24: Bursledon - Manor Farm Country Park - (Botley)

From a Priory church, walk beside the River Hamble to a chapel in the grounds of a traditional working farm, then on to a little market town.

Starting Point: Bursledon Rail Station **Map:** OS Explorer 119 **GR**490096
Terrain: A short section on roads then riverside and woodland tracks.
Distance: 5 Miles (Can be extended to Botley, adding 1½ miles).
Note: Bring a compass to find your way through the grounds of Manor Farm Country Park where many extra paths exist that are not shown on OS map.
Local Information: The buildings, including the chapel of **Manor Farm Country Park** are open April – October (10 – 5) and Sundays only in winter (10 – 4). Phone: 01489 787055

Early in 19th century **William Cobbett**, the radical farmer lived near Church Lane, Botley, 'the most delightful village in the world'. He should know! He travelled on horseback to explore the English countryside and is famous for his book: 'Rural Rides'. (See also Walk 7 and Walk 32).

For details of the **Hamble River Bus,** phone Blue Star Boats 023 8045 3542.

The Churches

St Leonard`s, Bursledon is at least 800 years old. As at Hound, Netley, a church was probably first built here by monks from The Priory of Hamble. Unlike Hound, Bursledon Church has undergone many changes over the years. All that remains of 12th century church is a blocked doorway north in the nave. The large font may be from the first church here. It has a strange mixture of carvings; partly Norman arcading and partly pointed gothic arches. The chancel arch is Early English. It has human heads at the base on either side. From the 13th century there is a blocked doorway south in the nave and a little lancet window north in the chancel. In 1391 the crown seized all foreign owned possessions. Hamble Priory and the churches of Hound and Bursledon were given to Winchester College. The east window, much restored was designed in 15th century and has fleur de lys pattern on the inside arch. Images and paintings were destroyed during the Reformation The Victorian architect, Sedding preserved much of the old church when the building was enlarged in 1888 and the transepts of 1830 were remodelled.

St Bartholomew is the original church of Botley, attended by country folk. It is now a chapel in the grounds of Manor Farm Country Park. A tree fell on the old church and only the chancel is left. The west doorway has simple Norman stones. This can be seen from the footpath. To see the deep-set 13th century lancets, the Perpendicular windows, the little box pews and the glass bier, you will have to visit when the farm is open. See above.

All Saints, Botley is the new church, built in 1836, in attractive cream coloured brick. It serves a village that had drifted northwards. The traditional tower presides over the wide High Street. The clock came from the home of William Cobbett. The ancient font with cable moulding at the top and arched panels at the sides came from the old church. The base was damaged and has been replaced. The font was rescued in 1740 after it was discovered abandoned 'in a field', 'on a farm', 'in the river'! Also from the

Bursledon - Manor Farm Country Park - (Botley)

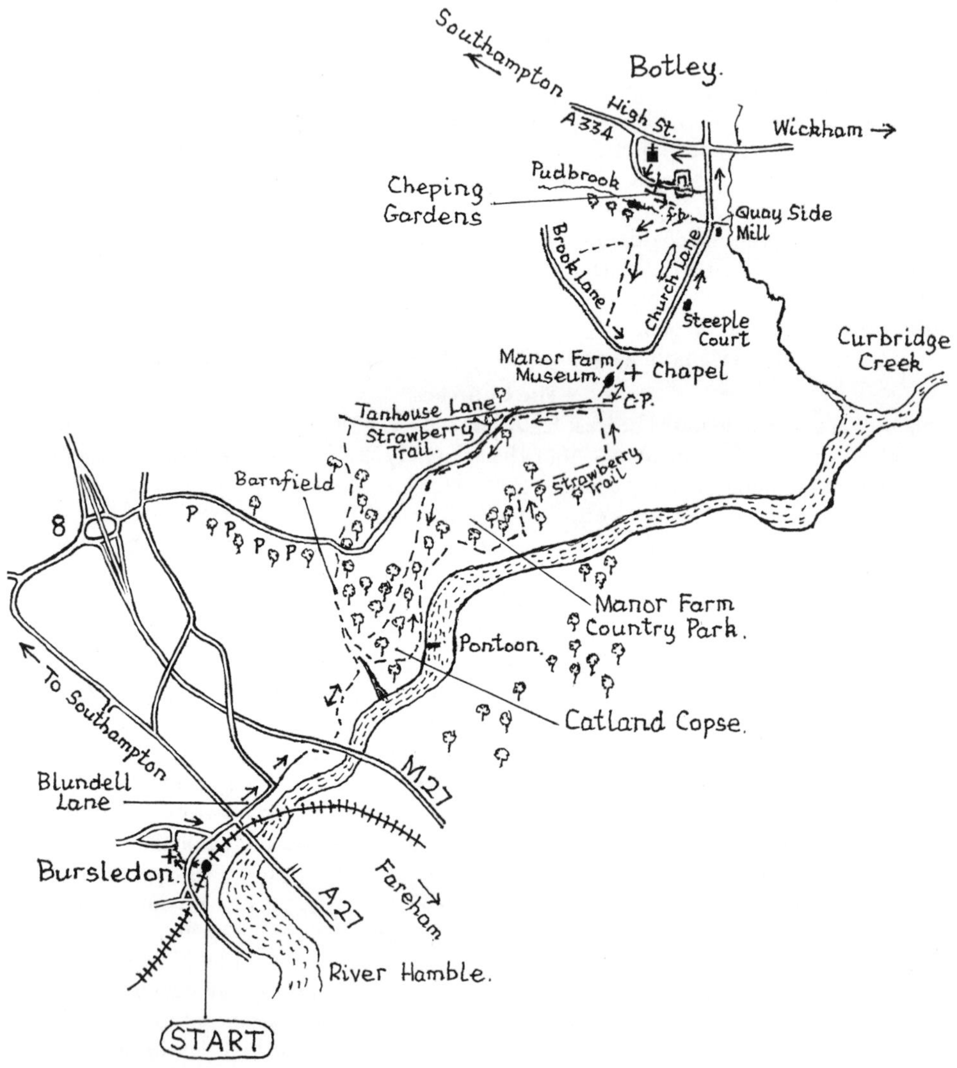

Botley St Bartholomew

Botley All Saints

old church, the tomb of John de Botele, Lord of the Manor 1260 has been set in the south wall. All Saints has grown over the years. In 1892 the north aisle was added with timber arcading. The wooden roof was built to cover the aisle and nave. There are dormer windows in the roof. In 1856 the tiny chancel was added. The modern church room is really impressive. It has a curved stone turret with rainbow cross set in the wall It is warm, spacious, light and welcoming – you may even find someone serving hot drinks 10 – 12 a.m.

The Walk

From Bursledon Station go to the exit. Station Road is to the right. Turn left into Station Hill. Almost immediately turn right into an enclosed path that leads up to the church. On the way up the slope you pass a recently opened piece of wooded parkland on the left.

After visiting St Leonard`s Church, continue along the path on the right. It crosses a small green to a suburban road. Turn right and go down to T-junction with Station Road. Turn left and you are walking away from the station. In 100 metres you come to the A27. Blundell Lane is opposite.

Go to the traffic island on the left to cross this busy road and walk along Blundell Lane for 200 metres as far as a sharp bend to the left. You go straight on along tarmac through an assortment of boats and past a chandler`s den. You are on Strawberry Trail. Look for occasional markers.

Go under the motorway then turn immediately right onto a rough footpath on the shore of the Hamble. It bypasses Brixedore Farm on the left and brings you to the soft turf of the field sloping down to the bank of the river.

Walk on the turf, keeping the river at arms` length on the right. The path bends left to follow an inlet and enter a slight valley. At the head of the inlet, turn right and cross a narrow causeway to the woodland on the other side.

You have now entered Manor Farm Country Park at a T-junction. Turn right and walk along the wide **riverside track** through Catland Copse. *The undistinguished path on the left that you pass in about 75 metres is for the return walk. If you are very observant, you may notice some faded yellow bands near the top of posts on this walk.*

Meanwhile, continue on the riverside track still marked Strawberry Trail. You are heading north and pass a river pontoon on the right. *Under these waters lies the wreck of medieval naval ship, Grace Dieu.* At a wide bend in the river you have a glorious view over the tranquil tree-lined waters.

Burlesdon

The path climbs gently through woodland on the left then returns down to the river. At another inlet the path goes into the wood again at Dock Copse. Steps go down to the stream then you climb a bank on the other side where a Strawberry Trail sign confirms that you are still on route. But Beware!

There is a misleading path to the right. Avoid this and follow the path to the left, heading north through the wood. In 250 metres it veers right (east), taking you out to an open plateau. Keep on course along a straight path beside a hedge. In 100 metres turn left into another straight path following another hedge on the right. Sheep and cattle graze in the flat field on the left.

You are heading due north to Manor Farm. At **cross tracks** go straight on avoiding the car park on the right. Keep on the track, passing the farm entrance, picnic tables and toilets on the right. You continue down to the nearby chapel, passing a pond on the way. *See below to continue to Botley.*

***From St Bartholomew`s Chapel** return to the **cross tracks.** *Avoid the path opposite that brought you here.* Instead, turn right, into a path towards 'Barnhouse'. It runs parallel with the farm road. You are heading west on another straight hedge-lined path. In ¼ mile you come to cross ways with a confusing choice. *Pass the path to the left (not shown on OS map). Avoid the road to the right, saying 'Goodbye' to Strawberry Trail as it heads that way.*

Instead, go straight on along the main trail with large signposts. You are now heading southwest and may catch a glimpse of the distant River Hamble after a while on your left. In 500 metres you come to the edge of the wood. *Avoid the farm road that veers right here and do not be tempted on the path on the left, leading along the edge of the wood.*

Instead follow the middle way into the wood. (You may notice that spaced posts have a faded yellow band around the top). Pass a distant car park on the right and keep heading gently downhill for ½ mile to emerge at the familiar **riverside track.**

Turn right and retrace you streps, crossing the causeway on you left now, over the field, under the motorway, through the boatyard, over the A27 and back to Bursledon.

To extend the walk to Botley, *keep heading north on the track from St Bartholomew, outside the bounds of Manor Park Farm now. At the nearby T-junction with Brook Lane, turn right and follow Church Lane. (Also the route of horse buses in the summer). The lane bends left and leads northeast for ½ mile to Botley. On the way you pass Steeple Court Manor,*

At the edge of Botley, cross the Pudbrook stream near Botley Mills and turn right for a short diversion to Quay Side. The Hamble is narrower here.

Return to Church Lane and continue past houses to High Street, Botley. A Bathroom Centre is on the corner. Turn left and stroll along the High Street, Passing the Bugle Inn, the Dolphin and the Market Hall.

In 250 metres you come to All Saints Church. As you leave the church, turn left on the path around the new room and through the cemetery at the back. Go out by a gate in the right hand corner.

Turn left on an estate road and walk past bungalows. Take the first turning right and go down to more bungalows on Cheping Gardens overlooking woodland above Pudbrook. Turn left then cross the green on the right to go down to the far corner where a footpath follows the stream on the right.

In a few metres you come to a strong metal footbridge. Turn right here to cross the stream and climb up to a track that serves as a driveway. Turn right and stop! Immediately after a pair of brick houses there is an uncultivated pocket of land. Turn left here and cross to the footpath with Strawberry Trail Marker.

You now have a pleasant elevated path over fields heading southwest. In 300 metres at a path junction, turn left. Hug the hedge on left for 350 metres to Brook Lane. Turn left to return to the entrance to Manor Park Farm on your right now. ***Follow instructions above* to return to Bursledon.***

Walk 25: Portchester Station to Portchester Castle

From a grand church in the spacious grounds of an ancient castle, we leave by the Watergate to view the harbour and Naval fortresses across the water.

Starting Point: Portchester Railway Station: **GR**617058
OR Car Park at Portchester Castle: **GR**624047
Map: OS Explorer 119 **Terrain:** Flat, Harbourside
Distances: Harbour Walk 3 ½ Miles Castle Grounds ½ Mile
Railway Station Walk 2 Miles Total Maximum 6 Miles

Local Information: 1. The old village of Portchester offers a nostalgic version of 18th century life: handsome houses on a spacious harbour road and extensive views to Portsdown Hill before the advent of suburbia.
2. Portchester Castle is a Roman fortress, converted into a medieval castle in 13th century. Richard 11 had a fortified palace here in 1399. In 15th century it was a depot and a prison for distinguished prisoners. Today it is in the care of English Heritage.

The Church

St Mary`s is a magnificent huge barn-like building. It was built of stone from the Isle of Wight in 1120s. Saxon graves have been found outside the church, suggesting the presence of an earlier church here. Henry 1 founded an Augustinian Priory here in 1133 and handed the church over to the monks. The Priory moved to Southwick 1144-53 (see Walk 5), perhaps to escape the noisy activities of the fortress. The church stayed in place and has changed little over the centuries, apart from the removal of the south transept. Nearly all is Norman including the fine carved entrance at the west end and the central tower with inside arches. The north transept still has recesses in the wall where the monks could sit. The east wall has carvings of a mouse near the capital of a pillar. The wooden beams in the transept roof are Elizabethan. Two queens have been benefactors. Queen Elizabeth 1 sent Sir Thomas Cornwallis to Portchester, possibly to keep him out of trouble for he was a Catholic. One of his tasks was to repair the east end of the church. He shortened the chancel and fitted the east window in a simple Perpendicular style. He also had to close the Lady Chapel in the north transept. The effigy of Cornwallis to the right of his window is normally stone coloured but in winter he blushes as the damp seeps through the wall. The Norman nave is long and plain with no arcade and simple round-headed windows. There is a leper`s window or squint in the north wall. The font of Caen limestone may be the oldest in Hampshire. It has carvings of plants animals and flowers, in a style similar to the Celtic. Queen Elizabeth has her coat of arms on the south wall of the nave. Queen Anne has an even bigger coat of arms on the north wall. After a fire in 1705 Queen Anne helped pay for the nave roof and allowed the felling of trees in Windsor to make the beams.

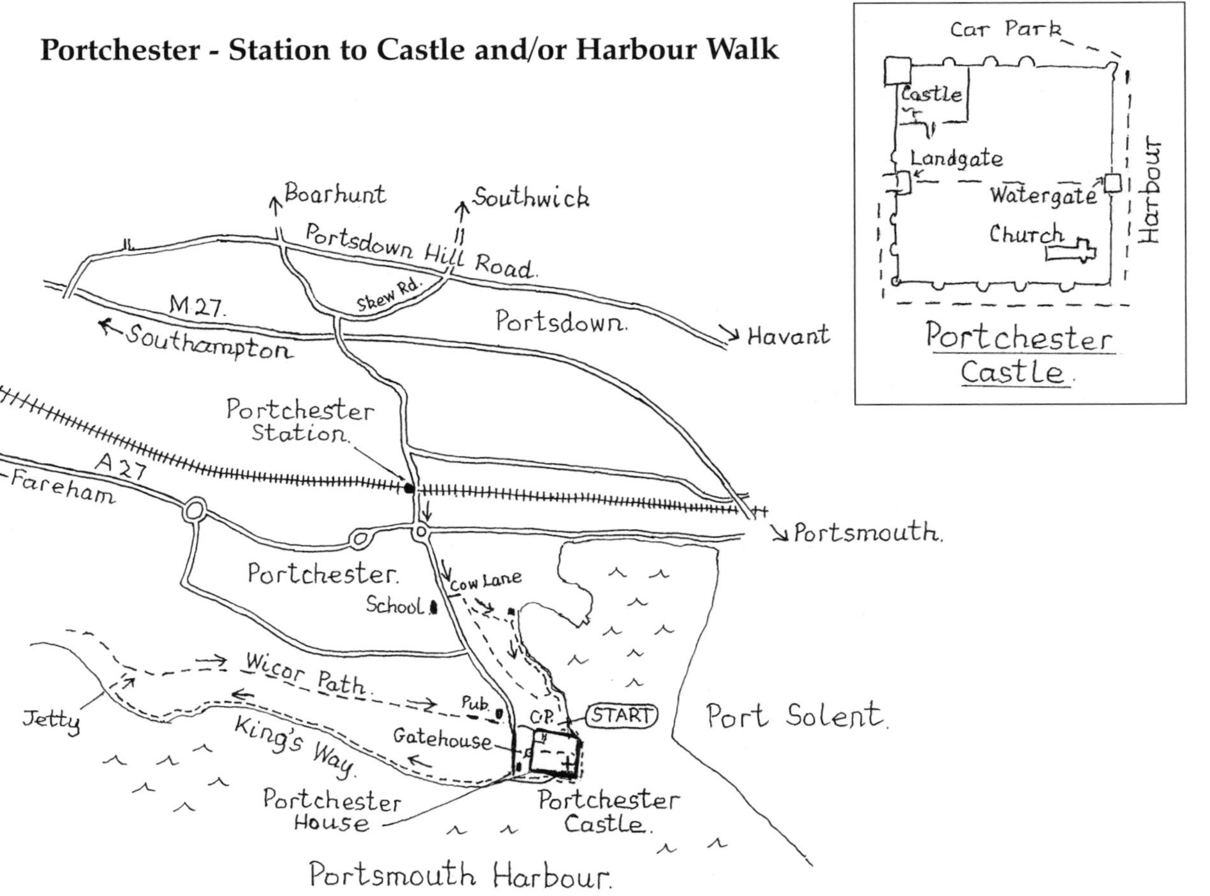
Portchester - Station to Castle and/or Harbour Walk
Car Park
Castle
Landgate
Watergate
Church
Harbour
Portchester Castle.
Boarhunt
Southwick
Portsdown Hill Road.
Skew Rd.
M27.
Southampton
Portsdown.
Havant
Portchester Station.
A27
Fareham
Portsmouth.
Portchester.
Cow Lane
School
Wicor Path.
Pub.
C.P.
START
Port Solent.
Jetty
King's Way.
Gatehouse
Portchester House
Portchester Castle.
Portsmouth Harbour.

Porchester

The Walk

Note: *we visit only one church in this walk. It is inside the grounds of Portchester Castle. Exploring the castle and walking around the Roman walls will occupy some time. I have added a harbour walk, described below.*

If you arrive before 3 p.m. you may be in time for ***Teas*** *served in the church.*

From the station head south towards the A27, and cross at a roundabout to the road opposite. It leads to Portchester Castle. Continue south along this road for 200 metres until you come to a school on the right. Turn left here into Cow Lane. The path soon forks. Avoid the enclosed path on the right. Instead, keep straight on along the track that becomes a twisting path up to the water front. Turn right and follow the path along the embankment. The water and mud is down on your left and recreation fields on your right. In ½ mile turn into the castle car park and follow the instructions below.

From the car park take the wide path beside the castle walls towards the nearby water front. You pass toilets on the left. At the harbour you join the long distance footpath, 'King`s Way'. Turn right around a corner in the walls. You head westwards keeping close to the castle walls. There is a view over the water to Portsmouth`s historic dockyard and beyond there to the Spinnaker Tower, a new landmark.

The Watergate entrance on your right allows you into the outer bailey of the castle where you will find the church on your left.

After visiting the church, return through the watergate to the harbour and turn right to continue your tour of the Roman walls. At the next corner of the walls ***either*** *turn right to circumnavigate the castle walls to the Gatehouse and return to the car park.*

Or for the harbour walk keep straight on. Go over a short stretch of rough terrain, then along the concrete wall. *Hospital Lane on your right leads past Portchester House and back to Castle Street and the old Village.*

St Mary's Porchester

Keep on the concrete wall and avoid the private drive to a detached house. After passing the house and crossing a bridge, continue over grassland in front of a housing estate on the right. Despite the proximity of human life, there is also an abundance of wading birds: oyster catcher, curlew and sanderlings to name a few.

In 1½ miles you reach a bit of rough common then emerge to a jetty. the path twists away from the water then crosses a field to a T-junction. Turn right. You have reached Wicor Path. It leads back eastwards past the field to the housing estate.

There are several side roads to take if you prefer the water front.

Wicor Path is not well signposted, but if you go straight on for 1 mile along suburban roads, passages and past a cemetery, you reach a lane back to Castle Street. The castle and the centre of Portchester village are to the right.

Turn left for pubs and the station. Turn right for the castle and the car park.

Porchester Castle

5 Walks
Near the River Test

River Test at Romsey

The Test is another of the great chalk streams of Hampshire. It rises in the centre of the county, near Ashe and flows through Whitchurch. Tributaries join the Test near Longparish. They are Bourne Rivulet and River Swift. The clear waters make the river suitable for watercress growing. It also supported many mills with a wide variety of activities: corn, paper, silk. There is even a tide mill at Eling near Totton. Several chalk streams rise in the northern hills and the long distance footpath, The Test Way starts at Inkpen Beacon. These streams are water bournes that dry out at the end of winter and fill up again with the spring rains. The Test has a good share of pretty villages, (Walks 28 and 29). Other tributaries join further south, including the River Anton from Andover and the Wallop Brook that has three villages named after it. Yet further south the Test passes through the parkland of stately homes, Mottisfont and Broadlands (Walks 27 and 26). Finally it flows through salt marshes and nature reserves before entering Southampton Water.

Walk 26:
Romsey Abbey, The Abbey United Reformed Church, The Baptist Chapel and Romsey Town

A short walk through a country town that bought its own Abbey church for £100 and a stroll by the river once famous for its salmon leap.

Starting Point: Romsey Rail Station **GR**357216 **Map:** OS Explorer 131
Terrain: Flat, mainly through the town **Distance:** 1½ Miles
Local Information: King John`s House probably built in 13th century and the Tudor Tearooms are behind the Tourist Information Centre. In 1306 King Edward 1`s knights on their way to Southampton were billeted in the house. The gardens and tearoom offer a pleasant respite.

The Churches

Romsey Abbey, The Parish Church of St Mary and St Ethelfleda

King Edward, son of Alfred the Great founded a nunnery here in 907. His daughter, Elfeda was the first abbess. Despite repeated attacks by the Danes, the Saxons kept the nunnery going. In 960 King Edgar re-founded this and other monasteries, insisting on the Rule of St Benedict. After an invasion in 990s, when the nuns fled to Winchester, the church was restored and extended. The nuns returned and kept up their work; praying, looking after the sick, giving shelter to the wives of knights and educating their daughters. Matilda, daughter of the Queen of Scotland had the protection of her aunt, the nun Christina. She rejected William Rufus as a suitor for her niece, then, when he died, accepted the more scholarly brother Henry 1. Matilda was a pious queen who endowed further priories. Two Saxon roods have survived at Romsey. On the outside wall of the south transept, a carving of Christ holding out his arms in welcome, has the hand of God above. Beside this rood is the intricately carved Norman entrance, used by the nuns. Inside, in St Anne`s Chapel in the chancel, another Saxon rood of 960 shows the Crucifixion with soldiers at the base of the cross. When the Normans began work on the Abbey in 1120, they started at the east end and took over 100 years to build the cruciform church using stone from Binstead on the Isle of Wight. It encloses the smaller Saxon church. There are several chapels in the chancel and transepts. The great glory of this building is the simple three tier internal structure and fine Norman arcade. As you walk from the entrance towards the crossing, you are going back in time. The builders started here and the first two bays have plain round Norman piers. The style evolved as they worked their way westwards. The carvings on the capitals are varied and give an insight into the humour and genius of the masons. There are so many treasures in this church, I cannot describe them all. I can only recommend you visit. The volunteers welcome you with an informative leaflet and there are more detailed guidebooks. No pressures are put on the visitor. Romsey Abbey retains its blessed peace.

ROMSEY
Romsey Abbey, The Abbey United Reformed Church, Baptist Chapel and Romsey Town

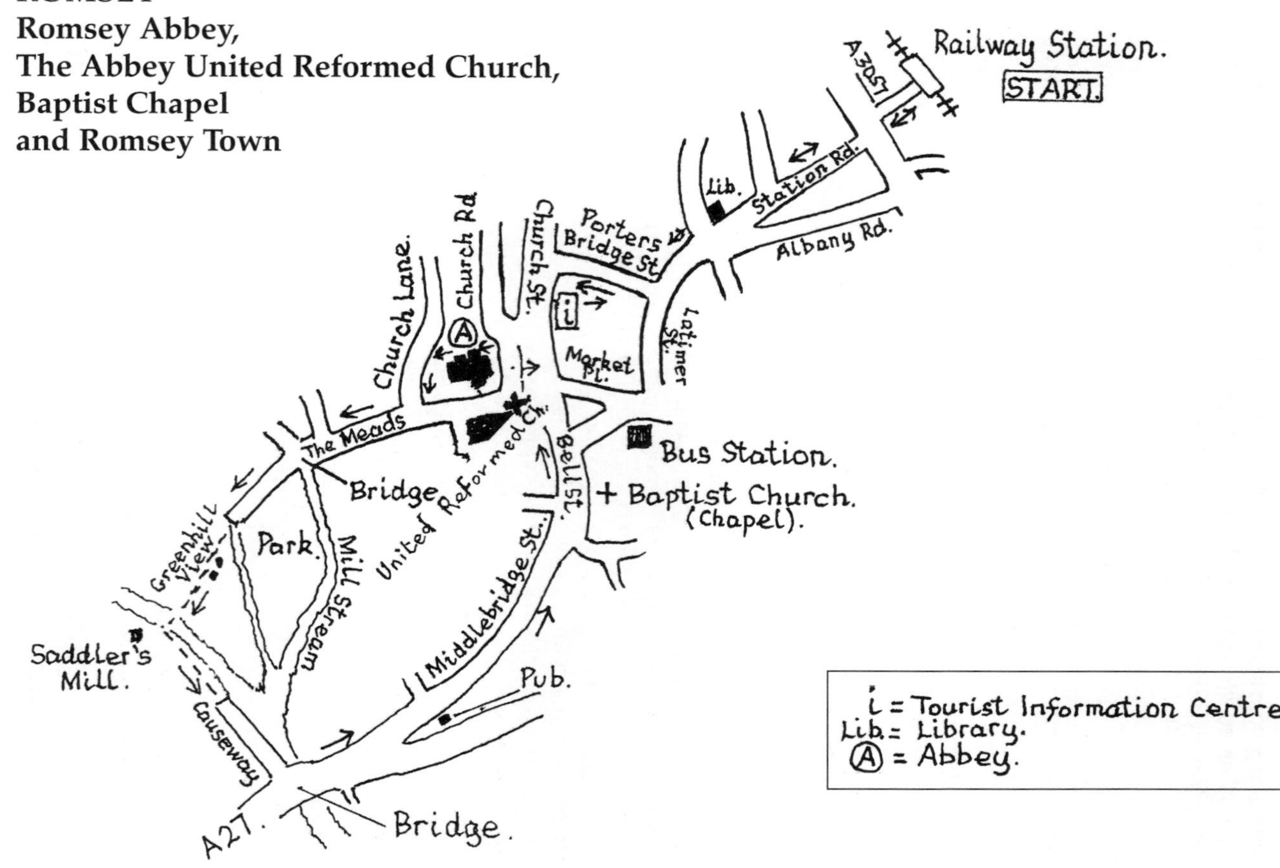

Abbey United Reformed Church is a fine building in Perpendicular style. This style and the facing of local flint match the 16th century archway into the Abbey precincts. Architects Paull and Bonella of Chancery Lane, London are responsible for the design, completed in 1888. Their contractors had had difficulties excavating for the foundations and had to damn a stream. The final building was so grand that the then council requested a notice be placed at the entrance 'This is not the Abbey' – they were refused! Inside the church is spacious. The focal point is a massive organ, replaced in 1975 by a Staffordshire one. Nave and aisles have Perpendicular windows.

Romsey Baptist Chapel (1811) has a plain white façade with windows in three bays below and arched windows above.

King John's House, Romsey

The Walk

From Romsey Station cross the main road, A3057 to Station Road opposite and head towards the town. Follow the finger post to the Tourist Information Centre. On the way you pass the public library.

When you reach a Car Park, turn right into Portersbridge Street. At the end go through the arch to Church Street. The Tourist Information and Heritage Centre is on the left. The Abbey is opposite.

Cross Church Street and go to the right of the Abbey. Pass Church Road. The north porch is the main entrance to the church.

When you leave the Abbey via the north porch, veer to the left, avoiding Church Lane on the right. Behind the Abbey, you pass quiet houses to a nearby T-junction. Turn right into the Meads, another quiet residential road leading to 'White Bridge'. This dark bridge crosses an offshoot of the Test.

On the other side of the bridge you find the War Memorial Park. The road, still the Meads follows the edge of the park. Enter the park and walk parallel to the Meads on your right until you reach the narrow exit back to this road. (Or keep going along this road).

Romsey Abbey

Find the twitten at the end of the road and cross another stream. You now have a pleasant view to open country. Pass two or three houses on the lane, aptly named Greenhill View.

The lane leads to the River Test at sluice gates and Saddler`s Mill, once used in the treatment of wool. *The clear waters form a wide pond here, known as 'Saddler`s Leap'. Autumn salmon make their way upstream back to their breeding ground. There are now fish ladders to help the few salmon who still make this journey. We watched the long twirling reeds instead.*

Pass the mill on your right and turn left to walk beside the river as far as the main road, A27.

Turn left on the pavement and re-cross the river to Middlebridge Street. *It stands on a line of gravel above the marshy land that used to cover this area. The water course on the right was once used in the tanning industry. As you walk along this street, you pass many old houses including a pub believed to date back to 17th century and a master stonemason`s house.*

At the end of Middlebridge Street turn left into Bell Street. Pass the Baptist Chapel on the right. Just before you reach Market Place, seen ahead, turn left at the gate to the Abbey United Reformed Church, also known as 'The Church by the Arch'.

Go through this arch, 'Abbey Gateway' to an enclosed lane. In a few metres turn right to walk through gardens to the South Side of the Abbey itself. Turn right to return to the Tourist Information Centre and retracc your steps to the station.

Walk 27: Mottisfont to Michelmersh

Lively activities at the National Trust Centre at Mottisfont contrast with the quiet country walk to a church off the beaten track. Return to an ancient church in Mottisfont village and the River Test.

Starting Point: Unofficial layby beside Oakley Road behind Mottisfont Abbey. (The Test Way, a long distance footpath runs along this road).
GR324273 **Map:** OS Explorer 131 **Distance:** 5 Miles (can be shortened)
Terrain: Mainly flat, 1 steep uphill, 1 long gentle slope down.
Local Information: Mottisfont National Trust house and gardens are open for much of the year. For times of opening, telephone 01794 341220.

The Churches

St Mary`s Church, Michelmersh. Nothing could be lovelier than this spacious church with 'beautiful views of rich pastoral and woodland scenery'. It was thus admired in 1867 and again in 1908 and thankfully still today. In 985 King Aethelred gave land in and around 'Miclamersce' to his friend Aelferd. The oldest part of the present church may be the 12th century door jambs of the south doorway. The Victorians cleared out much clutter in 1846/7 and have been criticised for destroying ancient features. The church on the other hand has gained space and light. In 13th century the chancel was probably lengthened. There is medieval glass in a window on the south side of the chancel. The glass, now in fragments, may have been in the east window originally. This three-light window now has glass of 1873. The 13th century font, re-cut so that it looks more recent, has a bowl decorated with human heads and fleur de lis. There is a 14th century recumbent

Michelmersh

Mottisfont to Michelmersh

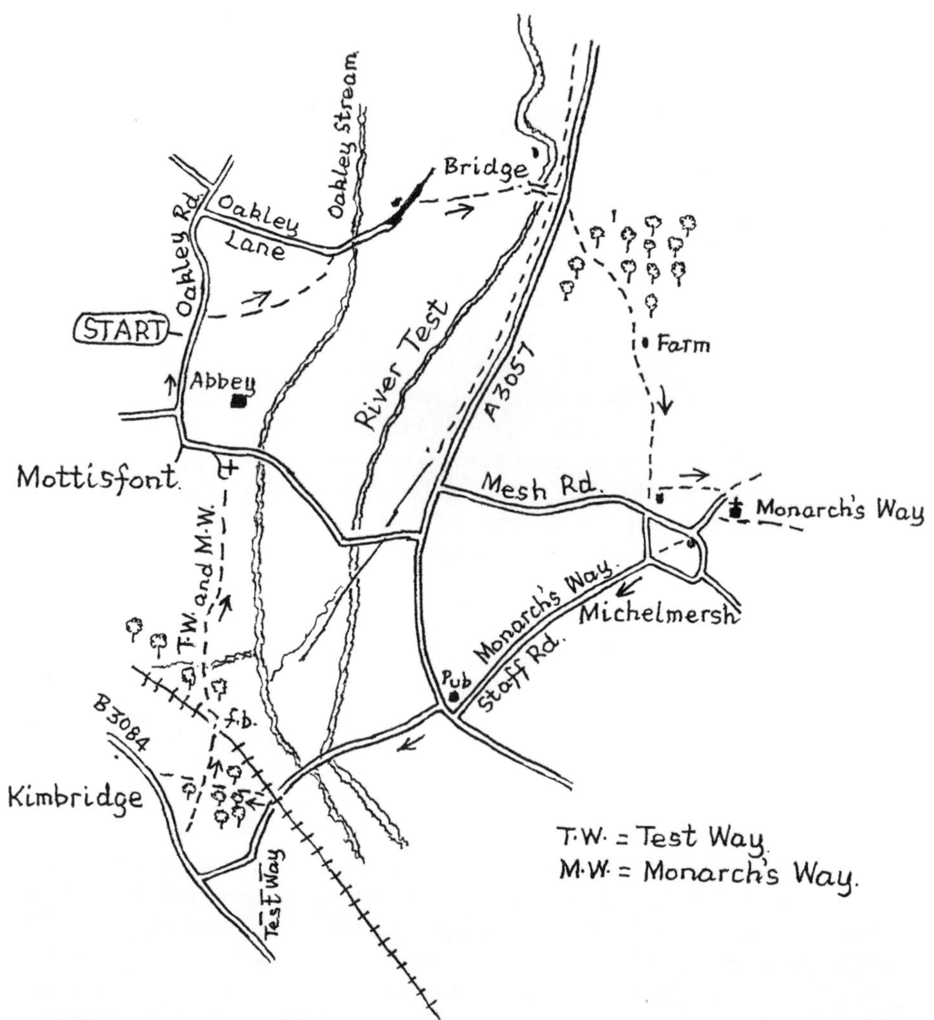

effigy in the chancel. He may have been a forester; his feet are on a stag. Angels are at his head. In 1888 the ceiling was removed from the chancel, revealing 14th century timbers. The wooden tower is probably late 16th century. Although close to the church, it is quite detached. In 1420 the Archbishop of Canterbury required all churches to have bells. This tower may have replaced an earlier one that was built in haste to house the bells.

St Andrew`s Church, Mottisfont was here before the Abbey. Vestiges of a Norman church include the fine chancel arch with its three orders of carving, the plain south door and the font. It has Perpendicular and Decorated windows. The chancel windows contain more medieval glass than any other church in Hampshire. The 15th century east window has restored glass and the original glass that first fitted into the frame. The side windows also contain medieval glass. There are several monuments, including one of an Elizabethan family of 1584 near the altar.

Mottisfont Abbey Cellarium

Mottisfont Abbey was built as an Augustinian priory in 1201. Monks chose this site as there was a deep pool of spring water and the nearby River Test supplied trout. The priory lasted for over 300 years until Henry V111 dissolved the monasteries in 1536. William Lord Sandys then acquired the priory and converted it into a Tudor house. Ever since it has been a private house until 1957 when Mrs Russell gave the estate to the National Trust. Parts of the original priory have survived including the Cellarium which has stone columns and a vaulted roof.

The Walk

Head north along Oakley Road (away from the Abbey). In 50 metres turn right into a field. Signs for Test Way and Monarch`s Way are on a post.

Follow the clear path eastwards across the flat field, passing a small copse on the right. Then veer left passing another copse on the left. You come out on Oakley Lane, a distance of about 500 metres from the starting point.

Turn right and walk along the lane to cross a bridge over Oakley Stream. Do not be tempted down the riverside path on the left. Instead, keep straight on along the pebble track to cottages.

Immediately after the cottages, turn right into a large flat meadow. Again the path is clear and has white marker posts at the far end. You can see the cliff ahead has a chalk quarry.

Shortly after the last marker, you cross a bridge over the River Test.

If you wish to shorten the walk *(omitting Michelmersh) turn right onto the disused rail track, now a cycleway. This leads back to Mottisfont).*

To continue to Michelmersh, keep on course for another 50 metres to the main road, A3057. (You have now departed from Test Way and Monarch`s Way). Cross with care to the path opposite. *You may prefer to walk a little to the right, away from the blind corner on the left.*

Once you have arrived safely on the other side of the main road, do not be tempted up the gently sloping valley ahead. Instead, turn right and southeast towards the tree covered cliff. At an inlet in the wood, you find the fairly steep path up through trees. Towards the top, a handrail has been provided.

Come out high up on an open field with extensive views south. Continue southeast towards more woodland. Go through a clearance at the corner of the wood. Park farm is hidden somewhere nearby.

Cross another elevated open field for 400 metres. You may glimpse the tower of Michelmersh over to the left and find the footpath leading to the church.

If you miss the path, continue to a copse where you pass an idyllic thatched cottage and emerge to Mesh Road. Turn left and climb for ¼ mile. At a road junction veer left into Church Road and pass Michelmersh Barns on the left. The church is on the right.

From Michelmersh Church return down Church Road to the road junction. Cross to the track opposite, passing a cottage on the left and continue southwest on Monarch`s Way which you rejoined at the church.

The track becomes a quiet hedge-lined lane, Staff Road. It leads downhill for 1 kilometre in a straight line to the pub at the bottom, the Bear and Ragged Staff.

Go to the nearby A3057. You have a safer crossing place here. Cross diagonally right to Kimbridge Lane. You are still on Monarch`s Way.

Walk with care along this lane for ½ mile. It passes a popular garden centre and crosses over branches of the River Test. The main river pours down a rapid on the left. Just after the river, you go over a level crossing then turn immediately right. You have now rejoined Test Way and Monarch`s Way shares the route.

After a small field, you enter woodland.

The long distance paths now take you due north for nearly 1 mile. First, you re-cross the railway line on an enclosed footbridge to more woodland on the other side. Veer left then right. Your path is still enclosed to guard you from the deep pit below. Emerge from the wood and cross a bridge over the little River Dun. Do not be tempted to the riverside path. Instead, keep heading north over a little meadow to a hedge-lined track. This brings you to the Village Church of Mottisfont.

You are now in Church Lane and continue to a T-junction. *Turn right for the entrance to Mottisfont Abbey – take care the road is narrow!*

To return to the starting point, turn left through the little village to a junction. Turn right and walk along Oakley Road. You are still on Test Way and Monarch`s Way. In ¼ mile you are back at the layby.

Walk 28: Longparish to Hurstbourne Priors

Climb gently above the villages that nestle close to the Test and its tributary, the Bourne Rivulet. Pass patches of woodland, part of old Harewood Forest.

Starting Point: Car Parks, B3048, southwest edge of Middleton **GR**424439
Map: OS Explorer 144 **Terrain:** Gentle slopes and good paths. Some road walking to and through Hurstbourne Prior **Distance:** 6 – 7 Miles
Local Information: Longparish Church is in Middleton. The original village of 'Middletune' is named in Domesday. As the village grew, it acquired a new name!
Note: Few paths on this walk offer a view of the river. Our map shows some diversions for walkers who wish to get a closer look. See instructions below*

The Churches

St Nicholas, Longparish stands near the River Test and its fine Perpendicular tower is a landmark for walkers on the Test Way. It is built of large blocks of stone and flint. The material probably came from Wherwell Abbey, dissolved 1513. The church has retained its medieval character; Transition Norman nave arcades, Early English chancel, Decorated windows. All have a fresh, clear cut appearance as if they were newly built. Two restorations in 1830s and 1850s would account for this fresh look. Only the chancel priest`s door shows the weathering of c. 800 years. In 1833 the church lost its clerestory windows when the aisle roofs were replaced and given a steeper pitch. Henry Woodyer is responsible for the new chancel roof and the south porch, 1851-2. At that time the Easter Sepulchre may have been moved from the north to the south wall of the chancel. Most of the church windows are filled with colourful glass. The east window has glass by J.H. Dearle of Morris and Co. 1912. It depicts Mary and Child with angels and the stables amongst trees. A window in the

Longparish

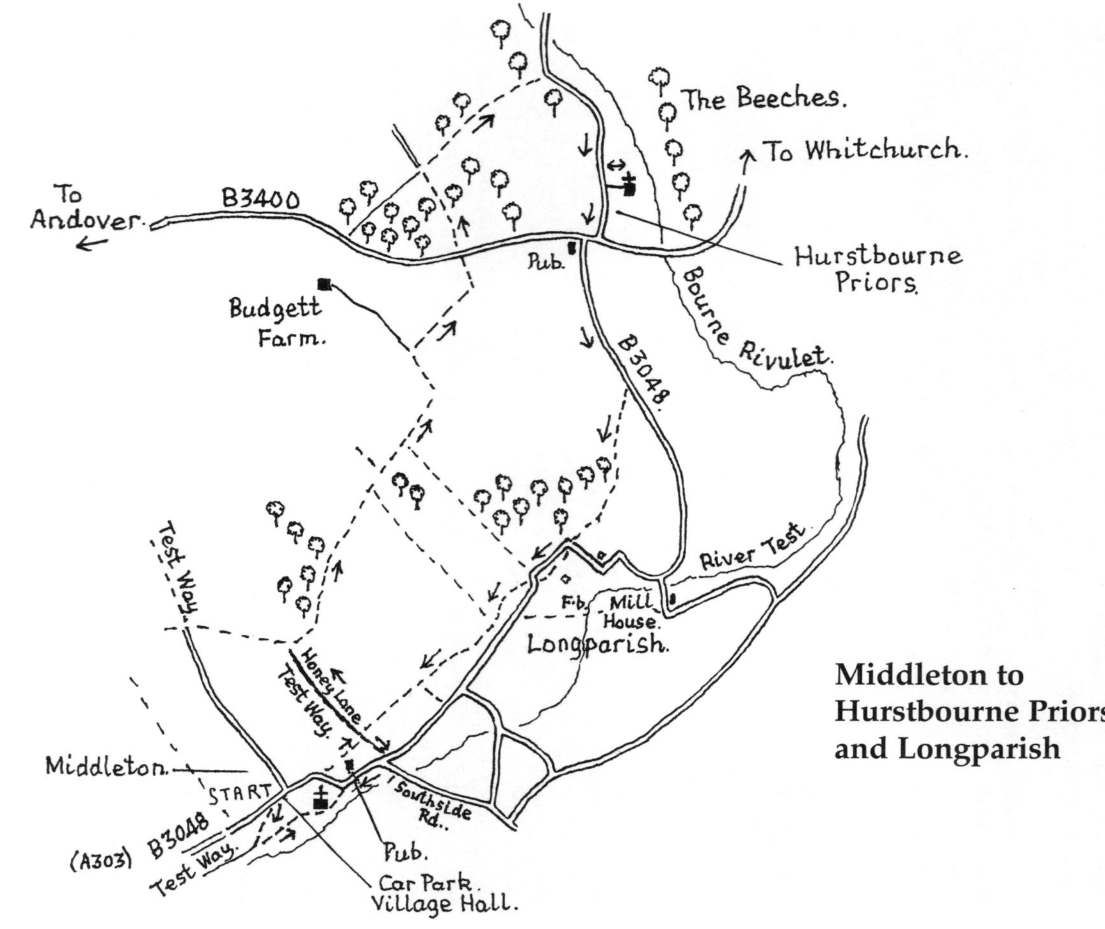

Middleton to Hurstbourne Priors and Longparish

northeast aisle of 1968 commemorates the aviator Major L.G. Hawker who lost his life in aerial combat with the Red Baron.

St Andrew, Hurstbourne Priors has a lovely setting near the Bourne Rivulet with the wooded hill behind. This hill is all we see of Hurstbourne Park. The original church was probably much smaller. It was consecrated in 902 when it probably separated from the mother church of Hurstbourne Tarrant. (See Walk 29). The west doorway has late Norman carving. The tower in Norman style was built in 1870. The cream coloured brick gives the appearance of stone. Another original arch leads to the 16th century north chapel whose straight headed windows are best viewed from the outside. Inside there is a tomb chest of 1574 to Robert Oxenbridge with kneeling children on either side below. In the churchyard lies Hippisley Cox who wrote 'The Green Roads of England' at his house in Hurstbourne Park.

Hurstbourne Priors

The Walk

Turn away from Middleton to turn left into a nearby footpath. It crosses a rough meadow diagonally right. Turn left for the riverside path along the Test Way.

Enter the churchyard and pass St Nicholas` Church on your left. You return to the village road at the Primary School. Turn right and walk past village houses as far as cross roads.

Turn left into the cul de sac, Honey Lane. The Test Way also takes this route. The lane becomes a farm track. Follow it gently uphill for nearly ½ mile to a T-junction. The Test Way departs to the left.

Turn right. You still have the benefit of a firmly based farm track but no footpath signs confirm your right of way – just the occasional 'Private' sign on a divergent field path!

Your track bends left and heads northeast gently uphill for nearly a mile. It hugs woodland on the left then gives a slight lurch to the right. Now you have a hedge on the left and a sloping field on the right. Climb to pass a footpath then a coppice on the right. Avoid paths to left and right.

Meanwhile, continue along the farm track on an open elevated route. It curves to the left towards Budgett Farm. In 250 metres a notice forbids us to go further. Fortunately there is an alternative route.

Turn right into a straight track, thickly enclosed with trees and bushes with just the occasional glimpse to the wooded hills to the right. In ¼ mile you have to turn left. The path is still enclosed and narrower but you soon reach the road B3400. *Hurstbourne Priors is down to the right but I have chosen a quieter walk adding 1 mile to the distance.*

Cross the road to the track opposite. Again the way is enclosed with hedges and then woodland. In ¼ mile you emerge to pleasant open country. *Avoid the tarmac lane ahead leading to Harrow Way. Alas, not our route!*

As soon as you reach the lane, turn right and head northeast gently down over open fields. You have a good view across the valley of the Bourne Rivulet to Hurstbourne Park and the presiding white Mansion. In ½ mile the path goes through woodland to reach the B3048 at a layby. This road is somewhat quieter but take care!

Turn right to walk along the edge of the road to Hurstbourne Priors. After the first few village houses, you reach the handsome drive and avenue on the left leading to the St Andrew`s Church.

Behind the church the Bourne Rivulet flows. Beyond is a hill with some magnificent trees, 'The Beeches'.

As you reach the church tower (also the entrance) turn right and go through the churchyard to the gap in the wall. Go through to the cricket ground and turn right towards a children`s play ground.

You pass the playground and come back to the road again. Turn left and walk to nearby staggered crossroads. The short cut on the right leads to a pub on the opposite corner.

Cross to Longparish Road. Pass the pub on the right and continue south for over ¼ mile. After the last house on the right, cross Drury Close to the footpath in the neighbouring field. Turn into this path.

Cross a riding track with the help of metal gates. Then go diagonally left uphill through the field towards woodland. Re-cross the riding track before entering the wood, *having escaped galloping horses and a phantom bull!*

The path in the wood turns left and soon comes out at a field where you see cottages in the far corner. Keep to your side of the field and avoid going down to the cottages. Instead cross their track and keep on course in the next field. You come to the Longparish Road again. Longparish House is ahead on the left.*

For the most direct route to Middleton, go straight on along the road then cross the next field to a residential part of the village. Turn left at the first road. Just before a thatched cottage, turn right.

Here is a grassy swathe between houses. Follow this grassy path for a ½ mile back to Middleton. The last bit crosses a field to a kissing gate on Honey Lane!

Turn left then right into a twitten to the pub in Middleton. Go through the pub garden to the village road and turn right to return to the car park.

***If you wish to extend the walk to see more of the river,** follow the footpath across the field in front of Longparish House and then continue on the village road. As you enter Longparish, a footpath on the left leads down to the River Test. Then find lanes back to Middleton (see the map).*

Walk 29: St Mary Bourne to Hurstbourne Tarrant and Stoke

Walking is the ideal way to see these pretty villages in the valley of the Bourne Rivulet. As pilgrims, you see fine churches in their rural setting.

Starting Point: St Mary Bourne recreation ground and car park for the shop and toilets. **GR**422503 **Map:** OS Explorer 131
Terrain: Gently undulatiing **Distance:** 7 Miles
Local Information: 1. Hurstbourne Regis (now Tarrant), Hurstbourne Priors (Walk 28) and St Mary Bourne were part of a royal Saxon estate. Hurstbourne Regis, the mother church was a royal manor until 1266 when Henry 111 gave it to the Cistercian nunnery at Tarrant Crawford (Walk 37, Dorset Church Walks). The nunnery has long since gone; the name 'Tarrant' persists.
2. In more recent times, Jane Austen knew these villages well. She often went to stay with her brother James at Ibthorpe House. He had married Mary Lloyd at Hurstbourne Tarrant in 1797. The vicar`s daughters visited Jane when she was there but she did not enjoy their company. She may also have walked over to Netherton House. The family here probably inspired her novel, 'Mansfield Park'.

The Churches

St Peter`s Church, St Mary Bourne was often called just 'Bourne' after the rivulet that runs through the village. It may have been dedicated to both St Mary and St Peter. There was once a long narrow Norman church here. The chancel arch survives from that time but it has been widened. Nothing remains of a possible Norman south tower, apart from the thick walls. The arcades show the extent of the Norman nave. The Pillars are staggered, maybe to fit in with a northeast entrance. The arcades themselves are Early English, added in late 12th century. The south aisle was extended in 14th century. The south chapel was completed in the middle of that century. It contains the tomb of a crusader, believed to be Roger des Andelys who fought 1209 – 1217 and died in battle. Vandalism to this image was probably the work of the

St Mary Bourne

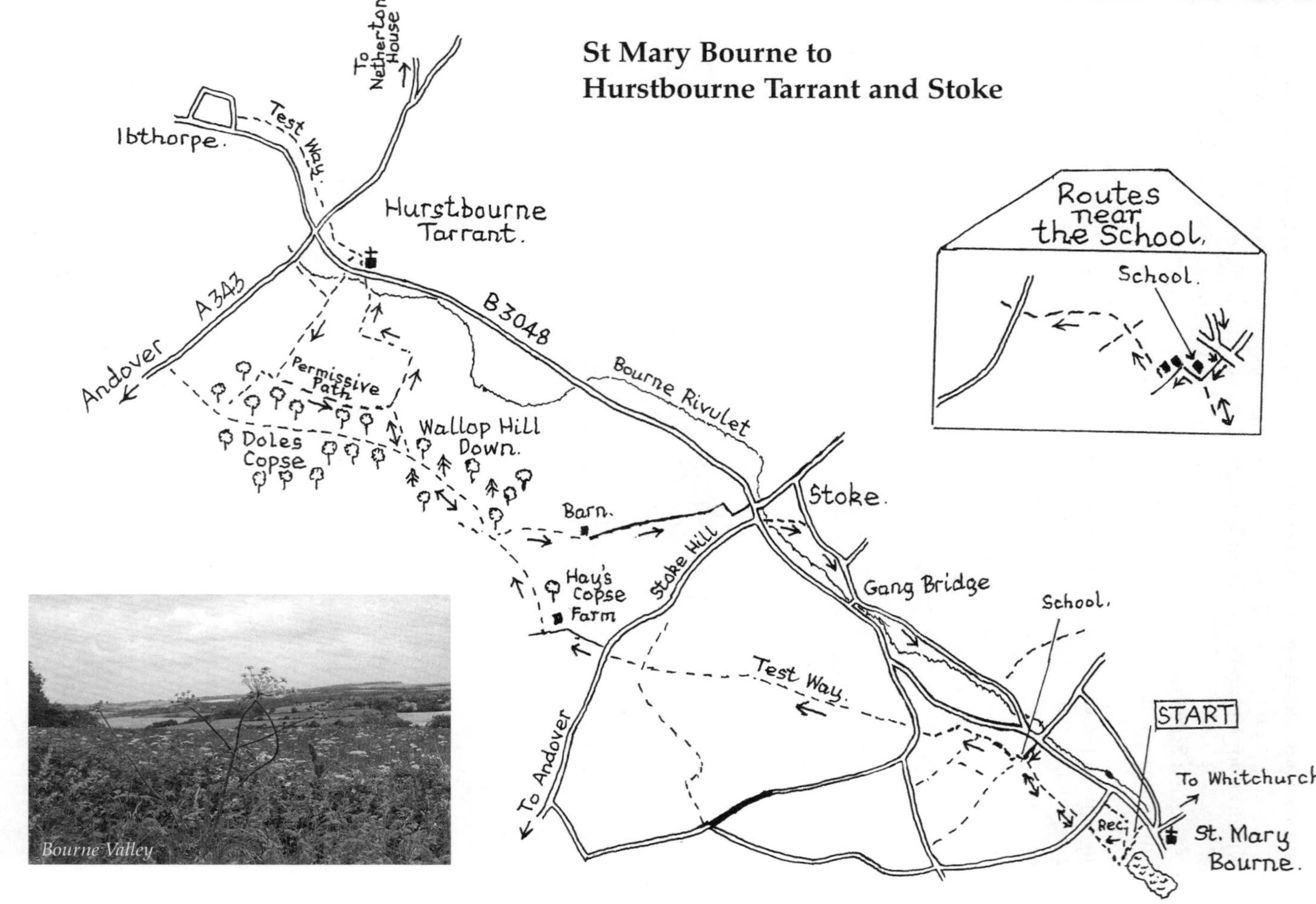

Bourne Valley

King`s Commissioners 1538 – 53. The chancel is late 12th century with original 14th century side windows. The east window was the gift of organist M.A.H.White in 1928. In 1855 the chancel was restored and the roof raised. The 15th century tower has thick walls with flint outside. St Mary Bourne did not have rich villagers. Nevertheless, this is a spacious church. Fortunately, it is well able to house the magnificent Tournai font, the largest in Hampshire. The other three are in Winchester, Southampton and East Meon. The black stone comes from Tournai in Belgium where the fonts were cut and carved. This font is less ornate than the others. On two sides there are carved arches; on two sides vines are depicted. Bishop Henri de Blois (1129 – 71), who founded the Hospital of St Cross was 'most earnest in beautifying churches' and doubtless gave this font to the church.

St Peter`s Church, Hurstbourne Tarrant appears from the outside to be a long, low building with a modest brick porch and a small bell tower. Only when you enter, do you get the true size and value of the church. The porch is medieval, strengthened in recent centuries with brick. It covers a late Norman doorway which has columns with capitals on either side and a zigzag arch. The nave arcades are also late Norman. The church is lofty with a clerestory added to the Perpendicular roof, probably around 1450. The huge round columns of the south aisle show that it is slightly older than the less heavy north aisle. Arches throughout the church are pointed in the Transitional stage from Norman to Early English style. The church has a variety of windows. The oldest (1220) is next to the tower. Starting at the west end, the north aisle has a double Early English window now filled with engraved glass by Tracey Sheppard (2000). Next is a fine 14th century window of three lights and Victorian glass of the Tree of Jesse. Then there is a 13th century window with modern glass (1907) depicting Jesus` miracles. The south aisle has a Perpendicular window. The chancel was rebuilt in1890 and the old windows restored. The east window of four lights is 15th century with modern glass (1935), In their new roof the Victorians installed corbels that give every appearance of being medieval. They are thought to represent King Alfred. Truly medieval is the 'Green man' or head on the south side of the chancel arch. Also of interest are the murals on the wall of the south aisle. The oldest artefact in the church is the stone bowl in the north aisle. It was discovered in the old vicarage garden in 1900 and is believed to be the original Saxon font of an earlier church on this site. For more details, see the excellent church guide.

The Walk

Go to the Sports Pavillion and look out for the Test Way sign in the field boundary on your right. There are in fact unusual metal gates instead of stiles in this part of the Test Way.

Go through the first gate and you are on the 'school run'; pupils` comments have been posted up at each gate. You have a good firm path heading northwest on the edge of agricultural land.

After crossing a tarmac lane, keep on course until you come to the Primary School at Batsford. Pupils from the village have a walk of about ½ mile.

Avoid the lane to the right. Instead, cross to an apparent cul de sac, and pass the

Hurstbourne Tarrant

school on your right. Go to the bungalow facing you and you find that the track bends to the left. Follow it to the second bungalow and turn right into an enclosed path behind houses.

Just before the end of this straitjacket, you can turn left into a field. The horses here were curious but we were able to shoo them away. Climb to the top right hand corner of this field and turn right to the narrow lane.

Cross to the footpath opposite, still the Test Way and still enclosed. You can at least enjoy the view on the right over the Bourne valley. This elevated path leads for 1 mile to Stoke Hill. Just before the road there are crosspaths. Ignore these and keep straight on to the road.

Cross the road to the track opposite which joins the leafy private lane to Stokehill Farm. Walk along the lane to the entrance to the lovely red brick farmhouse. Turn left here into a restricted byway, then sharp right so that you go behind the house. Here is a recreation area with pens for pigs and cockerels. The trig. point is nearby on the left.

Head towards Hay`s Copse and follow the field boundary around to the left until you come to the gate into the next field and the Test Way sign. The path ahead is clearly defined along a field`s edge towards woodland. There are uninterrupted views across the valley.

You enter the wood on Wallop Hill Down. **Note** the path on the right for the return walk, but keep going through the centre of the wood where deciduous and coniferous trees grow together.

In 500 metres the path divides. The Test Way forks to the right and starts descending through woodland for another 500 metres. Suddenly it emerges to a cultivated field slope overlooking Hurstbourne Tarrant.

Turn left to the nearby post with arrows pointing the way. Avoid the permissive path straight ahead (this is for the return walk). Instead, turn right and go down the rough grassy track on the edge of the field. Turn left at the bottom corner and head towards a barn. Turn right and pass the village sports field. You come down to B3048 just opposite the church.

After visiting Hurstbourne Tarrant Church, climb a little way up the graveyard slope at the back. Turn left to go through a squeaky gate to a small field. Pass behind a thatched barn on the left, then turn sharp left and go down to gates onto B3048 again.

We went unchallenged along the unmarked footpath opposite, on the drive between houses. *You may want to turn right and see a bit more of this most picturesque village.* Return to take the unmarked path through the houses to a flat field at the back. Then climb up the slope towards the wood.

Turn left just before the wood. This is the permissive path. It skirts the hillside and has open views to the village below and the rising slopes above the Bourne Rivulet. In ½ mile you return to the post with arrows. Pass it on your right. Retrace your steps along the Test Way into the familiar wood.

Climb up through the wood to the point where a path joins from the right. Turn left here and continue until you can see the gate at the edge of the wood. Just before the gate, turn left on the **noted** path. (The waymarker is hidden in undergrowth in the summer).

You soon come out of the wood to enjoy another open view over the valley. This time the hamlet of Stoke can be seen below beside the Bourne Rivulet.

This is our destination. Cross diagonally left as you descend through the field ahead, making for a decrepit barn – it may not last much longer as a landmark but there is a shabby brick building beyond it.

Pass the barn on your left then turn left into a pleasant tree-lined lane that takes you gently down to Stoke and the B3048 again.

Turn right and walk along the road for 50 metres. At a little footbridge turn left to cross the Bourne Rivulet towards a cottage. Turn right in front of the cottage and a kissing gate takes you into a wide flat meadow. Follow the path that veers right towards the nearby hedge.

Here you join the hedge-lined back lane and turn right. Walk along the lane for ½ mile. Just before the main road, you come to Gang Bridge. Do not cross the bridge but continue along Gangbridge Lane.

Now you have a delightful step-back in time as you pass an assortment of thatched cottages and barns and walk beside the clear little stream.

In ½ mile you again reach the B3048. Cross diagonally left to the little lane 'Batsford' to the Primary School. Pass the school on your right and find the familiar gate on the left into the Test Way. Retrace your steps to the recreation ground at St Mary Bourne.

Walk 30: Broughton to Nether Wallop

One long straight footpath above the Wallop Brook links these two ancient villages in chalk downland.

Starting Point: School Lane, Broughton. Informal laybys on the south side. **GR**306333
Map: OS Explorer 131 **Terrain:** Flat with some gentle slopes **Distance:** 6 Miles
Note: This is a 'pan handled' walk; you start and return along the same path.
Local Information: At the time of Domesday, 'Wallope' was a thriving rural community.
In 1547 Sir William Paulet bought the Manor of Nether Wallop but he and his heirs lived away.
Tenant farmers worked the land. In 1757 **Berry Court Farm** had 954 acres growing wheat, barley, oats, sanfoin, rye and rearing sheep.
Wallop Brook had 9 mills serving Wallops and Broughton, hence the name, '**Nine Mile (Mill) Water Farm'.**
Airports were here in World War 1. Middle Wallop Airfield is famous for its daring pilots in World War 11.
**Nether Wallop`s** picturesque lanes amd Tudor cottages made it the ideal setting for the television filming of Agatha Christie`s Miss Marples in 1980s.
Danebury Hill takes its name from the Celtic 'Dun burh' meaning a fortified place. Beaker folk are buried here, 2000 B.C. Iron Age people from Europe built a 27 acre hill fort, 400 B.C. When the Romans invaded in 43 B.C., Vespasian took the hill fort apparently without a battle.

The Churches

St Mary`s Church, Broughton was a chapelry annexed to Mottisfont at the time of Domesday. Remains of the Norman chapel can still be seen in the nave. In 12th century the north then the south aisle were added. Three bays of the north arcade have round pillars

Broughton

Broughton to Nether Wallop

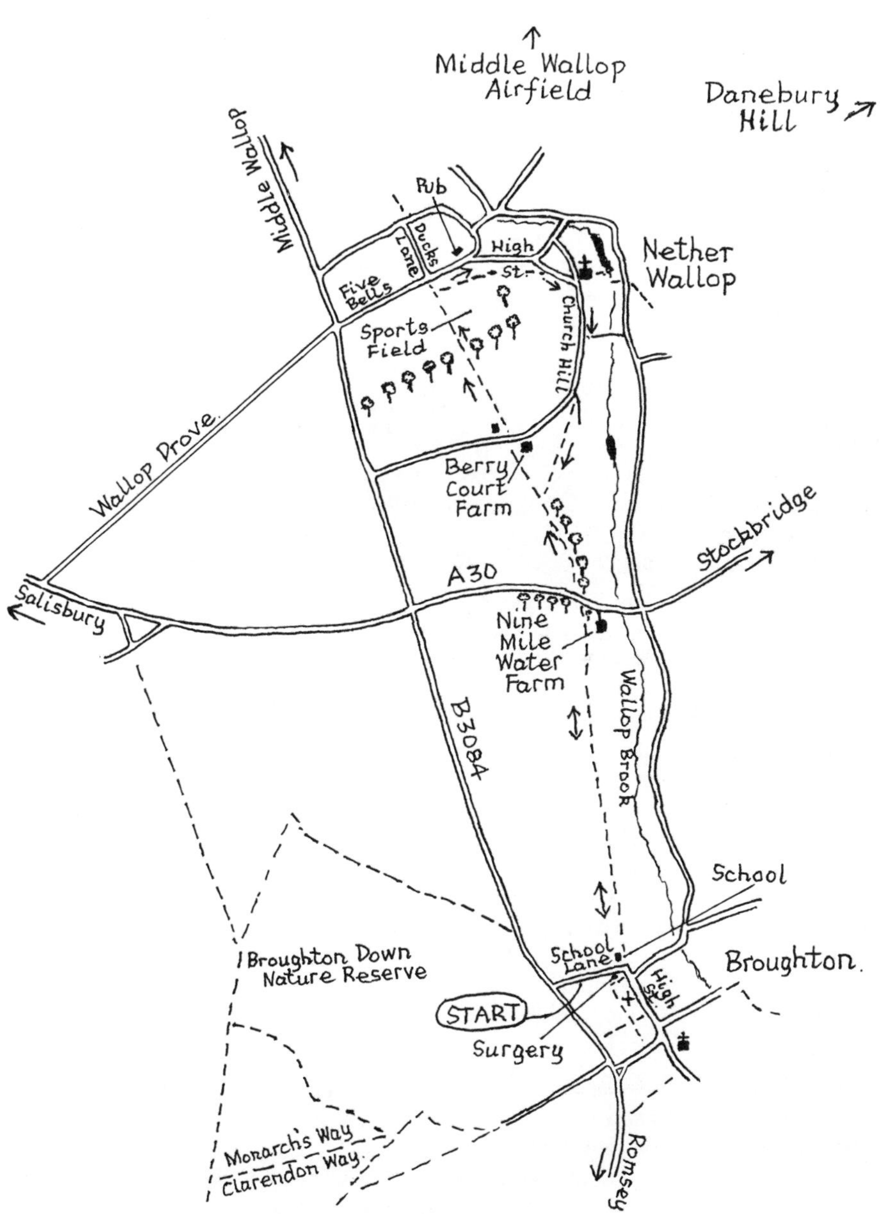

and pointed arches. The chalk arches and the capitals have been damaged by fire. In 13th century the nave was extended westwards and a fine west door fitted. In 15th century the short tower was added and the west door moved to join it. The clerestory windows on the north side are original, those on the south were designed to match. The chancel window by Kempe (1904) depicts the Nativity. There is a large pillar piscina with some carving of roses around the bowl and grotesque figures below. Broughton has had a dovecote since 1341. The present brick circular dovecote in the churchyard is 17th century.

St Andrew`s Church, Nether Wallop is amazingly built into the side of a hill above the Wallop Brook. Water from springs below seep into the floor and walls and yet it has survived many centuries. If you climb further up the hill, still inside the churchyard, you can see the sections of roof covering the different ages of the building. The crossing is the oldest, Saxon part This church was cruciform. Saxon kings owned 'Wallope'. The name 'Waela Hop' is Saxon for the valley by the stream. Saxons were the first inhabitants to live in valleys and so this site suited them. Above the chancel arch a wall painting, dated around 960, shows Christ in Majesty with angels. Succeeding generations have added to the church, making it a very long building. Normans added the south aisle and extended the chancel. In 13th century the north aisle, north chapel and a tower were added. In 14th century the nave walls were raised, larger Decorated windows added and the clerestory built. The chancel was enlarged yet again in 15th century. Most of the wall paintings were made in this century and they are very fine indeed. On south wall of the nave is a morality painting of Sabbath Breakers. Nearby, St George and the Dragon are watched by a wary King and Queen. Above the tower arch you see a dramatic painting of a bell as you turn to leave the church. In 1177 Henry 11 granted the royal estate of the Wallops to Amesbury Priory. In 1436 Maria Mary Gore, former Prioress was buried in the nave where her fine brass can be seen in the floor. The first tower did fall down in 18th century and was rebuilt without a steeple. Francis Douce, died in 1760 and is buried under his pyramid near the tower. He must have inspired his relative, Mad Jack Fuller (East Sussex Church Walks Page 99).

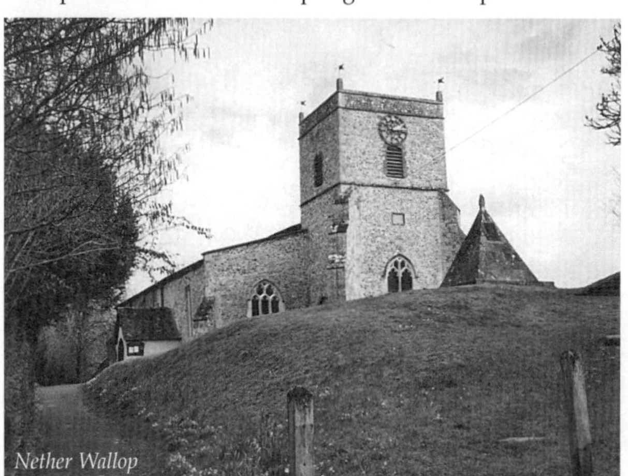
Nether Wallop

The Walk

Before setting off across the fields, walk southwards along the Broughton High Street to visit St Mary`s Church next to the Post Office. On the way, you pass one of the earliest Baptist Chapels built in brick in 1655.

Return to School Lane and the new surgery. Cross to the unmarked footpath and walk through the short alley beside the school on your left to the wide fields. The clear path hugs the field boundary on the right and heads straight to the north. Below, also on the right runs

Wallop Brook.

In one mile you pass farm buildings on your right. Keep heading north across the field to trees that line the sunken road, the A30.

Nether Wallop

Beware! The descent to this main road has no steps, just a mud slope. Cross with care to a small dirt layby opposite and veer left to climb the bank on the other side. Pass the fenced enclosure round a mast on the left. Keep on course along a rough farm track. You now have a tall hedge on the right where ash trees have grown to their full height.

In 600 metres pause to examine the arrows that mark a parting of the ways. The farm track veers to the right. ***We shall return along this track.*** Meanwhile, cross the open field on the left heading northwest towards the boundary hedge. If you fail to find the narrow overgrown path through the hedge, head up towards the large converted barns of Berry Court Farm. Here there is a wide gap and you can cross through the hedge.

Pass Berry Court Farm on your right. Avoid the farm road to the right and follow the finger post to the footpath beside an old barn opposite. Continue the walk northwest across a large flat field. The farmer has marked the way with his tractor. You have a good view to the right to Danebury Hill.

Seclusion appears complete until in 450 metres you cross the next hedge boundary and find a sportsfield. You can now look ahead to the right to see planes on Middle Wallop Airfield. Walk between the hedge on the left and the football ground, then the tennis courts on the right.

You come out on the west side of Nether Wallop at a residential close, Aylwards Way. Follow the access road to the left down to Five Bells Lane.

This map shows a route over the downland back to Broughton. Sadly, I have not tried it myself but keen ramblers may be tempted – if they have time!

Meanwhile, turn right, pass Ducks Lane and individual houses, some thatched. In 200 metres you come to Five Bells Pub. Turn right into the High Street where you pass further fine cottages. In another 200 metres, the High Street makes a cunning turn down to the left. You keep straight on up Church Hill. Pass cottages with a good view over the village. When you come to the church, you have to slip down the slope on the left.

From Nether Wallop Church, slip back up the slope and continue south along Church Hill. *If you have decided to explore the downland way back to Broughton, you will have to return to Five Bells Lane – Good Luck!*

Church Hill takes you above the Wallop Brook, on your left now. In ¼ mile at a finger post turn left into scrub and trees. Veer right to find the field leading to the highlighted track above.

Retrace your steps along the farm track, keeping to the hedge on the left. Pass the enclosed mast and go down to recross the A30 with care! Then return along the straight, elevated path south to Broughton. You now enjoy views to Broughton Down where there is a Nature Reserve.

5 Walks Near Basingstoke

River Dever

Mary Russell Mitford, who spent her childhood in Alresford, describes an idyllic 19th century countryside in her book, 'Our Village'. One chapter is devoted to Haymakers and I have selected a small extract:

'Our good neighbour, farmer Bridgewater, set six men on to mowing by a little after sunrise, and collected fourteen efficient haymakers by breakfast-time. Fourteen active haymakers for our poor three acres! Not to count the idle assistants; we ourselves, with three dogs and two boys to mind them, advisers who came to find fault and look on, babies who came to be nursed, children who came to rock the babies, and other children who came to keep the rockers company and play with the dogs… Nobody could imagine the joyous din of that little place.'

Walk 31: Bentley to Crondall

Step it out through woods, agricultural land or along quiet lanes past farms and country homes to the churches where their owners worshipped.

Starting Point: The recreation and sports field near Bentley Primary School, School Lane **GR**788443
Or Bentley Railway Station **GR**784447 **Map:** OS Explorer 144
Terrain: Gently undulating **Distance:** 10 Miles
(Add another 3 miles if you start from the Station)
Local Information: Bury Court belonged to the Winsor family in 17th century. George Windsore placed in the church a marble memorial to his wife Margaret who died in 1631. A kiln on the north side of the house is a reminder of the hop gardens here. Bury Court is now a centre for weddings and conferences.

The Churches

Bentley, St Mary stands on a hill above the village. The original Norman church was at the centre of the village. In 17th and 18th centuries people and their homes gravitated towards the turnpike road below. In 19th century they headed towards the station. The early church was one of four chapelries dependent on the Manor of Farnham. A monk from Waverley Cistercian Abbey was appointed curate of Bentley. The oldest parts of the church are the round Norman pillars on the north of the chancel and the slightly later north chapel, also the low tower. They are 12th century. The south chapel came a century later and completed the cruciform shape of the church. In 14th century this region suffered from the Plague and the church was neglected. Greater prosperity came in 15th century and the church benefitted.

Bentley

Bentley to Crondall

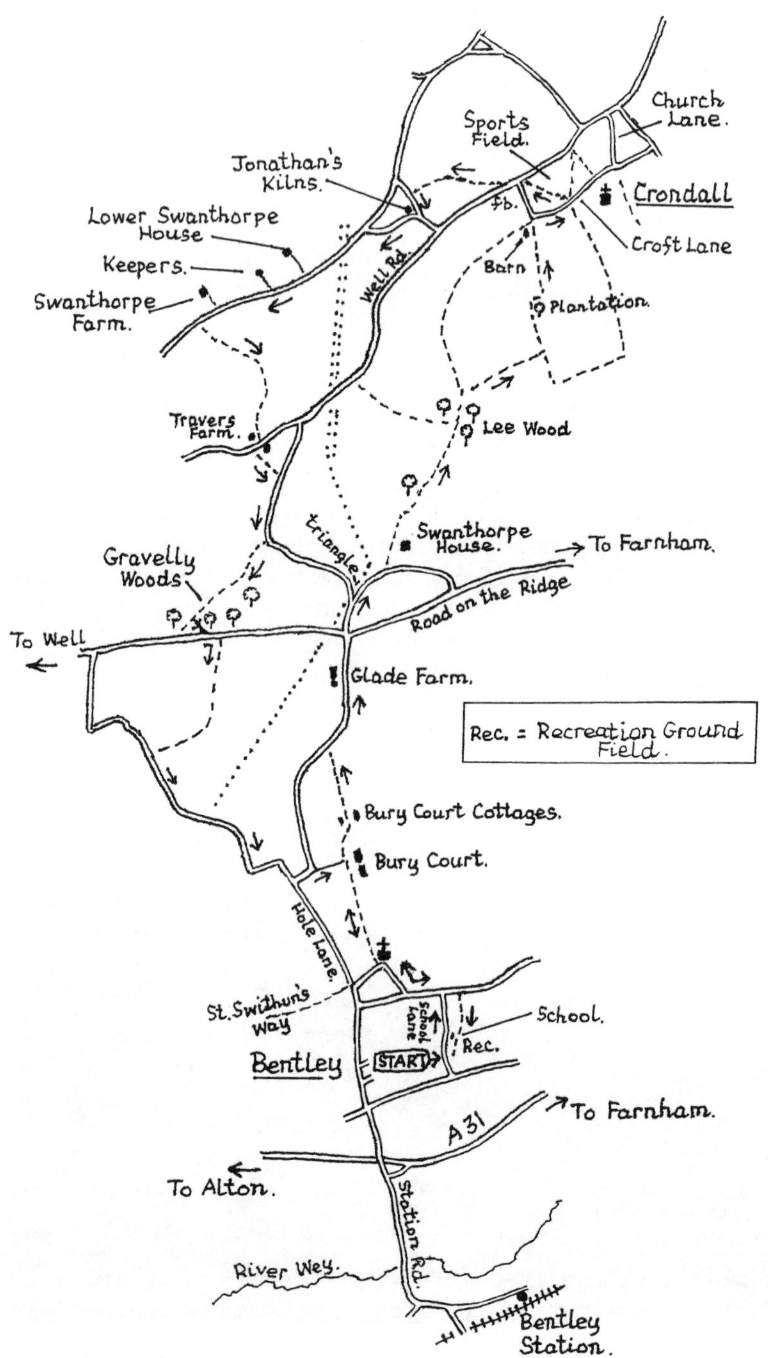

The clerestory windows were fitted in the chancel and the Perpendicular east window was added then. Most of the original glass has been destroyed, but fragments have been retained and included in the Victorian window. In 1890 later 15th century glass was put into one of the south clerestory windows. Early in 18th century the tower was heightened and 6 bells were installed. Rev. Henry Thomas Austen, brother of Jane Austen was the 'Perpetual Curate' of Bentley 1824 – 1838. At that time the village had problems with disorderly drunks and a request to the Bishop of Winchester was made for a cage to restrain the miscreants. In 1835 the south aisle was added but did not last long. In 1885 a major restoration included the replacement of the south aisle and porch. The north aisle in 14th century style was added to make the church rectangular. The Norman font was rescued from a farm and restored on a Victorian base.

**All Saints` Church, Crondall** is a very handsome country church. The original 9th century church was on a more modest scale. St Augustine brought Christianity to 'Aet Crundellan', the Saxon name for the village of chalk pits. Today`s village still has its Saxon shape. The church has changed radically. Only a blocked doorway, seen outside the south transept and the plain font recall the first stone church. Even the Norman church has left few marks: chiefly the south doorway and a blocked window in the north transept. The nave was built around 1170 and has Romanesque pillars. The chancel, a little later, is in Early English style. It has beautiful vaulted roofs with bosses such as those at Canterbury. The central tower was found to be unsafe and replaced with a separate brick structure in 1659. It was a great achievement to build the brick tower in three months. However the design, based on that of St Matthews, Battersea is better suited to a town church in my opinion. Victorian restorations in Norman style have been so subtle that even Pevsner has had difficulty in sorting one age from another. Parson White, the great nephew of Gilbert White was curate here early in 19th century. His diary is in the Oates Museum, Selborne. In 1971 the organ was moved to its place above the west door. Two Millennium windows have glass designed by students, Debbie James and Mia Hegnoj of the Surrey Institute of Art and Design, Farnham.

The Walk

From the recreation ground, walk along School Lane past the school to the T-junction at the end and turn left. Take the first turning along to the right, Church Lane. The church is at the top of the lane

From the station, *walk up Station Road and keep heading north for over a mile on pavements. On the way you cross the bridge over the A31 and the old turnpike road through the village. After that you climb Hole Lane. Go under a footbridge over the lane then turn right for the church.*

From Bentley Church head north on the track that runs beside the churchyard, passing the tower on the right. The avenue here may have been planted in the early 19th century. It is a pleasant shady walk across the hill and down to Bury Court.

Pass the garden and house on the right and the **driveway** on the left. Keep straight on down to Bury Court Cottages. The path goes between cottages then

Bentley, Jane Austen walked here

Crondall

veers left. Follow the hedge on your right up the sloping field to a road.

Turn right and continue up to pass Glade Farm with a triplet of oast houses on the left. When you reach the road along the top of the ridge, turn to admire the view behind.

Cross to the lane opposite and pass a post box and bungalows on the right. Walk as far as a road junction with a grass triangle in the middle. Go under overhead cables here. Fork right and go down the narrow lane as far as the entrance to Swanthorpe House.

Turn left into a good track and head north with glimpses into the garden of Swanthorpe House on the right then walk past well spaced cottages. After the last house, at present guarded by stone dogs, the path narrows and veers right into a strip of woodland. Avoid the unofficial path on the right and continue northeast through this wood.

When you leave this strip, you enter another bigger wood and continue on the path northeast for ¼ mile. Avoid a path to the left, halfway through the wood. Avoid another path to the left just before you leave the wood.

Instead, veer right to open fields and a view ahead to the North Downs. Nearer, more to the left you can see the pinnacled tower of Crondall Church. In another ¼ mile, at a T-junction of paths, turn left towards the church.

You are heading northwest on a farm track for over ½ mile. Midway at a bend in the track you pass a new tree plantation. Continue to a large barn on the left. Turn right and go through the farm gate to the road.

Keep straight on up the road into Crondall, Croft Lane. On the way you pass Farm Lane on the right and a sports field behind the hedge on the left. You also pass a large house next to the church. I am told this was the Manor and is now divided into flats.

From Crondall Church

If you wish to see more of the village of Crondall, continue along Croft Lane to the nearby junction and turn left into Church Lane with its venerable houses. At the end of Church Lane turn left towards the village of Well. In ¼ mile along Well Road, join the shorter route.

For the shorter route, retrace your steps along Croft Lane. Just past the sports field, turn right into a path that crosses a small sloping field diagonally left to Well Road. Turn left.

Both routes: pass the lane on the left to the familiar large barn. Continue along Well Road for 25 metres. Turn right, crossing a concrete footbridge over a ditch and enter a wide sloping field.

Follow the hedge on the left for ¼ mile. After a bend to the left, you come to a quiet lane. Turn left and walk up to Jonathan`s Kilns, a row of little cottages. At the end of the row, turn sharp right and pass the front of the cottages.

You are in another lane and, as it bends to the left, you find a lovely newly planted hedge including spindle berry, hawthorn and field maple. At a T-junction turn left into a no through road, heading southwest for 1 kilometre.

This hedge-lined lane goes under double power cables, passes the drive to Lower Swanthorpe House then Keeper`s Cottage on the right. When you finally reach Swanthorpe Farm with its red tiles, the road becomes a stony sunken track.

Walk up the track for 100 metres then turn left. Climb up steps to an open field and a view again to the North Downs. The footpath leads across the field to a tall thick hedge. Follow the hedge on your right for ½ mile. It bends to the right twice and leads to a lane and the cottages of Travers Farm.

Cross the lane diagonally right to a footpath beside a large shed. Cross the short distance over a field to another lane. Turn right here and walk uphill beside trees that screen the field on the left.

Go under power cables at a bend then turn right into an enclosed, overgrown path. As soon as the path enters Gravelly Wood, obstacles disappear and you have a clear way southwest through the trees.

You come out at <u>the top road along the ridge</u>, about ½ mile west of your earlier crossing. Turn left to walk under arching trees and glimpse the views on the right across farmland to the South Downs and Hindhead.

In 200 metres turn right to enter an unmarked track heading due south. In ¼ mile this track curves to the right and makes a steep descent into Hole Lane.

Turn left and follow the lane southeast for ½ mile to a junction. Turn left and walk along a little way, then turn up the **driveway** to Bury Court ahead. From there turn right and retrace your steps to Bentley Church.

Walk 32: Micheldever to Stoke Charity

Quiet villages in the Dever Valley still allow walkers to find a peaceful landscape where the church is the focal point.

Starting Point: Church Street, Micheldever **GR**514392
Map: OS Explorer 132 **Terrain:** Flat with some undulating ground, open lanes with verges **Distance:** 5 Miles (Add 2 miles each way for the station)
Local Information: Micheldever Wood to the east of the village was once part of Pamber Forest. William Cobbett described it as 'one of the finest oak woods in England'. Today there are forest trails. Trees hide the foundations of a large Roman villa.

The Churches

St Mary the Virgin, Micheldever is on the site of a Saxon church. In 903 King Alfred`s son gave Micheldever to the Abbot of Hyde Abbey, New Minster in Winchester. In 1538 Henry V111 sold the Abbey and its possessions to Thomas Wriothesley (see Introduction under 'Reformation'). He built a house here. He also built the church tower in 1544, possibly using stone from the Abbey. The church has three distinct sections: the handsome tower with bell openings and gargoyles and some interior arches of 1380; the extraordinary octagonal nave with stark walls and high windows, the work of George Dance in 1806; and the more conventional chancel added in1881. The Victorians did much to repair and renew this church. Today, the work continues, especially in the huge churchyard where footpaths abound. In the chancel there are memorials to the Barry family, one at least by Flaxman. Under the tower a tablet remembers Henry Marquis of Ruvigny, a Huguenot who fled from French persecution and fought in battle for the British where he was 'maimed and covered with honourable wounds'.

Micheldever

Micheldever to Stoke Charity

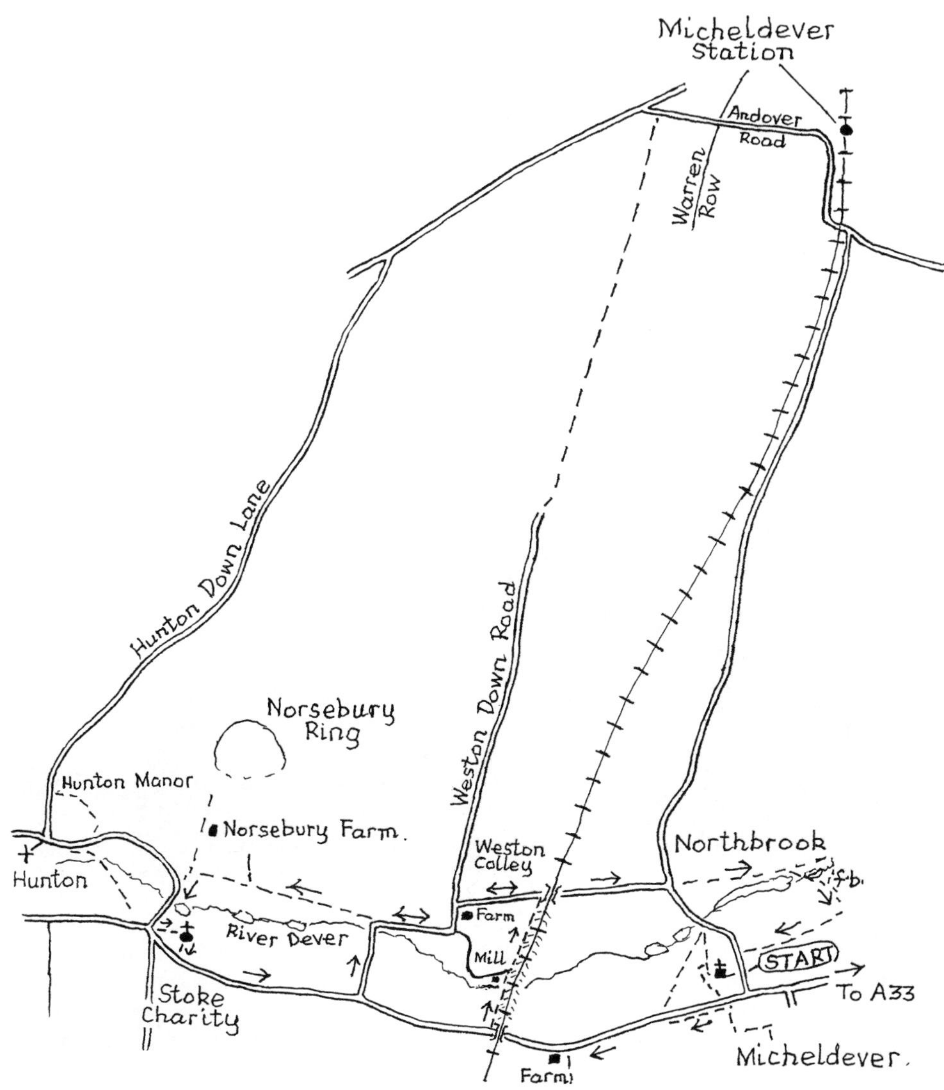

St Mary and St Michael, Stoke Charity is a perfect place. Here is a Norman church set among fields and lakes where village houses keep a respectful distance. Yet William Cobbett in 'Rural Rides' (see Walk 23) said that it was a 'half-starved place'! The manor house had already gone and there were no Victorian lords to interfere unduly. Conservation work in the 1990s has been sensitive to the age-old beauty of this church. The north aisle may have been the original Saxon church and the Normans added the present nave and chancel with lovely arches. The chancel arch is late 12th century. The little Hampton chapel was rebuilt in 15th century. Thomas Hampton, who died in 1483 has a family tomb here. The chapel is filled with ancient tombs also a corner carving of a 15th century revelation of Christ to Pope Gregory. According to a popular legend of the time, the Pope had prayed for the conversion of an unbeliever. This chapel also has a wall painting of around 1200, a carved head of around 1400 and encaustic tiles. Pieces of ancient glass are in several church windows. Outside by the south window, the marks of four 16th century dial clocks can be seen. See the Guide Book for more details of this fascinating church.

Stoke Charity

The Walk

From Micheldever Church walk up to the nearby road junction where a tree in the centre of the small green has a circular seat. Turn right on the road to Stoke Charity. The footpath soon mounts the verge bank on the left. Head westward on this straight lane for 1 kilometre. There are no hedges so you have a good view of the surrounding countryside.

Ahead looms the long, high track of the Winchester to Basingstoke railway line. Trees have grown on these massive slopes. Go through the long bridge, almost a tunnel and turn right into a footpath that hugs the railway on the other side. The footpath descends to cross three footbridges, one over the stream, the River Dever.

Micheldever

On the left the mill is one of the oldest, mentioned in Domesday. Using a broken stile to the access road to this mill, walkers have turned left here - not marked as a right of way. It leads to Weston Farm

You can also reach Weston Farm by continuing along the rail footpath for another 350 metres. Turn left when you reach the road. *At T-junction, the no-through-road to the right leads eventually to Micheldever Station.* Turn left for Weston Farm, pass the access road to the mill on a bend.

Keep heading west past cottages. At another bend in the road, you come to a private lane straight ahead. This is in fact a right of way for walkers. Go through the gate to a straight, flat sandy track past lakes on the left. This is the valley of the River Dever. There are scattered trees beside the track and views to the fields on the right. In ½ mile the track turns right to Norsebury House. You keep straight on along a footpath with a wire fence on the right and a ditch on the left.

In 250 metres you come to Hunton Lane. Norsebury Ring is to the right. Turn left for Stoke Charity. The church can be seen on the other side of ponds. The road crosses the river and climbs past one or two cottages to crossroads. Turn left into a footpath on the corner. Walk across the field to Stoke Charity Church.

From Stoke Charity Church go straight up the path opposite the porch. Turn left on the road back towards Micheldever. Again you are on a straight open road with views all around and a verge to enable you to walk safely.

In 1 kilometre turn left into the road that heads north down to the familiar private lane. Turn right and retrace your steps to Weston Farm. Avoid the no-through-road up the hill *unless you wish to return to Micheldever Station.*

Instead turn right and head northeast to the railway. Go through another rail underpass and emerge to a view over Micheldever. When you come to a T-junction, the station is to the left and the village to the right.

For the rural way back to the church, cross to the alley opposite. The path opens to a sloping field and heads up to a farmgate. In the next field veer to the right away from the main path and pass the narrow end of a lake. Take the wooden footbridge over the Dever and cross a narrow strip of meadow to a cultivated field. Here wide grassy paths lead to an unmarked junction. Turn right and walk straight along towards Micheldever Church. Your goal is in sight. You come out on Church Street.

Walk 33: Monk Sherborne to Pamber End

Quiet tracks and woodland paths lead from Norman church to Priory

Starting Point: All Saints Church, Monk Sherborne or in the village **GR**608558 **Map:** OS Explorer 144 **Terrain:** flat to undulating. Muddy in places after rains. Alternative roadside walk avoids mud. **Distance:** 5½ Miles, can be shortened by following roadside walk shown on adjacent map.

The Churches

Both churches are locked. Phone 01256 850434 to arrange to visit.

All Saints, Monk Sherborne, an early Norman church south of the village, would have been familiar to the monks of Pamber Priory. Herringbone stonework in the walls and some windows in the chancel are of this period. The north doorway with scallop and zigzag moulding is late Norman. The rustic medieval porch obscures the carving and would be better on the west side. There is a large medieval stair turret. The Norman chancel arch stands on slender pillars. The capitals have carved faces with pointed ears. The chancel screen has some 15th century carving. The Norman font has three heads under the bowl. The supports for the font are modern.

Monk Sherborne

Monk Sherborne to Pamber End

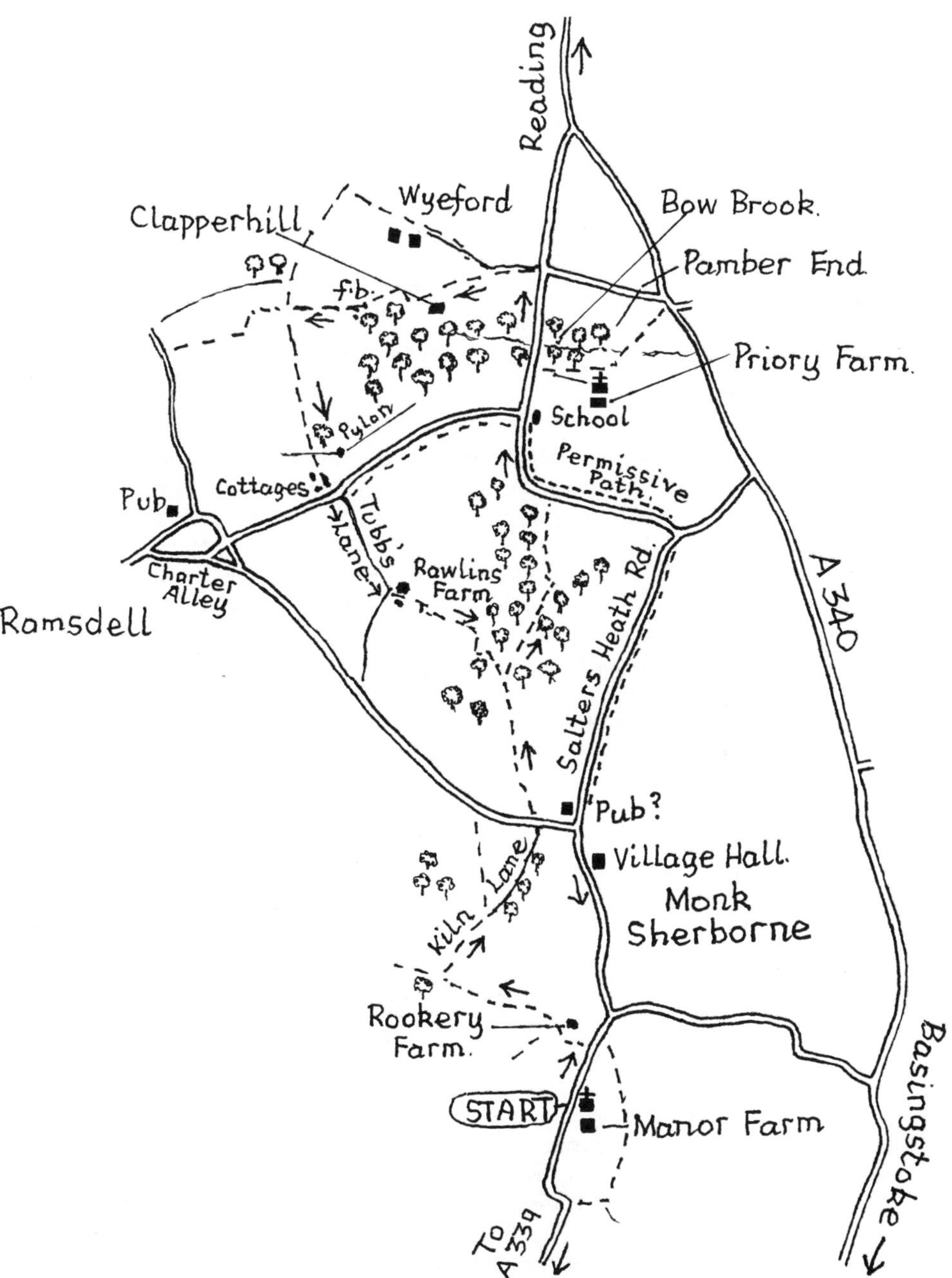

The Priory Church of the Holy Trinity, Our Lady and St John the Baptist, Pamber End was once central to one of the largest priories in Hampshire. This Benedictine Priory was founded in 1130 and enjoyed royal patronage. Monarchs stayed here on their way from Windsor to Winchester. The Priory survived Henry V`s suppression of alien houses in 1414. Henry V1 granted it to Eton College in 1452. The college evicted the monks and tore down much of the priory. Edward 1V gave it to The Hospital of St Julian, Southampton (see Walk 21) and both came into the care of Queen`s College, Oxford. Only the central tower and the chancel survive. As we approach the tower entrance, we are passing over the nave with transepts on either side. The chancel is big enough for a generous church building. It has rows of deeply splayed windows and two round Norman windows above them. The east end has three long, spaced Early English lancets. All the glass is plain. On the north wall are faint paintings of angels. Behind a grille on the southwest side of the church is a wooden effigy of an unknown knight, about 7 feet long, of 1310. The outer south side of the priory is inaccessible, as it is in the grounds of a private farmhouse.

The Walk

As you leave All Saints Church, turn right and walk down the road to nearby Rookery Farm. Turn left into the farmyard. Pass the farm buildings on your right. Then turn right to walk behind the farm.

Avoid the footpath to the left. Instead, fork right and follow the farm track uphill through fields for ¼ mile as far as woodland on the left that drops into a chasm. Turn right here to head north across the field to a tree-lined path. Soon after a bog on the right, the path becomes a track with spaced houses, Kiln Lane.

You come to the village road and cross diagonally left to the path through the alley. It heads northwest through fields to **Grove Cross Copse**. Inside this wood you fork right. The path is clearly marked through the heart of this wood, the haunt of deer. In nearly ¼ mile emerge to a flat field. Follow the edge of the wood on your left. You have a view ahead to the solid oblong Priory tower.

At the tarmac road turn left. *Note the permissive path opposite that leads to the right and back to Monk Sherborne. This is the short dry way back!*

First you have to proceed northwards along the road. At the Priory Primary School on the right you may be fortunate enough to be handed the key to Pamber Priory. *The road opposite the school provides another possible short cut. You walk up it for ½ mile as far as cottages and then turn left. Continue at Tubbs Lane * below.*

Meanwhile, armed with the key, you continue north for a few more metres and turn right into the driveway to Pamber Priory. Majestic oaks form an avenue. You enter through the tower and you can view the outside on the north. The south side, the domainof Priory Farm, is closed to the public.

From Pamber Priory return along the drive. *If you wish to follow one of the shorter routes, turn left.* For the longer route turn right and continue northwards along the lane. Cross the bridge over Bow Brook. In another 150 metres at crossroads, turn left into the private drive to Wyeford.

Walk gently uphill under trees and shrubs to a bend in the drive to the right. Immediately look for an arrow on the left. Turn left to enter a narrow path

Monk Sherborne

Pamber End

hemmed in with barbed wire on both sides. Watch out for rabbit holes further along. Pass a large house, Clapperhill on the left. In another ¼ mile you cross two footbridges over streams and then escape to a large open field.

Ignore the arrow pointing left on the post!

Instead, turn to the right and make for the furthest corner of the field where you can see a farmgate and the trees of Hog Park Copse. Inside the copse you come to crosspaths. Turn left and avoid the footpath facing you.

Turn left again and follow the hedge-lined path southwards. You are now walking on the other side of the hedge bordering the field you just crossed. In ½ mile you come out at cottages on the lane. *Priory School is to the left.*

*Cross to the tree-lined bridleway, Tubbs Lane diagonally left opposite. *Walkers who came up from the school turn left to enter this track.* Walk gently down for ¼ mile to Rawlins Farm. Pass the brook on the left.

Turn left onto the driveway through the landscaped gardens, pass the house then turn right. Walk between the smaller private gardens on the right and an arena for horse jumping on the left. After two sharp bends in the path, you enter **Grove Croft Copse** and follow the clear path back to the point where you first entered this wood.

Retrace your steps back to Monk Sherborne. Instead of the field route through Kiln Lane opposite, you may care to turn left and walk through the village. With luck the pub may have re-opened. Head south along the village street, pass the war memorial at the junction at the end and keep straight on up to the church.

Walk 34: Bramley to Silchester

We walk in the footsteps of Roman soldiers from a church on the edge of town to another on the edge of a Roman ghost town

Starting Point: Bramley Church on the Silchester Road **GR**645589
Maps: OS Explorer 144 and 159 **Terrain:** Flat fields, woods and lanes, few stiles. Instead there are several gates for pedestrians. **Distance:** 7 Miles
Local Information: Calleva Atrebatum (Silchester) was a Roman town built on the site of an Iron Age settlement. It was a well ordered, walled town on a grid system with a central forum, 4 temples, a possible church, houses, shops, squares and adminstrative offices.

Churches

Both churches feature in Simon Jenkins` book, 'England`s Thousand Best Churches'.
The Church of Saint James, Bramley has grown from a mixture of building styles. According to the succinct church history leaflet, 'It was built in 1160 on the foundations of the previous Saxon church with flints taken from the walls of the Roman settlement of Calleva (Silchester), and is unusual in that the chancel is the same height and width as the nave. The brick tower was added in the 1630s. The Brocas Aisle (south transept) was added by the architect Sir John Soane around 1800, to house the tomb of Bernard Brocas who died in 1777'. The mainly Norman nave has medieval wall paintings. On the south wall a vivid picture of the murder of St Thomas a Becket is believed to be an accurate portrayal made 50 years after the event. On the north wall St Christopher is painted (c. 1475) above mermaids and fish. The rood screen is 15th century. The east window by Victor Milner depicts 'Christ is King'. The large window of the grand Brocas Aisle has stained glass of the Liège school (1488 – 1540) and shows Biblical scenes in Flemish settings. The gallery was built in 1728 for the servants and young people. In 1884 fluted Corinthian style pillars were added to bear the weight of the organ. Church pews are larger at the front (for the gentry) than those at the back! The weather vanes outside are of a crowned moor`s head.
St Mary the Virgin, Silchester has developed from a simple nave and chancel to a varied building where all the sections fit to make one lovely whole. The Bluet family held the manor here in 1200 and added the north aisle. There are only two bays and a round pier with a Norman scallop capital. In 1230 the north doorway with hood-mould and dogtooth decoration was added. The south aisle was built at the same time. The last of the Bluets, Eleanor, who had married Edmund Baynard in 1323, continued to care for the church. The south aisle was then reconstructed in simple Early English style. The arches of the south arcade have a definite chamfer. Fine Decorated windows were inserted in both aisles and the west end of the nave, giving more light. The wall tomb in the south aisle has an effigy, believed to be of Eleanor. Late in 15th century, a large Perpendicular east window was fitted, replacing the triple lancets. One of the finest chancel screens in Hampshire is early 16th century. It has fine wood carving, a frieze of angels with a wide wingspan, pomegranates and roses are the symbols of Henry V111 and Catherine of Aragon. The Glastonbury chair beside the altar is made from Roman oak, part of a water channel. On the east wall a most striking wood carving of Cristos, painted in metal is the work of modern sculptor, Peter Eugene Ball. There is a rare pulpit made in the time of Oliver Cromwell. The sounding board above is 1639.

Bramley to Silchester

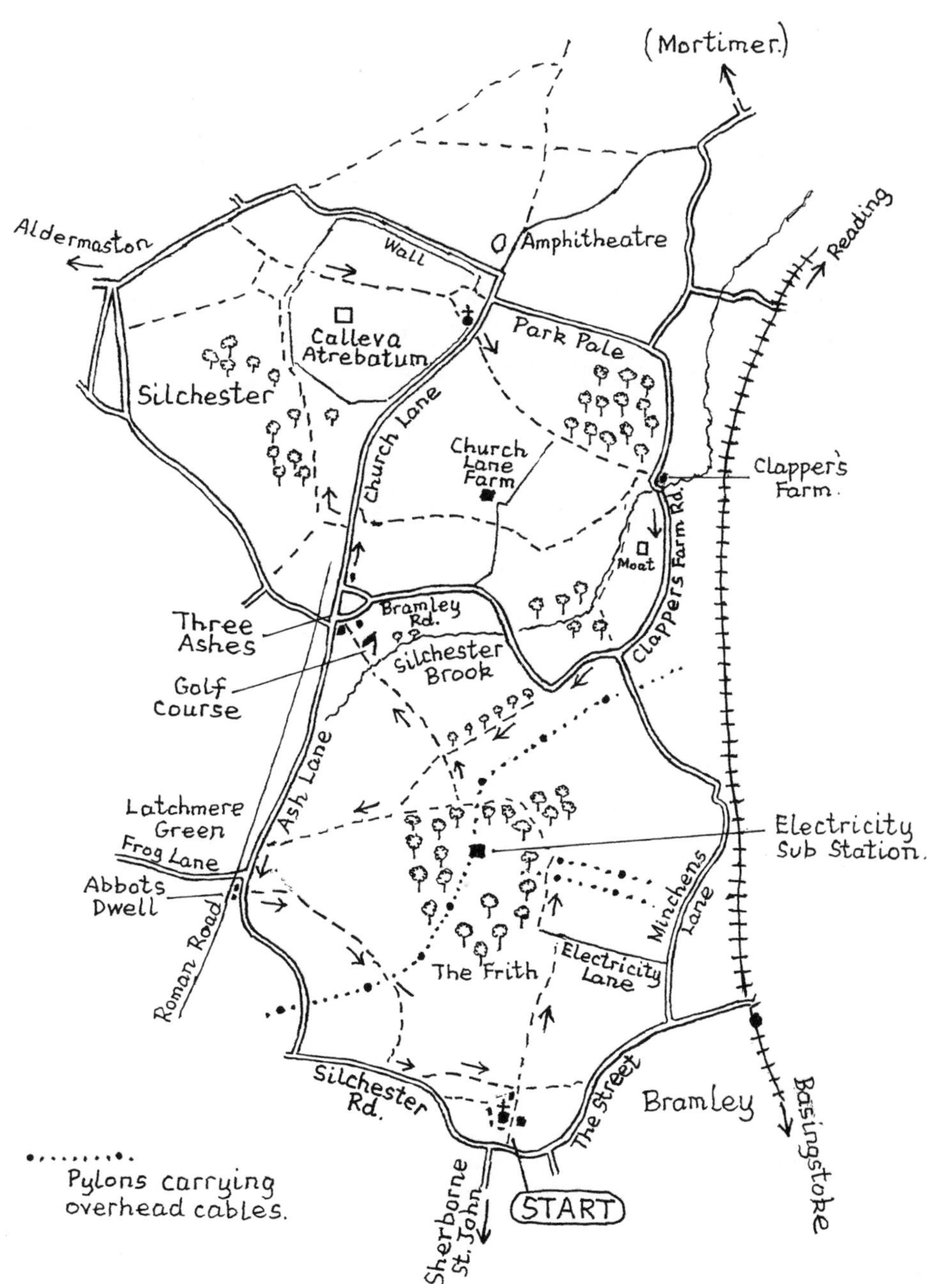

Bramley

The Walk

The footpath signpost points the way through the cluster of buildings in and near the churchyard. Pass the church on your left and the church hall on your right. Go past the school house to find the track heading north between fields

In ½ mile at Electricity Lane, turn left towards the entrance to an Electricity Sub Station. At the very gates, a path on the right takes you into the ancient woodland, known as the Frith. Bluebells, primroses and wood sorrel grow here. The path goes around the electricity station. You have glimpses of it on your left, as you walk around it for ½ mile.

The path curves to the left and the north side where you come to a gate out of the wood. Turn right here and emerge to open fields.

Pylons and cables are on your right. Walk straight on heading northwest across the wide open field. The path is well trod. In 200 metres you come to **crosspaths** at a tree-lined stream.

Go through this light barrier and continue northwest for ½ mile. On the way, you cross the footbridge over a stream overhung with willows, Silchester Brook. On the other side you find a little golf course, with daffodils under the scattered trees. Keep to the left on a narrow tree-lined path. The trees are succeeded by thick hedges and you come out to Three Ashes where roads meet and comfortable houses enjoy plenty of space.

Cross diagonally right to Church Lane opposite. In ¼ mile turn left off this lane and into a field. The path goes to the hedgerow on the left and follows it a little way westwards.

In 100 metres the path divides. Turn right and head north across the field towards Dickers Copse. Keep this woodland on your left as you make for the Roman Town of Calleva Atrebatum. The walls loom ahead. First you have to cross the boundary and earthworks, then a small field. Keep on course, veering slightly to the left to pass through more trees. Emerge to a field on the western edge of the Roman town. *The museum is to the left.* Follow the fence above the ditch on your right until you reach the gates into Calleva.

Enter the town then turn left to walk to the west gate. Turn right into the wide straight street through the town. Check on noticeboards to find where the buildings were. You pass the central forum on your right. Beyond it there may have been an early church.

The existing church of St Mary, Silchester can be seen ahead. Near the end of the street, take the path to the right to visit the church.

From Silchester Church leave by the north porch and turn right, following the main path to the car park. Go through to Church Lane. *The amphitheatre is to the left.* Cross diagonally right to the signed footpath.

It leads gently downhill through fields in a southeasterly direction for one kilometre. Halfway down you come to a farm track (to Church Lane Farm). Turn right then immediately left here. Pass a depleted copse on the left. You come down to the narrow east end of the field and find two paths.*

The path on the right is now part of the Silchester Trail (look for the sign). It follows the course of the brook, passing a moat and 13th century water meadows on the left. In ½ mile you cross a footbridge and soon come to a byway. Turn right on the Bramley Road.

Alternative road route:

*Take the path on the left and continue to Clapper's Farm Road. Turn right and walk along the lane. A square moat can be seen through the hedge on the right. In ½ mile you come to a road junction. Turn right on Bramley Rd.

Both routes: In ¼ mile the road bends to the right. You take the footpath to the left. It leads straight on southwest beside a stream on the right

At familiar **crosspaths** turn left to re-enter the Frith. Turn right and head east through the edge of the wood. You soon come to a footbridge and emerge to open fields. Keep to the right hand side and pass horse jumps.

In ¼ mile you climb a high stile and slip down a short slope to Ash Lane. Turn left and pass Latchmere Green Farm on the left then Frog Lane on the right. You come to two delightful little thatched cottages on the right.

Turn left opposite the second cottage, Abbots Dwell. Here a flat bleak farmtrack heads southeast for ½ mile. The only trees are in the Frith, away to your left. Soon after overhead cables, the public right of way ends. You have to turn right into a narrow footpath, hedged on the left and fenced on the right. It is almost a relief to reach Silchester Road – beware of traffic!

Turn left. In 100 metres, scurry into a private drive on the left where the footpath leads across pebbles to the back. Turn right into another fenced path behind houses then the field with the church nearby. Turn right for Bramley Church.

Silchester

Walk 35: Old Burghclere to Sandham Memorial Chapel and Burghclere

A sheltered walk mainly along tracks, including a disused railway line to an exciting variety of churches

Starting Point: Car park for Beacon Hill on west side of A34 **GR**463577
Maps: split between OS Explorer 144 and 158 or wholly on Landranger 174
Terrain: gentle slopes mainly on tracks **Distance:** 5 ½ Miles
Note: Sandham Memorial Chapel is open year round as follows:

28 Feb – 29 Mar, 1 Nov. – 20 Dec,	11 – 3	Saturdays and Sundays
1 Apr – 27 Sep,	11 – 5	Wednesdays to Sundays incl.
30 Sep – 31 Oct	11 – 3	Wednesdays to Sundays incl.

The Churches

All Saints Church, Burghclere has seen better days when it was the focal point of village life. Now, only at Christmas is the old church revived and folk flock here for this annual celebration. Despite the air of abandon and the rusty locks, someone slips in to make sure it is open to the persistent visitor – try the door to the chancel! The church was built around 1100. Outside, it reveals its age in the irregular stone and flint walls and two Norman doorways in the nave. The south doorway has a fish scale pattern on the tympanum above the door. The north doorway has columns and an arch carved with cylinder pattern. The west doorway, the north transept dedicated to St Katharine and the chancel are all 13th century. The chancel is Early English but much restored by the Victorians who must be responsible for the stained glass in the east window. Inside, the church is long and plain.

Sandham Memorial Chapel was completed in 1927. The Bishop of Guildford then dedicated this *Oratory of All Souls*. It is an oblong brick building, quite devoid of charm on the outside. It is a memorial to Lieut. H.W. Sandham who died in 1919 after the Macedonia Campaign. His sister and her husband, Mr and Mrs Behrand were greatly impressed with the art of Stanley Spencer who had shared some of the Macedonia experiences. Spencer was appointed Official War Artist in 1918. He wanted a 'holy box' to house his paintings. The Behrands supplied it when they commissioned this chapel by the architect, Lionel Pearson. Spencer moved in even before its completion and covered every inside surface with his inspired paintings The National Trust now manages the chapel and we are fortunate to enter and enjoy the artistic experience.

The Church of Ascension, Burghclere was built in 1838 to accommodate the shift in population. It is in Early English style with a tower and transepts. It was designed by G. Guillaume and remodelled in 1875 by W. G. Adey.

Old Burghclere to Sandham Memorial Chapel and Burghclere

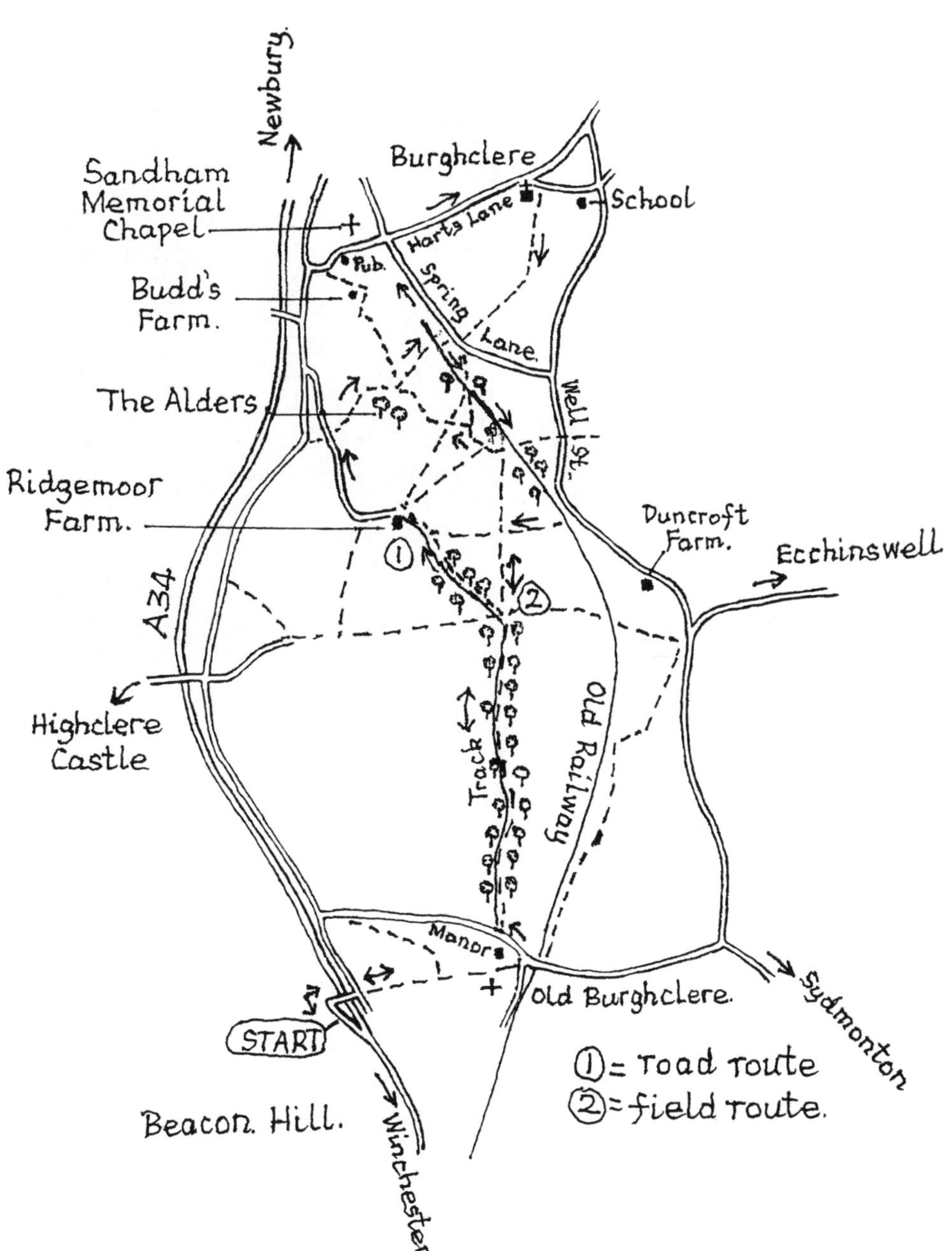

The Walk

Note: *If the maze of footpaths near The Alders is too confusing, follow the road route or find the disused railway line and take your bearings.*

Burghclere

From Beacon Hill car park cross the A34 on the quiet road bridge. At the T-junction on the west side, cross to the footpath facing you. The path veers right and descends the wooded slope. At the bottom turn left into a cultivated field.

Follow the hedge on the left towards Old Burghclere Church, seen among trees ahead. Up on the right you have a good view of Hampshire hills, Ladle and Watership Down.

At the field corner go through the narrow path passing the old church on the right. Continue along the driveway past the Manor and through gates to the tarmac road.

Turn left and pass Manor Farm on the left. After the bend turn right into a track described as a byway. It heads north between hedges for nearly 1 mile, rising gently at the end.

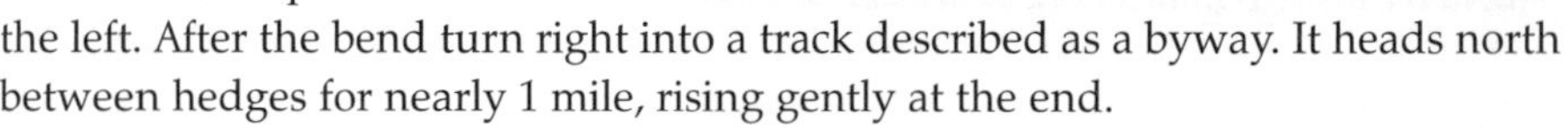

Once over the top, you come to cross tracks and have a choice:

1. The road route: keep straight on along the track as it descends towards Ridgemoor Farm. Pass this on your left and continue along the lane, West Street. After cottages, in ¼ mile a footpath crosses the street. Turn right and head northeast. (It is possible to avoid footpaths altogether. Keep on to the end of West St. then turn right to walk on a pavement beside busier roads)

The footpath northeast leads to woodland, 'The Alders'. After a gate you come to an opening with a seat in the gap on the right. A wonky finger post gives uncertain guidance. There is a rough uncultivated slope on the left.

The safer option is half left along a straight, narrow path northeast.

The path finally crosses planking then climbs up a sharp slope to the dismantled railway line. *The track to the left is blocked. We shall be taking the track to the right later.*

For now, cross to the path on the other side of the railway line and descend to the road, Spring Lane. Turn left and walk up to crossroads. Turn left for nearby Sandham Memorial Chapel and the pub, a little way further.

Sandham

The field route: *at cross tracks take the hidden footpath on the right. It heads due north down through fields. Go straight on at* **crosspaths***. In ¼ mile take the path on the left towards woodland. Cross a footbridge and enter 'The Alders' where you pass a seat on the right and a wonky finger post on the left. Veer right and head northeast on a straight narrow path to the disused railway line. Climb up to this elevated track and cross down to the other side. Turn left to walk along Spring Lane to crossroads. Sandham Memorial Chapel and the pub are nearby to the left.*

From Sandham Memorial Chapel return to crossroads but avoid Spring Lane on the right. Instead, keep straight on along Harts Lane to the new village of Burghclere. The church is on your right.

To return to Old Burghclere, go behind the church and head southwest on a footpath across fields. In ½ mile cross Spring Lane diagonally left to climb up onto the dismantled railway line. Turn left.

Keep on this straight elevated track for nearly ½ mile until you find it running parallel with the road, Well Street on the left. Avoid turning left to the road. Instead, turn right into a footpath through woodland. It brings you to the familiar **crosspaths** of the **field route**.

Turn left and retrace your steps to the cross tracks, go back down the byway to Manor Farm.

6 Walks in the New Forest or near the River Avon

The New Forest

William the Conqueror chose the New Forest as his hunting ground since the soil was not good for agriculture. The Normans made the first ever conservation laws. Men who lived in the forest, 'foresters', were allowed to release their animals and cultivate a portion of land but not to erect fences. William Rufus succeeded William 1 and was killed in the New Forest. This cruel and unpopular king died in a hunting "accident" in the forest. His courtier, Sir William Tyrell shot the fatal arrow and escaped via Ringwood to Normandy. The king`s brother, Henry hastened to Winchester to claim the throne. In medieval times timber from the New Forest was used to construct ships, including those of the Armada. William 111 introduced an 'Enclosures Act' in 1698. Despite this, the Forest was a refuge for fugitives and smugglers. In 1848 foresters, who gained rights to Common Pasture, were known as 'Commoners'. They elected 'verderers' to defend their privileges. The Verderes' Court is held at Lyndhurst. After the First World War, conifers were planted in the New Forest. There are still more native oaks and a great variety of trees including Douglas Fir, Redwood and Wellingtonia. New Forest ponies wander through the trees and over the heath land. They are owned by commoners who round them up every so often at Beaulieu Road and sell some for riding, some for meat. The New Forest is now a National Park.

Walk 36: Beaulieu to Buckler's Hard

A quiet woodland walk beside the Beaulieu River from a medieval refectory to a converted terrace house with a smugglers` cellar, both now churches

Starting Point: The Car Park, Beaulieu Village **GR**386022
Map: OS Explorer OL22, OL29 **Terrain:** A firm, flat woodland track, part of the long distance path, Solent Way. Avoid High Tide. **Distance:** 5 Miles
Note: This linear walk needs some preparation. **1.** The way near Buckler`s Hard may be flooded at High Tide. Consult a Tide Table. **2.** Beaulieu Abbey Church is usually closed to visitors from the riverside and open in the afternoons to those who have paid to enter the Motor Museum. You can arrange a free visit from the riverside by phoning Beaulieu Rectory on a Thursday Morning: 01590 612242 or attending a Service, Sundays at 9.30 a.m., Wednesdays at 10.30 a.m. **3.** You may prefer to find free parking and start the walk at Buckler`s Hard, reversing the order below.

The Churches

Beaulieu Abbey Church, the Blessed Virgin and Holy Child was part of the Cistercian Abbey founded in 1204 overlooking the Beaulieu River. After the Dissolution of 1538, the refectory became the church. It is the Parish Church of Beaulieu Village and can be approached from the river. The abbey ruins are in the grounds of the Motor Museum. The refectory was built around 1230 with a north-south orientation. It is a lofty building with a wagon roof of plaster and some original bosses. The lancet windows are irregular. In the west wall there are 18 steps leading up to a pulpit where, in the days of the refectory, readings were made to the monks eating in silence below. The pointed arches and Purbeck marble pillars of this wall are fine examples of 13th century work.
**The Chapel of St Mary, Buckler`s Hard** is a converted house in the middle of the west terrace of the High St. This street, flanked by terraces is unique. It is just a grassy slope leading down to the river. The houses here had a reputation as smugglers` dens. Since 1538 the Montagus have owned the estate. This house was home for shipyard workers. It became an infants` school 1846 – 1880. It was then converted to a chapel in 1886 when an altar was installed. In 1935 the Bishop of Winchester held a Dedication ceremony. Local people have endowed panelling, altar, statues and other gifts to this peaceful chapel. The little 'History of the Building' tells it all.

The Walk

From the Car Park in Beaulieu go through the wide pedestrian way past tourist board and café to the High Street. Cross diagonally left to the Post Office. Join the B3054 to cross the river.

Walk on the raised path beside the road on your left and the wide greensward

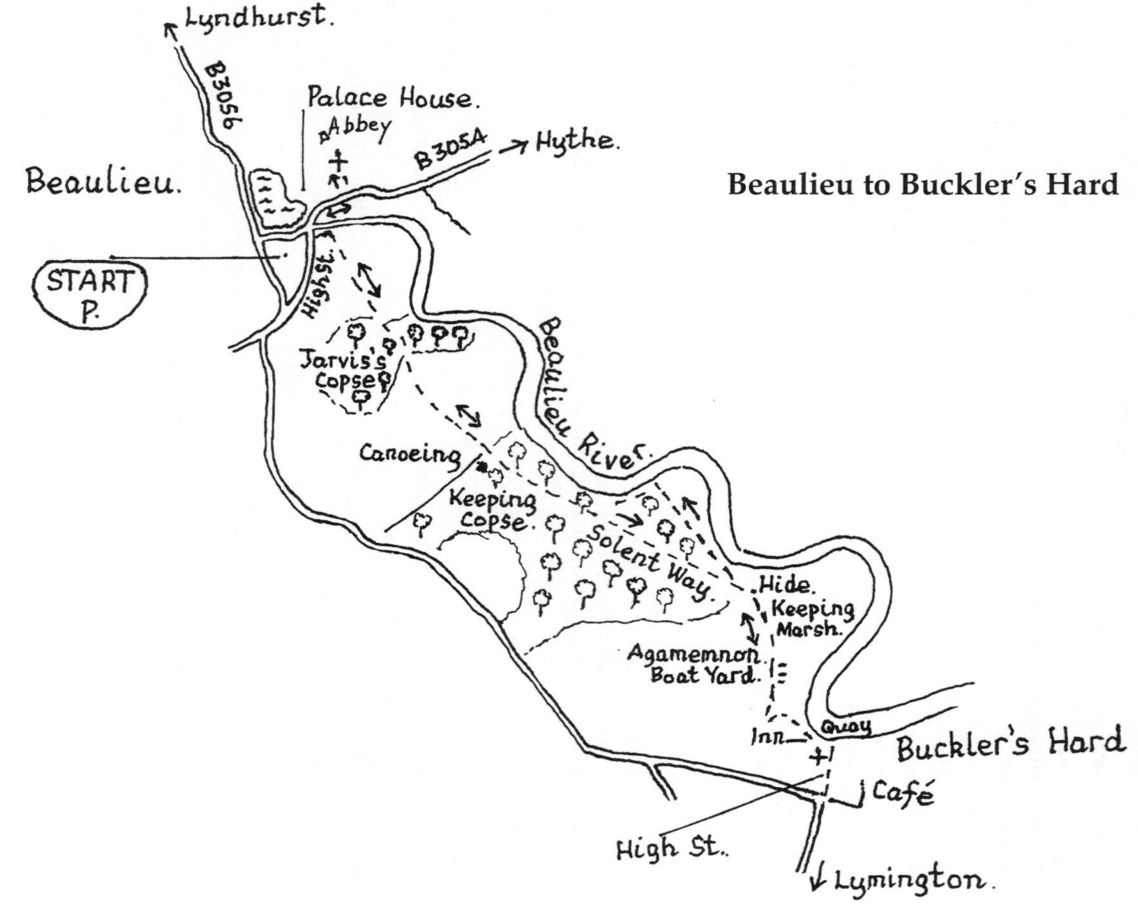

Beaulieu to Buckler's Hard

Buckler's Hard

beside the river on your right. In 150 metres, cross with care to the Abbey Church opposite. Approach the church by turning right in the small car park.

From the Abbey Church return over the river to the edge of Beaulieu. Here on the left the Solent Way is signed to Buckler`s Hard. Turn left into this wide alley and go between walls and gardens to a country path.

The route southeast is clear, across heath then into riverside woods. At Bailey`s Hard there is a centre for canoeing. The next landmark is a kink in the path where a track leads to a house on the left. Re-enter the woods as marked and continue on the straight path with conifers on the right and mixed woodland on the left.

In over 1 kilometre the path bears right and enters Keeping Marsh. There is a hide for bird watching here. I am sorry to report we only saw seagulls!

Assuming you have checked the tide and the river has not flowed onto the path, continue through the boat yard to the quay at Buckler`s Hard.

Turn right and climb the wide grassy slope between terraced houses. At the bottom of this slope on the right there is an inn. Halfway up one of the houses, number 82 has evolved into St Mary`s Chapel.

When you reach the top of the slope, the entrance to the Museum and the Car Park are to the left. There is also a café and gift shop here. *Solent Way crosses the road and heads towards East End and Lymington.*

To return from Buckler`s Hard to Beaulieu, retrace your steps and walk down the grassy High Street to the quay at the bottom. Turn left.

Follow the well defined path, Solent Way back to Beaulieu. There is a worthwhile variation on this walk, not shown on OS maps. Look out for a signed turning to the right. With the help of decking in places, you have a lovely riverside walk, running parallel to the main path. In about ½ mile you rejoin Solent Way.

Walk 37: Boldre Church to Brockenhurst Church

A walk through farmland and forest to visit two ancient lonely churches

Starting Point: The Car Park behind Boldre Church. **GR**324993
Map: OS Explorer OL22, OL29 **Terrain:** Flat or gentle slopes
Distance: 8 Miles
Note: For the return walk there are 1½ miles on lanes. Also you must cross the A337 and back again. If you wish to avoid this, retrace your steps to Roydon Manor and pick up the circular walk.
Local Information: 1. Peterson`s Tower, Sway is 218 feet high, built of cement blocks in wooden frames with a drum and dome on top. A retired Indian judge, Andrew Peterson was trying to evoke an Indian style in 1879.
Roydon Manor House, ensconced deep in the Forest, was the dwelling of William Henry Hudson when he wrote 'Hampshire Days', published 1903.
Brockenhurst Park was home of the Morant family, Lords of the Manor. The house was burnt down last century.
Brockenhurst was a Saxon village. When the railways came in 1847, it grew into a town.

The Churches

Boldre, St John the Baptist stands on an elevated, site, possibly pagan. Three Sarsen stones were found in the foundations. It stands on its own in the centre of its parish. Before William the Conqueror ordered the reforestation of this area, the Jute and Saxon inhabitants would have had a clear view of their church as they approached it climbing from all directions. A charter of 1100 mentions 'Boldra' Church and its chapel at 'Brokehurst' Boldre was the Mother Church of the southern New Forest. The Norman church consisted of nave, apsidal chancel, south and possibly north aisle. Three Norman pillars at the eastern end of the south aisle have survived. The north arcade is early 13th century and a south porch was

Boldre

Boldre Church to Brockenhurst Church

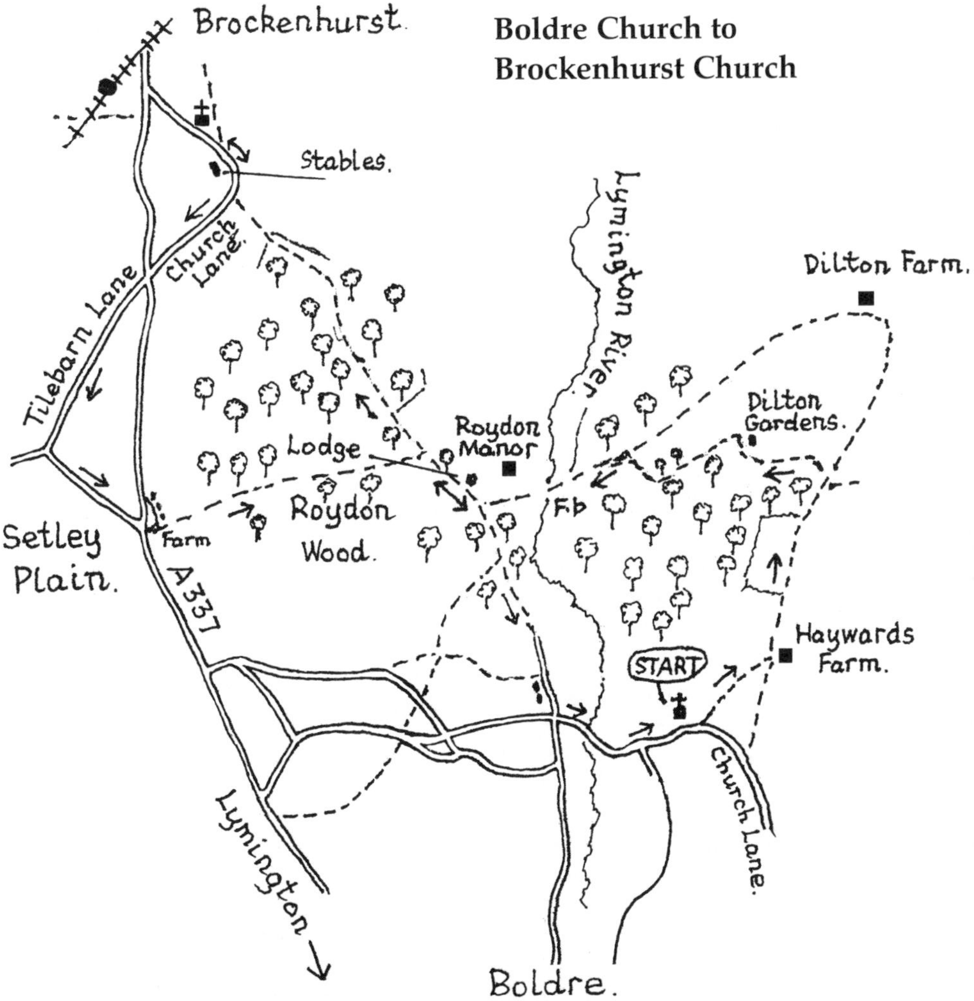

Brockenhurst.
Stables.
Church Lane.
Tilebarn Lane
Lymington River.
Dilton Farm.
Dilton Gardens.
Roydon Manor
Lodge
Roydon Wood.
Fb
Setley Plain.
Farm
A337
Haywards Farm.
START
Church Lane.
Lymington
Boldre.

Lymington footbridge

also added then. Later in 13th century the nave and south aisle with octagonal pillars were extended to the west. The nave has a barrel roof with carved bosses of 14th century. In the early 14th century the chancel was replaced and the tower was added to the south side of the chancel. The tower acquired its brick upper part in 17th century. A wall tablet in the north chapel remembers William Gilpin, vicar from 1777 to 1804. He sold his water colour paintings to pay for the education of his wild 'bandit' parishioners. The chancel was again rebuilt in 19th century. In the northwest corner there is a 'Hood' memorial. The Hood, flagship of Vice Admiral L.E. Holland was destroyed in 1941 by the Bismarck with the loss of 1417 lives. The modern glass of the east window and also the smaller west window of the south aisle enlivens the church. Both are by Alan Younger in colourful abstract design.
The Parish Church of St Nicholas, Brockenhurst is also on a lonely hill in the centre of its parish. It is mentioned in Domesday as 'Broceste'. Near the south doorway is some herring bone masonry in Saxon style. The doorway is Norman with zigzag carving and scalloped capitals. The Purbeck font is 12th century. The chancel is a complete Early English delight. Unusual flower designs on Victorian glass fit beautifully in the 13th century side windows. The east window has early 19th century glass of the four evangelists. The brick tower was built in 1763 replacing an older one. The octagonal spire was added later. The ground floor of the tower is Tudor. Another Tudor window is next to the south doorway. The two heads above this window may represent Henry Fitzalan, 12th Earl of Arundel and His son Henry, Lord Maltravers. The Fitzalan arms are above centre. Also east of the porch arch is a scratch dial, 5 feet above ground. The north aisle was added in 1832.

The Walk

The track to Boldre Church car park continues northeast as an enclosed bridleway through fields. Follow this path to a T-junction at Haywards Farm. Turn left on the wide track northwards towards woodland.

In ½ mile avoid the right fork. Keep straight on for 50 metres then turn sharp left away from the main track. There is no marker for this bridleway. It hugs woodland on the left and there are fields on the right.

You are now heading west northwest for ½ mile. Pass a large house, Dilton Gardens on the right then keep to the bridleway that turns left into mixed woodland. Oak and beech have holly under some of them.

You come to a fine wooden fingerpost at a T-junction. Turn left towards 'Brockenhurst'. You are deep in woodland and head downhill to the Lymington River. Fortunately a footbridge spans the river here as the waters are too deep to ford. Pass Roydon Manor (see Note 2 above) on the right and you soon come to a T-junction.

Turn right and walk along the straight forest track, heading northwest. Pass the Manor entrance and the lone brick lodge. Within ¼ mile of joining this track, you reach a **junction**. Avoid the bridleway to the left but keep straight on into thick woodland. The clear way takes you across narrow streams.

In 1 kilometre, you have a prospect of parkland. The path narrows and comes out of the woodland, veering left along its edge on the left. Come away from the forest to an enclosed path that passes a magnificent avenue of lime trees on the right. You soon come to stables on a T-junction at Church Lane. (**Note:** the return circular walk is to the left). First, turn right for Brockenhurst Church. Continue past the church if you wish to see the town.

From Brockenhurst Church return along Church Lane past the stables to the path on the left that brought you here.

***If you wish to avoid roads**, retrace your steps to the lodge and Roydon Manor then keep straight on heading southeast as below.**

For the circular walk, continue along Church Lane as it bears right, and heads southwest to the A337. Cross with care to the Tilebarn Lane opposite. At first you pass select detached houses. After the cattle grid you pass woodland. Go as far as the T-junction at the end of the lane.

Turn left and walk along a new lane with open heathland on either side. Over to the south, on your right you can see the top of Peterson`s Tower (See Note 1). You soon come to another cattle grid and the A337 again.

Cross to the road opposite. Do not pursue the road as it immediately turns left. Instead, veer right for the entrance to the bridleway to Roydon Manor. A cottage on the left bears the name, 'Setley Farm'.

Follow the bridleway, a forest track eastwards for nearly a mile when you reach the **junction** in the woods of the outward walk. Turn right and retrace your steps past the lodge and Roydon Manor. Pass the path on the left that brought you here and ignore turnings to the right.

*Keep straight on, heading southeast through the forest for a kilometre.

Your track becomes a country lane with the occasional thatched cottage on the right. At the end you come to crossroads at a green with a welcome long bench. Take the lane on your left that leads down to a bridge across the Lymington River and up to Boldre Church.

Brockenhurst Victorian glass

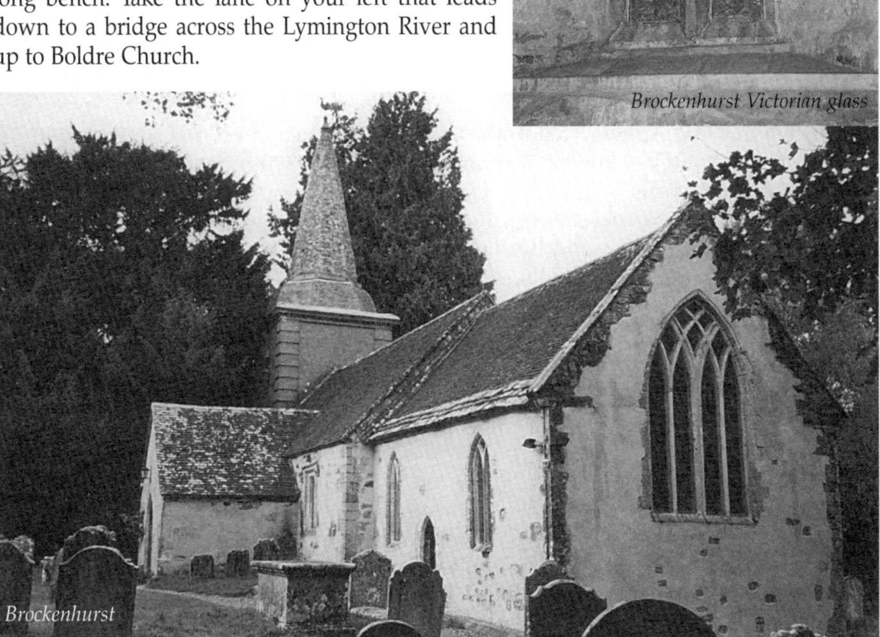

Brockenhurst

Walk 38: Minstead to Lyndhurst

Byways, heath and forest paths help us avoid traffic to the busiest town in the New Forest on our walk to two very different, unconventional churches.

Starting Point: Minstead Church **GR281109** **Map:** OS Explorer OL22
Terrain: heath, forest, gentle slopes **Distance:** 11 Miles (can be shortened)
Note: In the depth of the forest, we follow well marked and firm cycle routes to avoid going astray, but bring a compass!
Local Information: The Portuguese Fireplace marks the camp where a unit of the Portuguese Army stayed and worked felling trees for the war effort (1914 – 1918). The flint fireplace is from the old cookhouse.

The Churches

All Saints, Minstead owes its peculiar shape to the Georgian period when family pews in separate rooms were added without any reference to the basic medieval building. One of the rooms even has a fireplace, another has its own entrance. One is big enough to house the manor`s family and tenants. All are more in keeping with domestic buildings. The chancel arch, a lancet window and the north doorway are from the 13th century church. The bowl of the font with handsome carvings is earlier, possibly Saxon although Pevsner describes it as late 12th century. There is a 17th century pulpit in three tiers and a west gallery in two tiers. The brick tower was added in 1774 and the south transept in 1790. Sir Arthur Conan Doyle and his wife Jean were buried in 1955 in a horizontal position in the churchyard. They once lived in Bignell Wood. The famous author, a spiritualist originally chose an upright position for his 1930 burial in his garden in Sussex. .

St Michael and All Angels, Lyndhurst. A church has stood on this site for over 700 years. William White, nephew of the naturalist (see Walk 8) designed this colourful and lavish building in the 1850s. It took 10 years to build and contains works of art and craft of famous contemporaries of White as well as memorials from the former Georgian chapel. The spire of 141 feet is a landmark in the busy town. The contrasting red and yellow brickwork makes more of an impact inside than outside. The interior is spacious and lofty. The red brick nave pillars have stone shafts and carvings on their capitals by William Searle. The Gothic arches are finished with a pattern of zigzag brick. The roof corbels have carved heads and above them on brackets, the dramatic presence of full sized angels. Several windows are from the famous Morris school. The east window by Burne-Jones depicts the New Jerusalem. His is also the lively south transept window. R. J. Clayton and A. Bell designed the north transept window in reds and blues. In the north aisle the delightful Arcadian windows are by Powell. The later west window (1903) has a theme of angels. In the corner is the wheat sheaf signature of Charles Kempe. The chancel has a striking mural of the Wise and Foolish Virgins by Lord Leighton. There is much more of interest in this church. Buried outside in a plain grave at the back, lies Alice Hargreaves, the inspiration for Alice in Wonderland.

Minstead to Lyndhurst

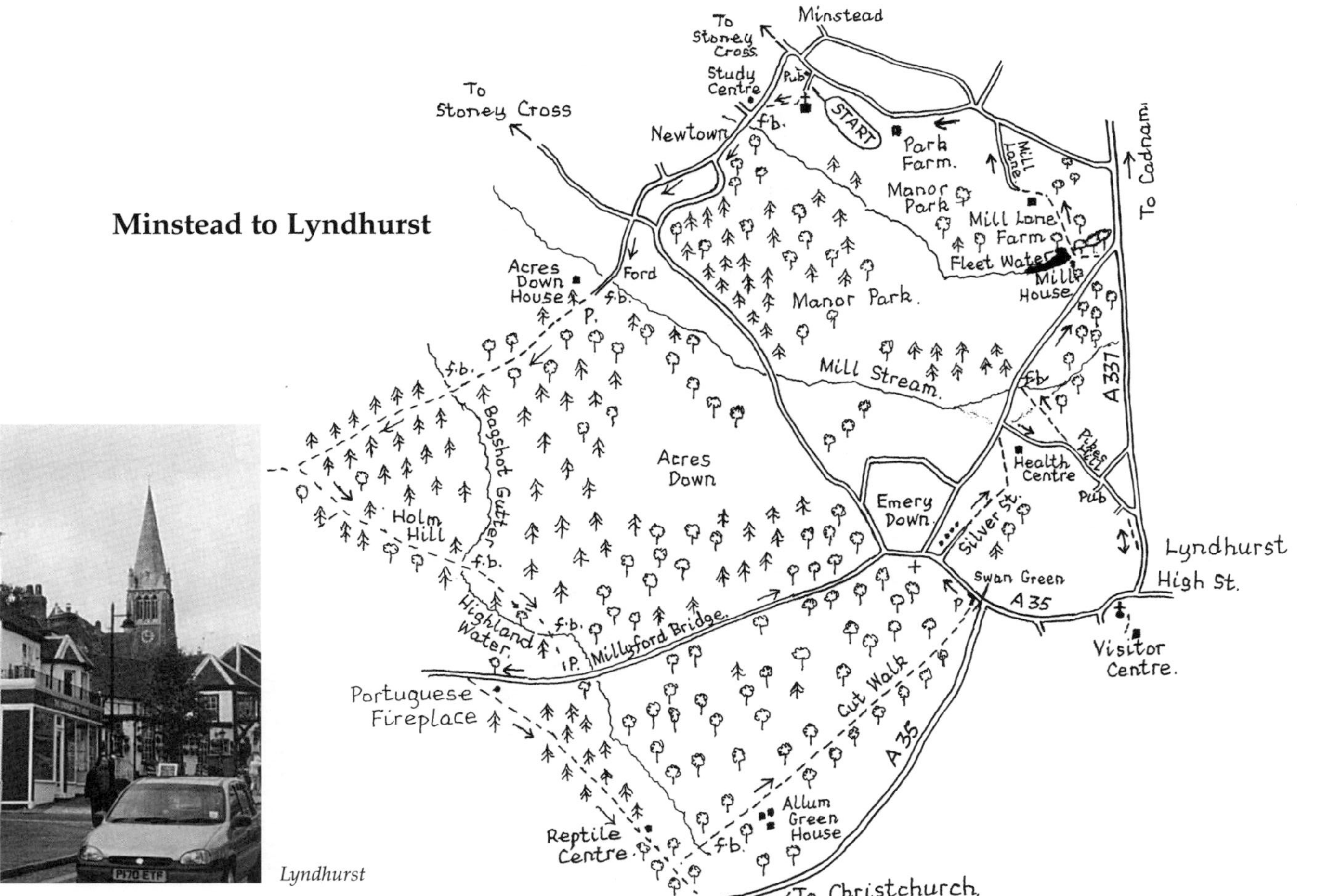

Lyndhurst

The Walk

Face Minstead Church and follow the enclosed footpath on the right. It passes the churchyard on the left and leads down through trees to Newtown.

Turn left onto the lane. Cross a footbridge over a stream and ford, passing a Rural Study Centre on the right. *Children were stream dipping as we passed.* Walk along lanes in rural Newtown for the next ½ mile.

At the first road junction turn right. At the second road junction at a grass triangle, veer left. You come to the main road to Lyndhurst. Cross with care to the little Lane opposite. Follow the lane down to the Mill Stream and cross the ford. You come up to a clearing in the forest with scattered houses.

The track ahead leads to Acres Down Car Park and access to heath and forestland. Head southwest on the firm gravel cycle way going gently down through woodland and crossing a stream, Bagshot Gutter. In over a mile, you come to a T-junction turn left towards woodland gates.

You are now on another quiet cycle track walking southeast for a mile and deep in woodland. In ¼ mile veer left at a slight opening where a track joins from the right. Go gently over Holm Hill and cross Bagshot Gutter again. It joins a wider stream, Highland Water which runs parallel to then goes under our track. Shortly after crossing Highland Water, you come to Millyford Bridge Car Park then a tarmac road carrying some traffic through the forest.

***For a short cut** turn left and follow the road heading east for over a mile. Soon after another car park you come to a byway at Emery Down. Turn right Pass New Forest Inn then Emery Down Church, both on your right Avoid a turning to the left. Follow the road round to the right and in 50 metres turn left into a little cul de sac, **Silver Street**. Continue below at*.*

For a traffic free route, turn right and walk for ¼ mile along the side of the road, passing the Portuguese Fireplace on the left. At more wooden gates on the left, turn into another gravel track. This leads through conifers to the Reptile Centre. Go through the centre to keep on course past a cottage. You are walking away from the centre on the access road.

In another ¼ mile turn left and head northeast into a straight unmarked path, 'Cut Walk'. Cross a footbridge over a stream, Highland Water again. In 200 metres the path divides. Fork right here. In another 250 metres, you reach a cluster of houses at Allum Green. Pass Corner Cottage and Caister Cottage on your right, then the garden of the main house. The footpath goes close to the wall then the open boundary. Stay on course, northeast through trees, silver birch and holly. At clearings in the forest, you may want to divert to avoid mud. Make sure to resume the path in its steady direction.

Cut Walk runs parallel to the A35 and you may hear the faint noise of traffic on the right. Soon after a cross track, the path climbs up through beech trees. Deep mauve violets grow under these trees. Towards the end of the mile long Cut Walk, you descend to Swan Green. Thatched cottages overlook the green. Cross the green diagonally left to the Car Park.

At Swan Green take the car park exit to the road and turn left. In ¼ mile turn right into Silver Street.

*After a few cottages the street becomes a slightly elevated track so that you can peep through trees on the left to the downland. The track narrows and veers left. Soon after passing the buildings of a hospital on the edge of Lyndhurst, you come out at the Emery Down Road.

Turn right then immediately right again into a lane, Pikes Hill. Pass the other side of the

Minsted

hospital buildings, a Health Centre on the right. Follow the lane down for 1 kilometre, passing a pub on the way. Just before the end of the lane, turn right and walk up across a green to a cutting, Gales Green.

You come to the main Romsey Road, A337 and turn right. Walk up on the pavement for ¼ mile to the centre of Lyndhurst.

Turn right at the junction with the A35. The imposing Church of St Michael is on a mound opposite. Take care forcing your way through the traffic and climb up the steps to the Church.

If you wish to go to the Visitor Centre, the path straight on along the south side of the church bears left and down to the Car Park behind the High Street where you will find the Library and Visitor Centre.

From Lyndhurst to Minstead retrace your steps along Romsey Road to Gales Green on the left and return up Pikes Hill but not to the end.

After the cattle grid turn right, passing cottages on the left. Enter forestland at a fairly open spot. Avoid the path straight on. Veer left on a slight path through a holly grove. You come to horse paddocks. A very narrow footpath between paddocks has stiles at either end. It leads to a small field. Go down to the left hand corner and cross a footbridge over the Mill Stream.

You emerge onto the Emery Down Road again at a more northerly point. Turn right and walk along the road for ½ mile. Soon after Mill House and a small caravan site on the left, you are coming to the end of this road and approaching A337. Look for a track on the left. It has no signpost at the time of writing. If you cross the cattle grid, you have gone too far.

Just before the cattle grid, turn left and follow this unsigned track through trees to the Mill Pond, quite a sizeable stretch of water.

At the Mill Pond, turn right and go down to a wide, dank, straight section of the track. In ¼ mile you come out of the trees as you turn left and the track merges into Mill Lane. Pass Mill Lane Farm on the left. Building is in progress here and I suspect that the track you have just followed will become more widely used.

Go to the end of Mill Lane and turn left. Follow the road to Minstead, nearly 1 mile ahead.

Walk 39: Milford-on-Sea to Lymington

Paths and lanes overlooking the Solent with views to the Isle of Wight and Hurst Castle, we pass the lagoons formed by salt pans on these flat lands.

Starting Point: Church Hill, Milford on Sea **GR**291922
Or Lymington Railway Station ½ *Mile from town centre* **GR**328958 *Go to page 193*
Maps: OS Explorer OL22 or 29 **Terrain:** Flat, coastal **Distance:** 12 Miles
Local Information: 1. Hurst Castle was built by Henry V111 (1541 - 1544) in a strategic position as a defence against the French. He is reputed to have used stone from Beaulieu Abbey. The castle stands at the end of a shingle spit into the Solent, 1½ miles from the mainland. Charles 1 was held prisoner here on his way from Carisbrooke Castle to execution in London.
2 The remains of salterns can be seen on the coast between Milford and Lymington. Salt has been evaporated from the sea since the Iron Age. As the technology developped, methods changed. In medieval times Quarr Abbey and Christchurch Prory benefitted from the extraction of salt here. The last saltern was closed in 1828. The whole area has been given over to wild life. Wetland birds enjoy the lagoons left by the salt works.
3 Once an old port with a boat building and also a smuggling history, Lymington is now a holiday town with a handsome High St, picturesque Quay Hill and a lively yachting haven.

The Churches

All Saints Church, Milford on Sea is mentioned in Domesday, suggesting that there was a Saxon church here. It was rebuilt in stone 1150 – 1175. This Norman church was enlarged in the 1200s. Two Norman doorways have survived. One in the north transept is best seen outside. It has a trefoil arch and carved human heads. The other is beneath the organ in the south transept. The tower, nave, crossing and chancel are 13th century. Inside is spacious with 20 arches. Two pillars near the entrance in the south arcade have capitals of that period. The north aisle has Early English octagonal columns. The Jacobean roof over the chancel dates from 1639. It has 54 carved oak bosses in the shape of strange human and mythical heads. A visitor today, who may be disappointed to see the dull pebble dash exterior, will be delighted on entry to find such a warm, well balanced and interesting interior.
St Thomas and All Saints, Lymington is a handsome light grey stone church at the top of an elegant High Street. The distinctive tower (1670) with Georgian cupola has become a

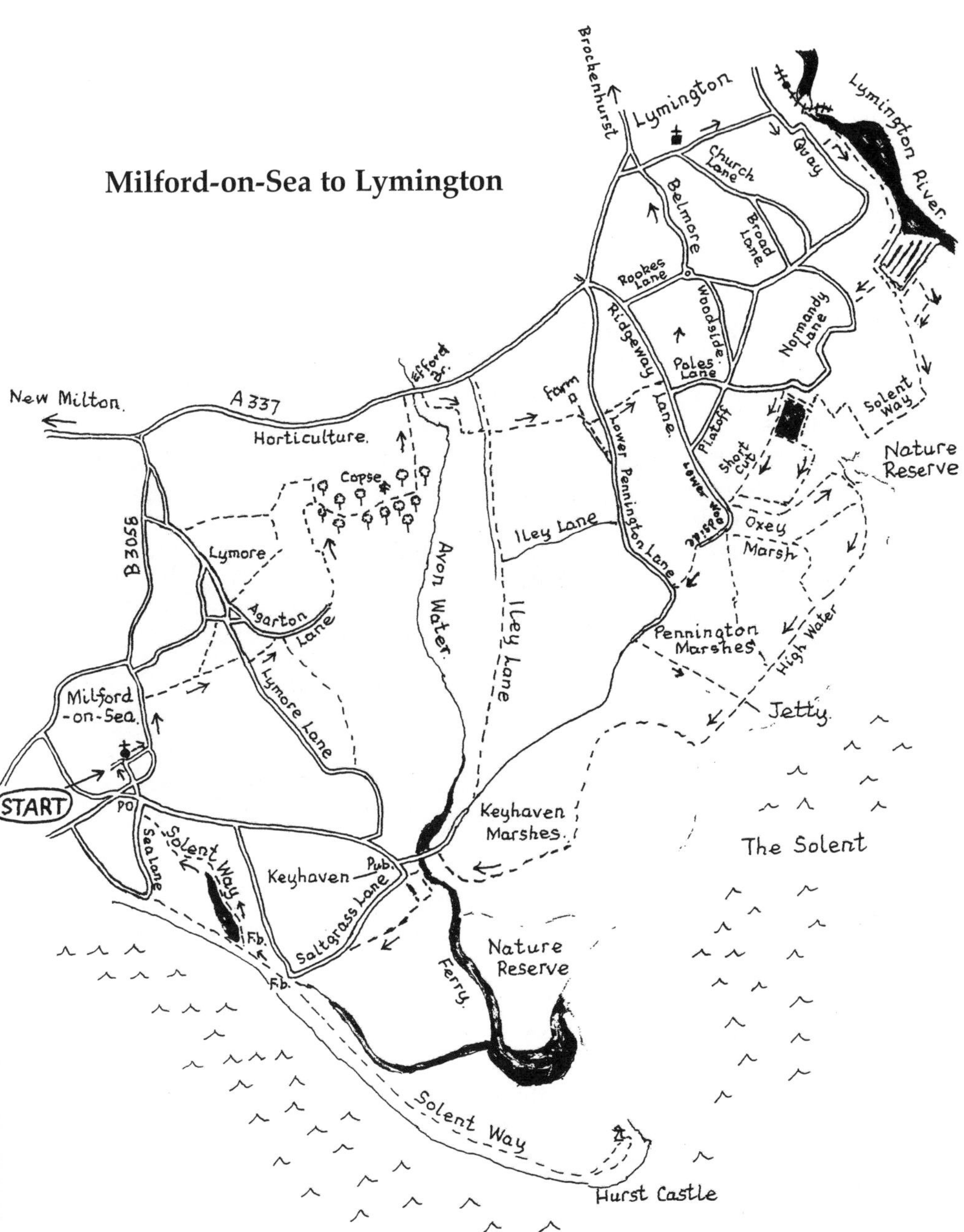
Milford-on-Sea to Lymington
Brockenhurst
Lymington
Lymington River
Quay
Church Lane
Belmore
Broad Lane
Rookes Lane
Woodside
Ridgeway Lane
Normandy Lane
Poles Lane
Platoff
Short Cut
Solent Way
Nature Reserve
Lower Woodside
Lower Pennington Lane
Farm
Efford Br.
New Milton
A337
Horticulture
Copse
Iley Lane
Oxey Marsh
High Water
Pennington Marshes
Jetty
B3058
Lymore
Agarton Lane
Avon Water
Iley Lane
Lymore Lane
Milford -on-Sea
START
PO
Sea Lane
Solent Way
Keyhaven
Pub.
Saltgrass Lane
Keyhaven Marshes
The Solent
Fb.
Fb.
Nature Reserve
Ferry
Solent Way
Hurst Castle

symbol of Lymington. Inside, the stone walls of the nave rise high to the plastered barrel ceiling. Tiers of galleries are supported by Tuscan columns. This grand classical building draws attention away from the remains of an earlier medieval church. As you enter the church through the narthex at the west end, on the left is a 13th century column. In the sanctuary, still to be seen, are some early lancet windows. The east window has been moved to the north gallery. It contains Flemish glass depicting the crucifixion. The new east window was presented by Lord Lennox in mid 19th century. It shows Christ commanding the waves and David playing his harp. The stained glass of the 14th century window of the Courtenay Chapel was inserted in 1936. Bosses from the old church are now in a showcase.

Lymington

The Walk

At Church Hill, walk past Milford Church on your left and continue towards the main road. Turn left onto B3058 and walk uphill on the pavement for a ¼ mile. At a postbox turn right into a footpath, marked to 'Lymore'.

You are heading northeast across fields. At cross paths, keep straight on to Lymore Lane. Cross the lane diagonally right to pick up another footpath to Agarton Lane. You are high above the Solent with views across to the Isle of Wight. In fact there is a Trig. point on your right just before you go down to the lane.

Turn right and walk along this quiet lane past the occasional detached cottage. At the end, a narrow footpath leads down to a footbridge into woodland. The enclosed path bends left and still has a cover of trees as it heads northwest for 500 metres.

The path then turns right into the woodland proper, Great Newbridge Copse. Go downhill to cross a stream and then up to a T-junction. Turn right and follow the path southeast. You are walking on the edge of forbidden territory on the left with notices warning of deep water. This is the Horticulture Experimental Station. Pass a private entrance and a glimpse of hangers on the left, keep on course along the main path through the wood. Avoid side paths to the left until you come to a finger post on stilts. Turn sharp left and head north again to emerge from the wood.

The path straight ahead along the edge of the field leads to A337.

Turn right at the main road and cross Efford Bridge over Avon Water Turn immediately right to resume your country walk on footpaths. Pass woodland on the left. Veer left and pass a small caravan site. Cross a footbridge to enter the next field. Turn sharp right then left along two edges of the field. You come to a lane. Cross the lane to a track signed to Muddy Creek Farm. About ¼ mile along the track you cross a flat bridge and only then do you find a little mud.

Join a wide private drive to the farm on the left. Turn your back on the farm to walk along the drive for 50 metres. Turn left at a finger post Go through a garden to a tarmac road. This is Lower Pennington Lane.

Cross to a track opposite and pass Oakhaven Hospice Trust and nursery on the left. You then have to go through a narrow enclosed path that veers left to a field. Turn right and follow the field boundary to kissing gates in a twitten beside a house. You emerge to Ridgeway Lane.

Turn left to find a sports field on the right. Cross the field diagonally left towards tennis courts, passing the sports pavillion on the right. (you may have to go round the edge of the field when there is a game in progress).

Milford-on-Sea

Follow the tarmac path at the edge of the tennis courts. You come to ornamental gardens and a path junction. Turn right and go through rhododendrons. The path divides again and you fork left.

You leave the gardens via a gate to the crossroads and a mini roundabout. Cross with care to Belmore Lane.This leads for ½ mile up to St Thomas`s Street. Turn right for the church and Lymington High Street.

***From Lymington Church** walk down the High Street to Quay Hill, leading to The Quay. Turn right and pass the car park to walk beside Lymington River on your left. On the far side of the river, trains take passengers to the ferry boats for the Isle Of Wight.

On your side of the river, you follow the green arrow marking Solent Way. Go past the Marina and then the Yacht Haven. Solent Way makes a loop to follow the contours of the coast.

If you wish to take a more direct shortcut, stick to the lanes. Normandy Lane takes you to the Salterns. You rejoin Solent Way to pass the Salterns on your left. Keep heading southwest to another lane, Lower Woodside.

Turn left here and follow Lower Woodside to the end where you continue on a footpath. You come to Lower Pennington Lane and turn left again.

The lane bends right and comes in ¼ mile to a junction where you turn left. A straight track follows one of the lagoons. You reach the Solent at a jetty. Turn right and continue southwest along Solent Way on the sea wall.

You have a good view of Hurst Castle ahead and the Isle of Wight on your left. You pass lagoons and marshes, now a nature reserve, on the right. In over 1 mile from the jetty you come to the harbour of Keyhaven.

The path turns right to the road. Turn left for benches on the bank overlooking the harbour. Keep straight on for the pub.

At Keyhaven go to the ferry point. *A seasonal ferry takes passengers to Hurst Castle. From there it is possible to walk to Milford via the shingle spit.*

Otherwise, continue heading southwest along the sea wall. In 1 kilometre you come to a footbridge below the spit. *Avoid the road on the right. It brings holiday makers and refreshment vans.*

Cross the footbridge and turn right to walk on the path in the flat area between the spit on the left and the stream on the right. In ¼ mile cross back over the stream on another footbridge. Walk beside a lake on the left. Pass holiday homes and houses on the right.

Avoid all turnings until you come to the car park at Milford on Sea. Cross to the shops by the village green. Pass the Co-op on your right; the village green on your left. Cross the main road to walk up Church Hill opposite.

***To return to Lymington Station,** go to the start of the walk.*

Walk 40: Christchurch to Sopley

Find road and river crossings to enjoy the River Avon and two very handsome churches.

Starting Points:
Waitrose Car Park near Fountain Way Roundabout on A35 **GR**157929
Or Christchurch Station, 500 metres away, off B3073 to Hurn **GR**153933
Map: OS Explorer OL22 **Terrain:** Flat, riverside, some urban
Distance: 8 – 9½ Miles – *can be halved if you catch a bus. Bus 175 leaves Sopley for Christchurch at 12.45pm, 15.57pm, and 16.52pm.*
Warning: 1. Avoid water meadows in wet weather.
2. The circular walk includes 1 mile along the Avon Causeway. This is a busy road with no footpath. A traffic calming scheme has forced vehicles to a slow pace. *If you wish to avoid this road, you will have to leave Sopley by the way you came or catch a bus back to Christchurch.*

The Churches

Christchurch Priory Three crypts are all that remains of the Saxon minster church that stood here from 7th to 11th centuries and was then demolished. In 1094 Ranulf Flambard, chief minister of King William 11, started building a new church. It contains a 'miraculous beam'. The carpenters realised they had cut the beam too short and left it on the ground overnight. The next day they found the beam was the correct size and had been fitted by a mysterious carpenter, believed to be Jesus Christ. As a result, the town changed its name from 'Twynham' to 'Christchurch'. The present nave and transepts have survived from that Norman church. The north transept is a great feat of Norman architecture. When the church was finished in 1150, an Augustinian Priory was established. The Norman nave with regular heavy columns and rounded arches is one of the finest in England. As you enter the church from the large west porch, you are struck by the wonderful view through the nave to the reredos. Simon Jenkins in his book, 'England`s Thousand Best Churches' describes this view as a 'coup de theatre'. Carved in 14th century, the intricate stone reredos behind the high altar has several panels. The central one of the Epiphany tells the story of Christmas. The blue mural above is of Isaiah`s Vision by Hans Feibusch. The Norman chancel and Lady Chapel were replaced in the late 15th century by the Great Quire in Perpendicular style. It is truly great with vaulted ceilings, roof bosses and carved capitals. For more details, including the various chapels and windows, see the picture booklet on sale in the Priory or join a guided tour. The new Lady Chapel has an unusual room above, possibly for training monks. The Victorians used it as a grammar school. Today it is St Michael`s Loft Museum. The west tower was built towards the end of 15th century. Christchurch is the longest church and has the largest porch in England.

Christchurch to Sopley

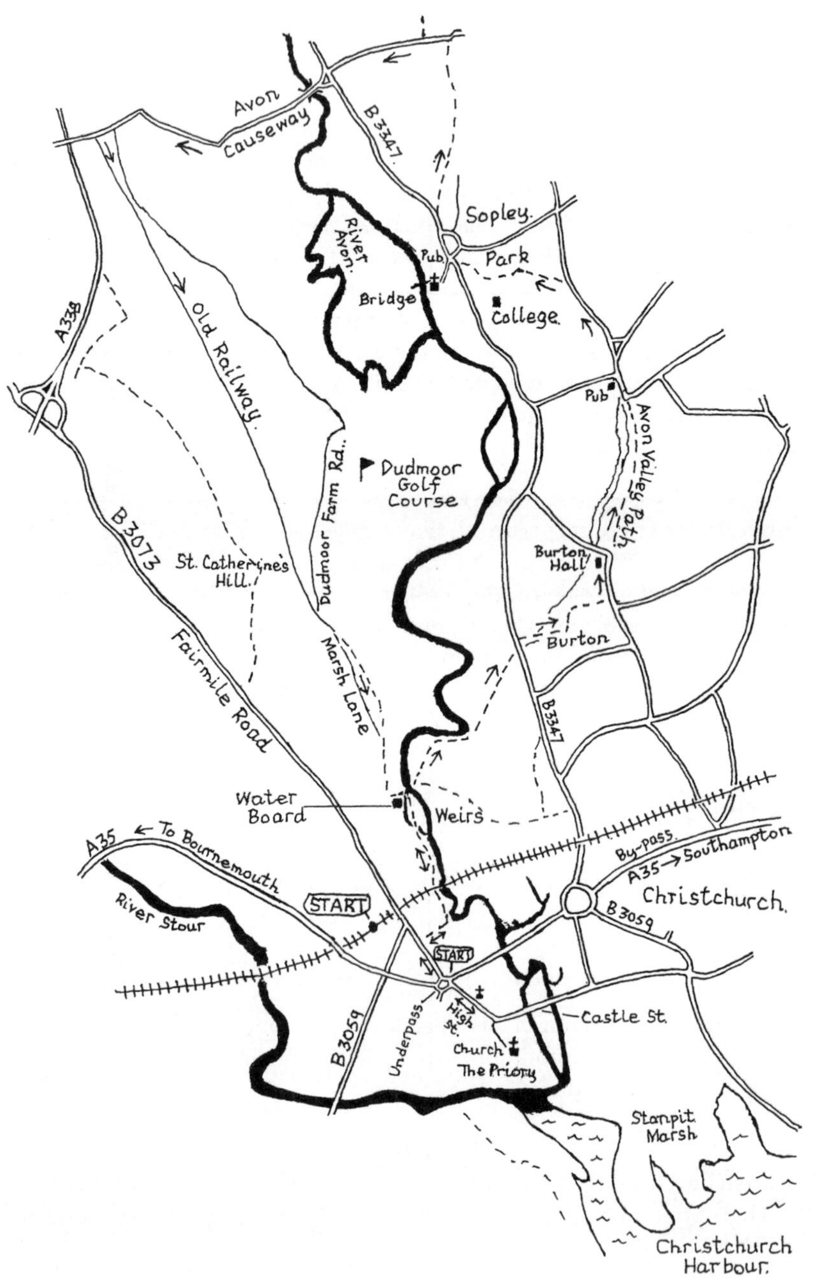

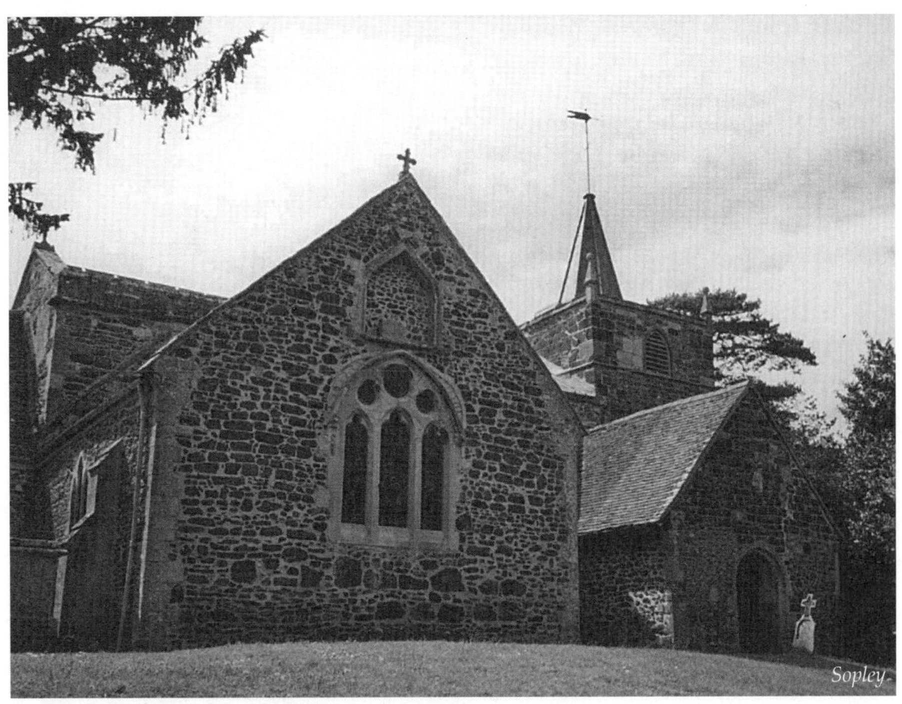
Sopley

The Parish Church of St Michael and All Angels, Sopley stands above the River Avon. The little lane to the church ends at the mill restaurant where a bridge enables tables to be placed on either side of the river. The mill is mentioned in Domesday when there may already have been a church on the hill above. This small Norman church took its place. It was enlarged in 13th century by adding transepts and lengthening the chancel. The north transept was the Lady chapel with an altar. It was decorated with a lily pattern mural. A large squint in the south transept enabled the chantry priest to keep in time with the high altar priest. It is now useful for the organist. The nave was rebuilt in 14th century with high wooden roof and stone corbels similar to those of Christchurch. Until 1539, vicars of Sopley were appointed by Priors from Christchurch. The north aisle is wider than the south aisle. The ornate arch at the east end has heads of a man and a woman on the corbels. The church has a beautiful ironstone tower. The church has benefitted from a Victorian restoration, exposing the fine timber roof and opening the Early English lancet windows in the chancel.

The Walk

To visit Christchurch Priory cross the A35 via the underpass near Waitrose. Go down the High Street, passing the TIC on the right. Keep on course along the narrower Church Street to the nearby Priory.

Christchurch

To walk from Christchurch Priory to Sopley Parish Church, retrace your steps and go back through the underpass. Then go behind Waitrose. Turn left to B3073 road to Hurn. Turn right towards the station. In 75 metres turn right at Avon Villas. Walk past pretty terraced houses to an enclosed path down to the river.

Avon Valley Path starts here. See the end of this book, long distance paths.

Continue along Avon Valley Path. The river is on your right and meadows beyond. Go under the railway bridge and you come to the Water Board buildings on the left. *Note: in ¼ mile a path on left for return walk.*

Keep heading north along Avon Valley Way which crosses the weirs here.

You come to water meadows and head northeast to a pylon at a bend in the river. Turn right to follow the river bank on the left. The river curves away to the left and you continue northeast over the wide meadow. (The path crosses these wide spaces for about 1 mile). There is a concrete way marker and a faint path on the ground enables you to find the way. The muddiest parts are covered with raised planks. Head towards a Trig. Point and pass it on your left. Go over a wooden bridge to an enclosed path on the right.

You come to B3347 and cross to the grassy bank by a stream opposite. Walk along the bank to a footbridge. Turn right to cross the stream here to an alleyway. This suburban estate is in Burton.

At the end of the alley, turn left and walk to Woodstock Road. Turn right. At the end of Woodstock Road you come to a lane on the edge of the estate. Turn left here and pass Burton Hall, a large brick house on the left.

At a bend in the lane, cross to the path opposite. Avon Valley Path is marked again. The tree lined path follows a stream on the left. In 1 kilometre you come to the pub, 'The Lamb'.

From 'The Lamb', continue north along the road, still Avon Valley Path. Fork left towards Ripley. Avoid the first path to the left. Take the second path on the left into an open field. Cross to Moorlands College. Pass this on your left. The path now has some very high stiles. It leads around the college to the driveway and onto the B3347 at Sopley.

Cross to the pub at crossroads then turn left for the church. *This quiet lane used to be busy with traffic to the mill at the end.*

After visiting Sopley Parish Church, you have 3 options:

1. return to the pub at the end of the lane to wait for a bus to Christchurch,
2. retrace your steps along Avon Valley Path to 'The Lamb', water meadows and river.
3. continue on the circular walk and brave the traffic on Avon Causeway.

For the circular walk, continue through the village of Sopley, passing the pub on your right. As you leave the village on the north side, you come to a footpath sign on the other side of the road. Cross to this enclosed path behind houses on the left and beside the stream on the right. The houses give way to fields and the stream stays with the path, passing through trees.

In 1 kilometre you come to a road. Enjoy the peace of gazing from the bridge to the stream below. Then turn left and walk along the road to B3347 at crossroads. Cross to the Avon Causeway opposite.

This road crosses over the River Avon and continues in a mainly westerly direction through water meadows for 1 mile. The traffic on this road is forced to slow down so you may admire the scenery.

In 1 mile, pass Pithouse Lane on the right and Bramble Wood on the left. In 50 metres, at the next driveway, turn left opposite Hurn Chapel.

Avon Causeway Hotel is a little further along the main road.

From the driveway you turn into the old railway line. It is an elevated track through trees and makes a bee-line back to Christchurch for 2 miles. You pass St Catherine`s Hill on the right, then Dudmore Farm and Golf Course on the left. You join Dudmore Lane and pass through a Nature Reserve.

When you come to a housing estate in the suburb of Fairmile, veer left along Marsh Lane. In 500 metres, at the end of the lane you enter a bridleway on the left. This path is enclosed with fences as it passes the backs of houses on the right and a water works` reservoir on the left.

You come to a grassy play area. Keep to the left hand edge as far as a metal bar. Come out to a tarmac road and turn right, Nearby on the left is the entrance to the Bournemouth and West Hampshire Water Board.

Turn left to go through their side gate where pedestrian access is allowed in daylight hours. Turn right for the riverside path back to Christchurch. You are on the familiar Avon Valley Walk at the noted turning. Retrace your steps back to Avon Villas. At the main road, Waitrose Car Park is to the left and the Station is to the right.

Walk 41: Hale to Breamore

Saxons once held this land where we enjoy a quiet walk to two very different estate churches on either side of the River Avon.

Starting Point: St Mary`s Church, Hale (approached along the drive to Hale House) **GR**179186 **Map:** OS Explorer OL22 and a little overlap on OS Explorer 130 **Terrain:** flat riverside and gently undulating parkland **Distance:** 7 Miles
Local Information: Breamore House was built by William Doddington in 1583, after he had acquired the Manor of Breamore. Since 1748 The Hulse family has lived here. A fire in 1856 damaged the interior.
The house is open to the public April to September Phone: 01725 512468
Breamore Mizmaze is a rare ancient turf labyrinth. It pre-dates the medieval times when penitent fanatics are rumoured to have shuffled round the maze on their knees.

The Churches

The Augustinian Priory, Bremmer was founded in around 1130 by Baldwin de Redvers on the west bank of the River Avon. It flourished and catered for scattered communities of Saxons. It acquired much land, worked by tenant farmers and was known as the 'Manor of Breamore Bulbarne'. In the late 13th century, the Priory was responsible for the building of three churches; two chapels for the hamlets of Charford, and one at Hale. After the Dissolution of the Monasteries in 1536, North and South Charford Chapels were deserted and dismantled. The Priory met a similar fate.
St Mary`s, Hale is half way up a steep wooded slope above the River Avon. It began as a simple single cell roughly thatched chapel. Patronage of local churches was given to Mrs Doddington, mother of Sir William above. She may have agreed to the maintenance of Hale. In 1630 the Penruddock family came from Northumberland to live at Hale Manor House and re-designed the church. Their connection with Inigo Jones is apparent in the extraordinary town church they created below the house. They rebuilt the nave walls with a stone bench for the infirm, added a chancel, a new roof and, as a final touch, they made a grand, ornate west entrance. During the Civil War, both house and church were vandalised by Cromwell`s men. In 1715 the London architect Thomas Archer bought the estate. First he extended the house and adapted it to Queen Anne style. He then enlarged the church, adding transepts and a new square chancel to match. He had all the outer walls lined with ashlar. He included Doric pillars and doorways. A large monument to Thomas Archer and his two wives stands in the

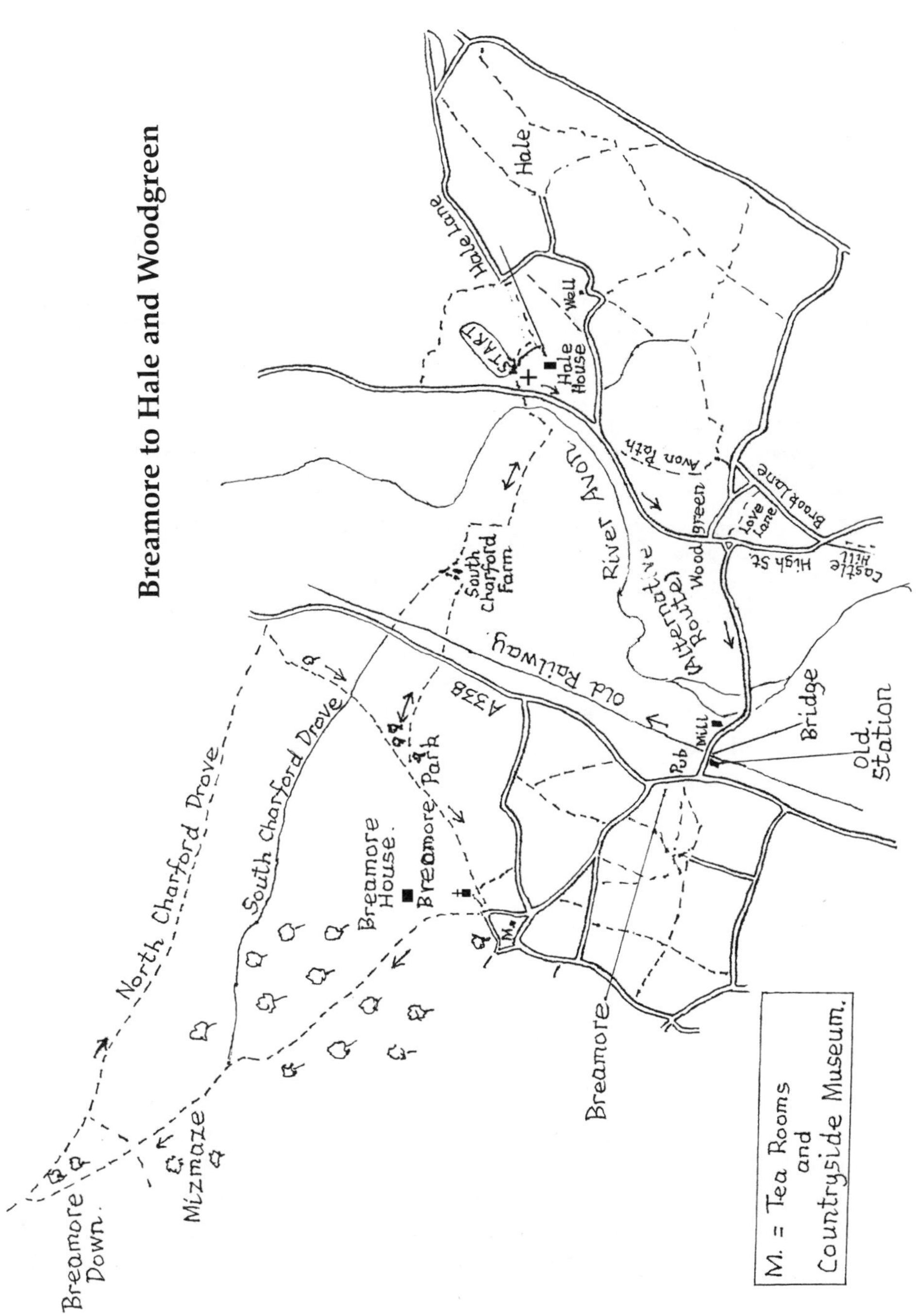
Breamore to Hale and Woodgreen
Hale Lane
Hale
START
Hale House
Well
River Avon
Avon Path
Woodgreen
Brook Lane
Love Lane
High St.
Castle Hill
(Alternative Route)
Old Railway
A338
South Charford Farm
South Charford Drove
North Charford Drove
Breamore Park
Breamore House.
Bridge
Old. Station
Mill
Pub
Breamore
M.
Mizmaze
Breamore Down.
M. = Tea Rooms and Countryside Museum.

Breamore

south transept. It has a Latin eulogy. Hale Park passed to the Goff family who lived there for three generations 1836 – 1920. In 1854, Revd. Joseph Goff became rector and modernised the church, making a new roof and windows. Victorian glass does not suit this Baroque building. Recent renovations have uncovered writings high in the wall of the nave, they are the Ten Commandments, Lord`s Prayer, and the Apostles` Creed and date from the Georgian period.

The Saxon Church of St Mary, Breamore was built around 1000 A.D. in the reign of King Ethelred the Unready (978 – 1016). It is a fine church fit for a king. The King would have chosen the priests. In Breamore, Baldwin de Redvers acquired the Manor around 1100 and passed the advowson to the Priory. The Prior appointed priests until the Priory was dissolved in 1536. The new Lord of the Manor, William Doddington then held the advowson. Originally a Minster or Mother church, responsible for several parishes, Breamore is now, in turn, administered from Fordingbridge. This is still the finest Saxon church in Hampshire. It is unusually large and well built for its period with a rare Saxon tower. The walls are of flint and stone with some long and short work. There are seven double-splayed Saxon windows. The north transept was removed in 15th century. The south transept survives with a memorable arch at its entrance and the inscription in stone: 'HER SWUTELATH SEO GECWYDRAEDNES THE'. Usually Anglo Saxons were unwilling to write and this is a rare exception. It is translated: 'But God hath in due time manifested to us His Word'. The south porch was added in 12th century. A large Saxon rood sculpture was removed from the chancel arch in 15th century and placed above the porch so that it was on the outside of the church. In 16th century the porch was given an upper floor, covering the screen. Sadly it was mutilated later in that century. Wall paintings in the porch were whitewashed also – all part of the Reformation! The chapel in the upper floor has since been abandoned and the floor removed. So now the rood screen can be seen as you enter the church.

The Walk

From Hale Church descend the steep wooded slope on the tarmac footpath, part of the Avon Valley Path. At the road at the bottom, Moot Lane, say Goodbye to Avon Valley Path that goes left. Instead, cross to the parking space opposite. Here is the River Avon with a fine humped concrete bridge beckoning.

If you wish to include Woodgreen with tempting pubs, turn left and follow the lane to that village. Turn right and follow the lane for ½ mile to the Avon where two handsome bridges span the divided river. At the railway bridge go down to the disused line and abandoned station. Go under the bridge on the newly opened footpath and head north for 1 mile. At crosspaths turn left and follow instructions below after the words: 'disused railway'.*

Cross the river and turn left. Go through a farm gate into flat meadows. Go over two flat wooden bridges then turn right before you reach the hedge. You are heading northeast. A low causeway runs parallel on the right of the hedge. A ditch runs alongside on the right for a while.

At the field corner turn left and go over footbridges to head due east for 200 metres. Turn right into another field and follow the hedge on the right. Go through an overgrown piece of wasteland for a short way then cross another footbridge to a farm track.

Follow the farm track as it turns right and heads north for 200 metres. The track turns north to South Charford Farm. *At the farmhouse, pause for a moment to look back and note the way you came for the return walk.*

Go through the farmyard, passing the egg house on the left then barns on the right. Open the stiff farmgate after the barns and continue eastwards across the field to cross the **disused railway line***. Pass through a small field, cross a footbridge and then a driveway to reach the nearby A338.

Hale

Cross with care to the footpath opposite. It leads to a small wood. Veer left and walk through the southern edge of the wood for 200 metres. You emerge from the wood to a **junction of paths**.

Turn left and go through the kissing gate into parkland. Follow the field boundary on the right and enjoy the view over rolling fields where sheep graze. Do not be tempted up to Breamore House on the right – that is for later. Instead, keep on course to trees where another gate lets you into the churchyard.

At Breamore Church go round to the south porch and turn left onto the main path. Leave the churchyard for the green outside. Turn right then immediately right again to re-enter the park. Follow the drive towards Breamore House.

Pass the house on your right and continue on the track up through Breamore Wood where clearings among the handsome trees make this a very pleasant walk. After 1 kilometre in woodland, you come to fields on the left. Another track, South Charford Drive joins from the right.

Keep heading northwest through open countryside. *Breamore Mizmaze and Giant`s Grave are on the left.* Carry on up to a junction of paths and turn right into a hedged track. This is North Charford Drive.

It takes you back down for 1½ miles to A338. Turn right before the main road. Follow a track that runs parallel at a field distance from the main road. In 1 kilometre, after passing woodland on the left, you come to the familiar **junction of paths.**

Turn left and retrace your steps back to South Charford Farm, over the River Avon and up the slope to Hale Church.

Hale House

9 Walks on the Isle of Wight

Tennyson Down

(All walks are covered in OS Explorer 29)

In Bede`s 'Ecclesiastical History of the English People' (731), the Isle of Wight was the last region to be converted to Christianity. St Wilfrid`s disciple, Eoppa was kept busy on the Island. Also St Boniface preached in Bonchurch (700). The Christian King Caedwalla annexed the Island in 686. In Bede`s time it was assigned to the Diocese of Winchester. Several churches on the Island have Saxon origins. Arreton and Freshwater even have some Saxon stonework. After the Norman invasion, William Fitz Osbern, overlord gave 6 island churches to the Benedictine Abbey of Lyra in Normandy. The Island suffered from French raids and the towers of churches, notably Shalfleet were used for defence. Pilgrims came to the Isle of Wight in the Middle Ages to seek health and Salvation at the holy wells. Pilgrim paths still exist and are marked with the scallop shell. There are 26 medieval churches. The island has made up for a slow start. There is also a netwark of beautiful paths where you are never far from the downs and the sea.

Walk 1: Brading to Yaverland (and Bembridge)

This is a varied walk over reclaimed marshes, downland and sea cliffs. The short walk is an easy linear. The long walk to Bembridge is more strenuous.

Starting Point: Brading Station **GR**609868
Terrain: 1 hill to Yaverland, several hills to Bembridge
Distances: Short Walk 3 Miles, Long Walk 9 Miles
Local Information: 1. Brading Marshes were under water 150 years ago. Brading was an island port. The haven silted over in 17th century. Now the marshes are an RSPB nature reserve.
2. The eastern River Yar passes through fertile land. The Romans appreciated this. Their mosaics in Brading Roman Villa portray Ceres, Godess of Fertility. Springs in the Yar were believed to be holy.

The Churches

St Mary the Virgin, Brading has an unusual tower built on piers so that it stands above open arches. The oldest part of the tower is 13th century. The nave has 12th century symmetrical rows of pillars. The oldest window of 1100 is at the back of the north aisle. Two fonts are in this aisle; the older (1200) is at the east end, the other has the date 1631. More recently a poignant statue of little Elizabeth Rollo graces the north aisle. The 14th century north chapel is dedicated to the de Alva family. The south aisle was re-decorated by John Oglander is 1500s. He also built the Oglander Chapel at the eastern end. It contains some of the tombs of this family who came originally with William the Conqueror. The figures of the family of the Knight, Oliver are depicted in prayer on the side of their tomb. Victorians rebuilt the east wall of the chancel but they left the rest intact, including the ancient piscina.

St John the Baptist, Yaverland stands close to the Manor House. It was the private chapel of the Norman de Aula family. There are two Norman arches: the chancel arch and the arch over the south door, now covered by a porch. The openings in the wall between the nave and the chancel are of interest. One led to the rood loft and one is a squint, allowing those in the nave corner to see the altar. Behind the altar there is an alabaster reredos with fine carvings of the four Evangelists and other saints.

The Walk – Brading to Yaverland and back

From Brading Station go out along the access road for 30 metres then turn right at a footpath sign to a housing estate. In 50 metres turn right again to cross the railway line. You come to a rough open meadow. Cross slightly left and in 450 metres you will find a footbridge over the tiny River Yar.

Bear right over Brading Marshes for 150 metres to a junction of paths. Turn right and a low hill confronts you. Climb up to a notice board and seat at the top. Ahead you can see Yaverland Manor. This is your goal. Bear slightly left over rough ground to find a farm gate and a stile. Keep on through the gate entrance to the main road, B3395.

Brading to Yaverland and Bembridge

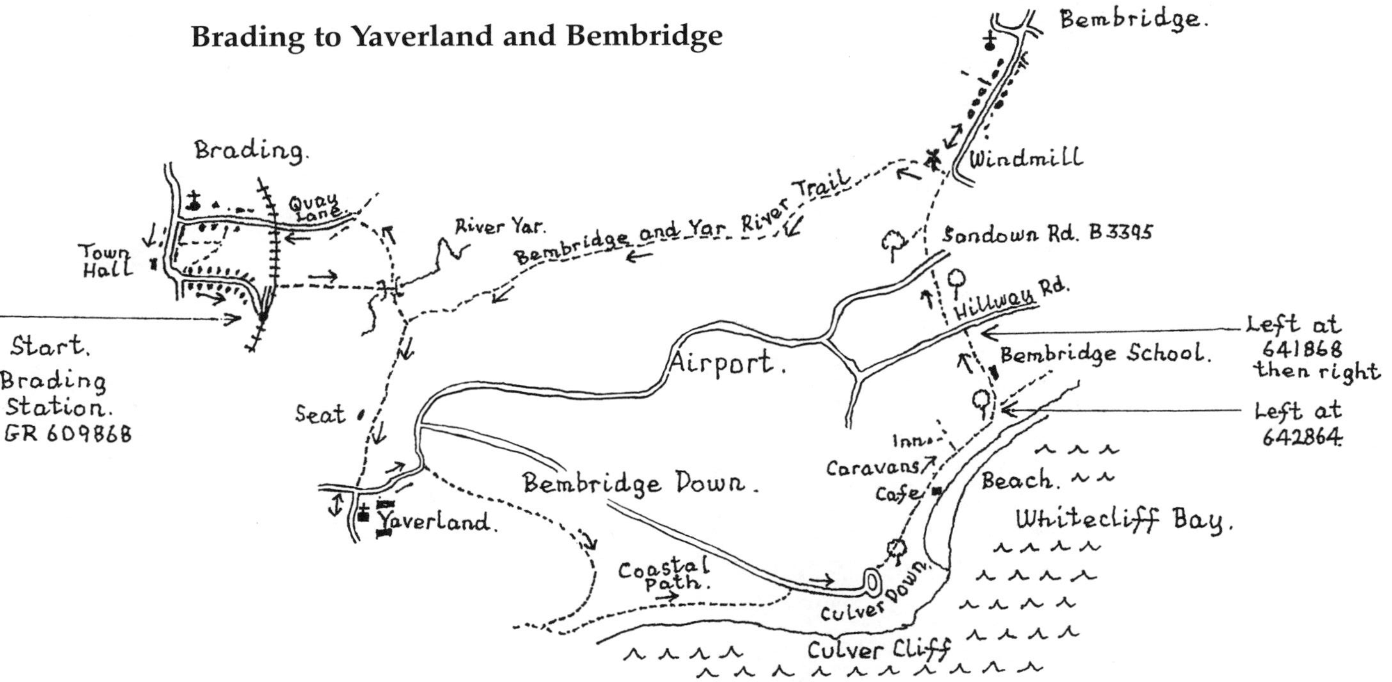

Brading

Yaverland

You have reached a road junction. Cross with care to the road opposite to Yaverland. Pass the Manor House on the left and the Church is next to it.

To return to Brading from Yaverland, retrace your steps.

Continuing from **Yaverland to Bembridge**

From Yaverland Church, return to the main road and re-enter the field of the low hill. Turn right to the right hand corner. A stile leads back to B3395. Cross diagonally right on a bend of the road and another footpath sign.

Follow the enclosed path along the base of Bembridge Down. In about 450 metres you reach open downland. Keep straight on up over an incline to find the sea with views to Sandown to the right and Culver Down to the left.

Make your way down to the Coast Path and turn left towards Culver Down topped by a needle. Climb Culver Down to the needle. *You can go around the headland on the right to the other side of the needle. You have a view over the flatter ground below. Pass a car park on your left then turn right.*

If you wish to avoid the headland, keep straight on passing the needle and the car park on your right and turn down the footpath on the other side.

The path takes a diagonal course to the right down towards woodland. Continue down through the wood to walk on the Coast Path along a lower cliff. Pass caravan sites on the left and a track down to a seaside café on the right. Keep to the Coast Path. It opens to a field and an inn away to the left.

Find the Coast Path in the right hand corner of the field and continue on an enclosed way through rough woodland for another 250 metres. Turn left at a sign describing Bembridge School in the trees on the left. You now have an enclosed way through sad trees with the cold wall of the school on the right.

It is with relief that you emerge to the road, Hillway. Turn left and walk down the road for 75 metres to a footpath sign on the right. Enter more woodland. Away to the left is Bembridge Airport. In 300 metres you come to B3395, known as Sandown Road here.

Cross to the footpath opposite through more woodland. At a T-junction of paths, turn right and start climbing on a bridleway between hedges. A climb of 300 metres brings you to Bembridge Windmill, a shop and café.

To return to Brading from Bembridge Windmill, turn left and follow the well marked path 'Bembridge and Yar River Trail'. It leads you downhill over several stiles for 1½ miles back to Brading Marshes, passing the airport on the left. When you reach the familiar junction of paths, retrace your steps as far as the River Yar. Cross the footbridge and, instead of veering left, take the track to the right towards Brading Church. You join Quay Lane, turn left and cross the bridge over the railway line to continue to the church.

From Brading Church follow the high street to the first junction and traffic lights. Turn left here for the railway station.

To visit Bembridge Church from Bembridge Windmill, *keep straight on along the bridleway for 150 metres to the road. Turn left and follow the road for 1 kilometre, turning left for the church. Retrace your steps to the windmill and follow instructions above to return to Brading.*

Bembridge

Walk 2: Ventnor to Bonchurch

We are never far from the coast on this walk. There are two fine Victorian churches in Ventnor and a little Norman gem in Bonchurch

Starting Point: Trinity Church on A3055, Upper Bonchurch **GR**569778
(Bus to Trinity Church on A3055 or roadside parking on Bonchurch Village Road)
Terrain: Hilly. Mainly lanes or seaside promenade. **Distance:** 4 Miles
Local Information: Bonchurch was a mecca for Victorian poets and artists and still retains an air of Romantic beauty. A short account of the 'literary characters' can be found in the little local booklet on Bonchurch.

The Churches

Holy Trinity Church was built on a prominent corner of the road down to Bonchurch when Ventnor was becoming established as a holiday resort in mid 19th century. Its tall slender spire on a northwest tower and generous proportions of nave and chancel, all make a statement of Victorian confidence in the perpetuity of Christian faith. Much of the style is Early English.

Holy Trinity

Ventnor Parish Church, St Catherine stands above the High Street, Ventnor, looking exactly as if it has been there from Medieval times. It is in fact another Victorian Church. The spacious nave, chancel and south aisle blend into a welcoming interior. Two galleries survive.

The Old Church, Bonchurch nestles into a leafy space at the head of the cliff near the Coastal Path. It is dedicated to Boniface, a Saxon saint. In Domesday the name given is 'Bonecerce'. 'Cerce' is Saxon for church. In 700 A.D. the monk, Winfrith from Nutcelle Monastery, Hampshire was named 'Boniface' meaning doer of good. Pope Gregory made him a bishop. He may have come to the Isle of Wight before going to Germany to be Bishop of Maine. 1000 years ago, monks from the Abbey of Lyra rebuilt the Saxon church. The nave, chancel and south door are early Norman. The windows

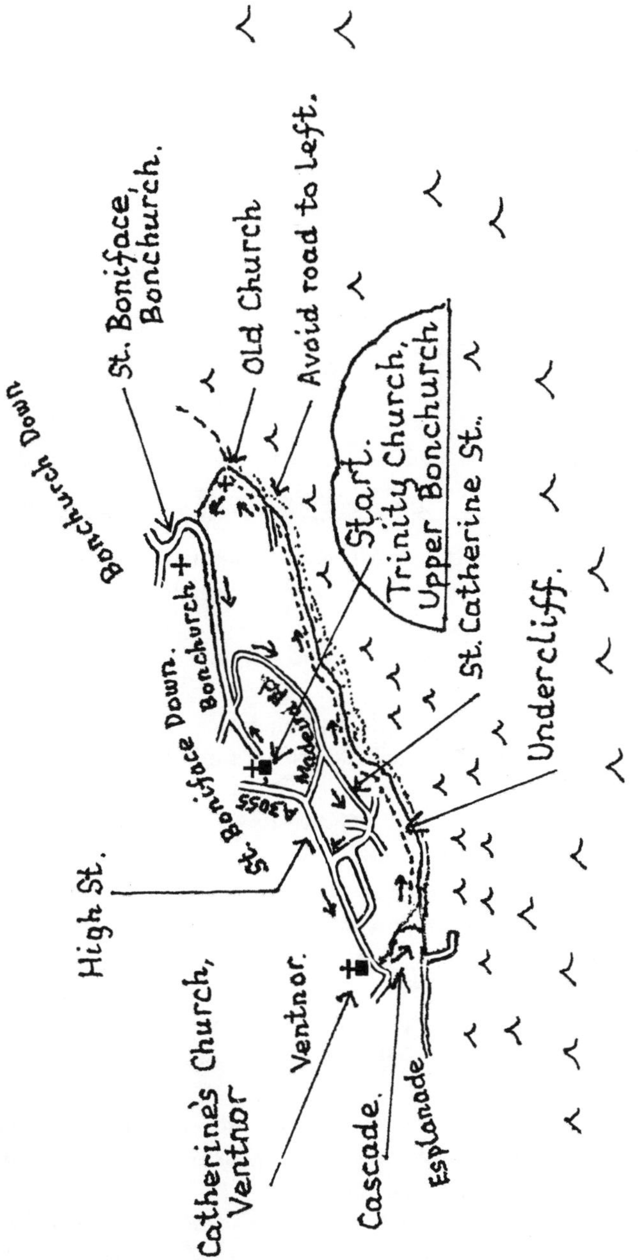

Ventnor to Bonchurch

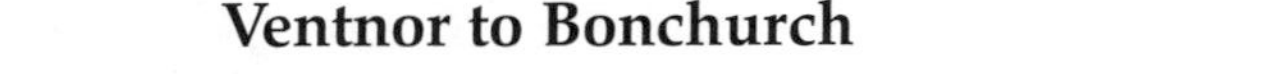

Bonchurch

range from 12th to 15th century. The porch and belfry are more recent. The Victorians managed to fit 102 people in the church, not enough for an expanding village. Fortunately it was decided to build a new church rather than extend or demolish the old one. The old church was left intact, a beautiful and holy haven for walkers.

The new Parish Church of St Boniface, Bonchurch was built in 1845 through the efforts of local benefactors. The village school, now the Church Hall was built at the same time.

The Walk

From Trinity Church walk down the lane towards Bonchurch. You are on Trinity Road and soon join Boniface Road. It enters from the left and the two roads merge to become Bonchurch Village Road. Bonchurch is for later.

Meanwhile, at nearby Madeira Road turn right and follow this elevated lane for 1 Mile to Ventnor. The lane curves through scattered houses with grand sea views. Housing becomes denser as you approach Ventnor. And finally you should turn right up to the High Street. Follow the High Street to the far end where St Catherine`s Church dominates.

From St Catherine`s Church cross to the post office and take the nearby lane down to the sea. When you reach the promenade, turn left passing the cascade on the left and the fish market on the right.

You are on the Coastal Path. Here a concrete seaside pedestrian road leads for 1 Mile to Bonchurch. On the way you pass the chalets at Wheelers Bay then the scrub of Undercliff and a restaurant as you approach Bonchurch. Avoid the first road to the left. Keep on the seaside road.

Bonchurch

Continue to a tarmac track leading behind stone cottages. It climbs steeply up to the Old Church, Bonchurch on the left.

After visiting the Old Church, turn left and walk along the lane to Bonchurch Village. (The Parish Church is just to the right, across the road.)

Turn left onto Bonchurch Village Road and walk gently uphill. You pass the Post Office on the left and the wild life pond, once a swamp on the right. Avoid left turns. In ½ mile at the top, you fork left for Trinity Church.

Ventnor

Walk 3: Godshill to Whitwell

From a picture book village we descend to the little River Yar and follow it to a place of pilgrimage where wells are 'dressed'. We return over the hills after our visit to two medieval churches.

Starting Point: Godshill Church GR527817

Bus from Shanklin or Car Park down in the village off the main road A3020

Terrain: flat riverside at the outset, open and undulating for the return walk.

Distance: 9 Miles

Local Information: Medieval pilgrims came to the holy wells on the island. We pass one of these wells at Whitwell. In the church there is a leaflet showing the pilgrim path. It is marked with scallop shells.

Churches

The Church of the Lily Cross, Godshill, set amongst thatched cottages is the subject of many photographs. It is a Medieval church dating from the early 14th century. If there was an earlier building, it has not survived. The tower is 14th century in the lower stages and 16th century in the upper stage. It has grotesque carvings, many below the southwest pinacle. One is bearded face with bared teeth and glaring eyes. The church has two naves divided by an arcade of six bays. In the late 15th century the Perpendicular style prevailed

Godshill

and saw the replacement of an earlier arcade. There is no division between nave and chancel. The south transept is dedicated to St Stephen. The Lily Cross is a mural painted in 1450 on the east wall of this transept. It depicts Christ crucified on a three branched lily. The lily was a symbol of purity. The north transept may have been a chantry chapel. In 1741 Sir Robert Worsley had it rebuilt in Classical style. The Worsley family became local landowners after the Dissolution of the Monasteries. Before their advent, Richard de Redvers gave the Manor of Appuldurcombe to the Abbey of Monteburg in 1090 A.D. In 1490 the manor was granted to the Nuns Minoresses. They leased it to Sir John Leigh. His daughter Anne

Godshill to Whitwell

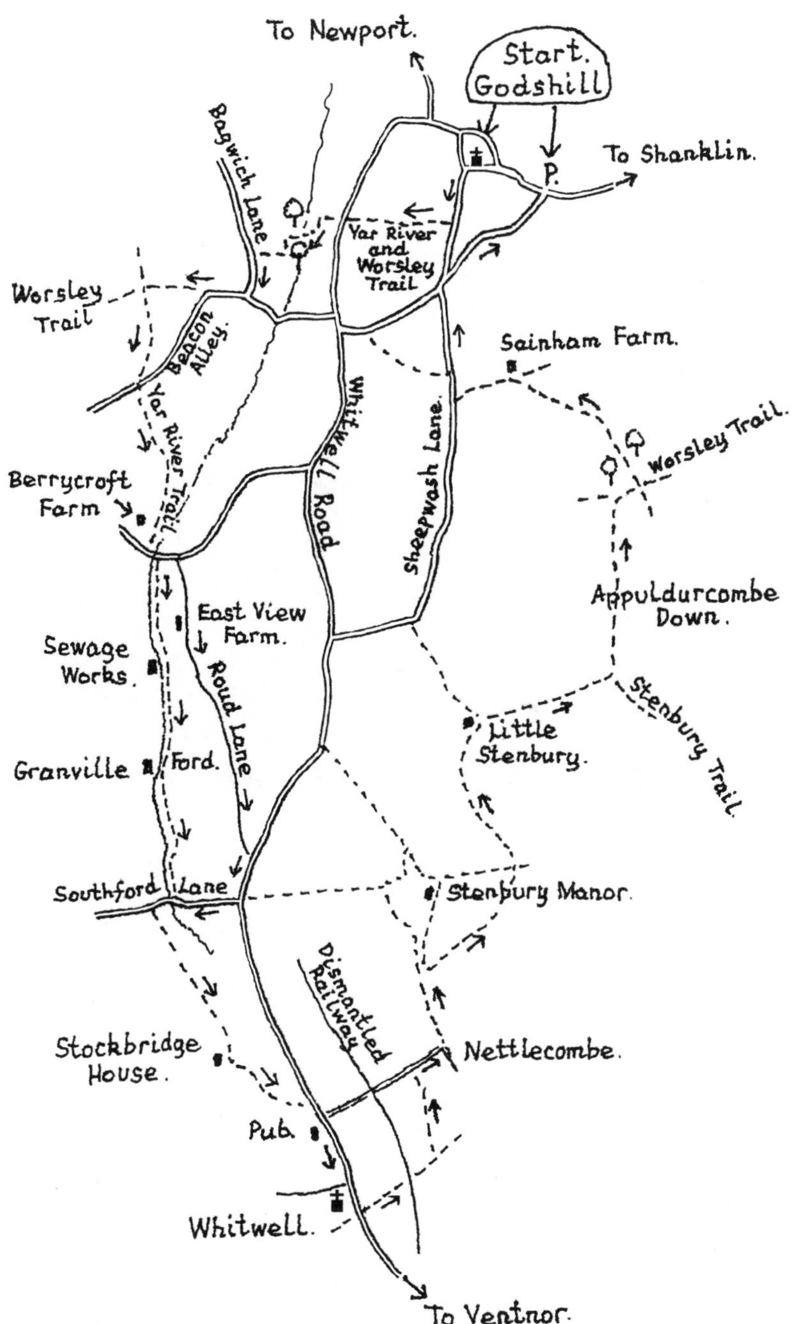

married Sir James Worsley. For 300 years the Worsleys held Appuldurcombe House. The weather vane on the tower is a Wyvern, the crest of the Worsleys. And now we walk on the Worsley Trail! *See 'Long Distance Paths' at the end.*

The Parish Church of St Mary and St Rhadegund, Whitwell also retains a deeply medieval character. It consist of two chapels. One St Rhadegund built in 12th century as a chantry for the de Esturs of Gatcombe, a Norman family. Their feudal tenants at Whitwell also worshipped here. The other separate chapel was built in 13th century by the Lords of Stenbury for the parishioners south of Godshill. Both chapels have wagon roofs with king posts and arched braces. In 16th century the dividing wall was removed and the south aisle became the St Mary Chapel. Only the east wall of the chancel dates from the divided time. North and south walls of the nave are 15th century. The south arcade was rebuilt. The south aisle has Perpendicular windows. The tower, unusually placed on the southwest corner of the church is also Perpendicular. The font is attached to a pillar of the tower. The heavy south porch has to support Swanage stone tiles.

Whitwell

The Walk

When you come out of the church porch Godshill, turn right and go down the path past a cottage offering water to drink. At the road turn left heading south between thatched cottages and walking along the straight, elevated lane. You pass the turning on the left down to the village. Next on the left is a little public garden with seats. In 300 metres turn right and eastwards across fields along the footpath on the Yar River and Worsley Trail.

In 400 metres you cross the Whitwell Road to the path opposite. It passes a pond, curves left then right through undergrowth. You cross the little River Yar and avoid the path to the right. In another 100 metres you reach the Bagwich Lane. Turn left and walk to a T-junction where you turn right.

You are now on Beacon Alley. Despite its name, this is quite a busy road so it might be worth doing the little detour to the right in 100 metres, still on the trail. In 200 metres the trails divide. *Worsley Trail goes straight on.* You turn left on the Yar River Trail and make your way back to Beacon Alley.

Cross with care to the continuation of the trail opposite. Follow the hedge on the left for 300 metres then veer left into the field corner over rough ground. Another path joins you here and you continue south with the river on your left.

You come to the open lawns of Berrycroft Farm then a tarmac lane. Turn left. You now have a choice of routes.

Route 1: *to continue on the Yar River Trail, turn immediately right and follow the river for 1 mile to Southford Lane. Here you turn right then left.*

Route 2: take the next turning, Roud Lane. This rejoins Whitwell Road at a more southerly point. On the way you pass East View Farm. At Whitwell Road turn right. In 250 metres turn right again into Southford Lane. In 300 metres you rejoin the trail on your left.

Both routes are now on a straight, flat, unenclosed bridleway. Pass a small stately home, Stockbridge House and turn left into the unmarked lane to continue on the trail. In 350 metres you join the Whitwell Road again. Turn right for the pub then Whitwell Church.

From Whitwell Church keep on course along the Ventnor Road for 100 metres. Turn left into a marked 'pilgrim' path on the left (see Local Information above). Head northeast across a field and over an old railway line. In the next field at crosspaths, turn left away from the pilgrim route.

Godshill

Follow a stony path north over the field to a tarmac lane. Turn right and walk up to a T-junction. Medieval Nettlecombe Farm is on the right. Turn left through a farm gate and along a bridleway to an open field.

The bridleway leads straight on to Stenbury Manor and farm. Instead, I have chosen a downland route. Turn right towards Little Stenbury. Hug the boundary on the right to the next field. Cross diagonally left to the far, elevated corner. On the way you cross a moat then climb to the next field.

Follow the hedge and enjoy the views over the River Yar. In ½ mile you pass a lone grey cottage on the left. This is Little Stenbury.

Turn right into an enclosed grassy path up to Appuldurcombe Down. Veer left to join the Stenbury Trail northwards. You are on the edge of the ancient estate of Appuldurcombe and pass some on the boundary walls on the right.

In another ½ mile avoid the path to the left and go on to enter a copse. There is a footpath signpost under the trees. Turn left to follow the Worsley Trail down to Sainham Farm on the right. Then continue to tarmac Sheepwash Lane. Turn right for Godshill. Keep on the lane for the church or *turn right in ¼ mile to walk down to the car park in the village.*

Walk 4: Newport - River Medina - Whippingham

A spring or summer time stroll beside this important waterway leads to a church designed by a monarch

Starting Point: St Thomas Church, Newport **GR**499893
Map: OS Explorer OL29 **Terrain:** Flat
Distances: 4 Miles (return by bus no.5, a frequent service to Newport)
Alternative routes back following the map: 6 miles partly on disused railway
9 miles by continuing to Cowes

Local Information: 1. Medina is the Latin for Saxon 'Medena' meaning 'Middle River'. It rises from chalk streams on St Catherine`s Down and is 17 km long. Marine industries grew up around the Medina. Newport was a centre of trade. Today there are still sail makers and chandlers but more leisure activities abound with sailing yachts and rowing boats, walkers and cyclists.

2. Quay Arts Centre is formed from two 18th century brewery warehouses. There are three galleries of contemporary art, cinema, and a waterfront café.

Note: Volunteers keep Whippingham Church open from Easter to October
In winter it is only open for services.
Newport Parish Church is also dependent on volunteers

The Churches

Newport, St Thomas stands in a pleasant square near the High Street. It was rebuilt in 1854 in Decorated style. The dominant tower rises above the roofs of the aisles. Inside, the font and the fine pulpit are both early 17th century. Most of the interior is in good early Victorian style.

Newport

Whippingham, St Mildred`s *(not open in the winter except for services).* Once a modest parish church by Nash has been transformed into a monument to the Victorian Royal family and attracts coach loads of visitors. Prince Alfred re-designed it in 1854 with the help of the architect, Thomas Cubbitt. It is a grand ornate cruciform church. Above the crossing is the high, impressive lantern tower with a replica of the Order of the Garter in the centre. The transepts have rose windows that are mini-versions of those of Notre Dame de Paris. Chapels and arcades on either side of the chancel include the Battenburg Memorial Chapel and the Royal Pew. Queen Victoria and her relatives lavished gifts on this church. After the death of the Queen, parishioners contributed the pulpit in her memory. The church is dedicated to an Anglo-Saxon Princess Mildred who died around 700. There is a Saxon carving set into the west wall of the porch.

Newport - River Medina - Whippingham

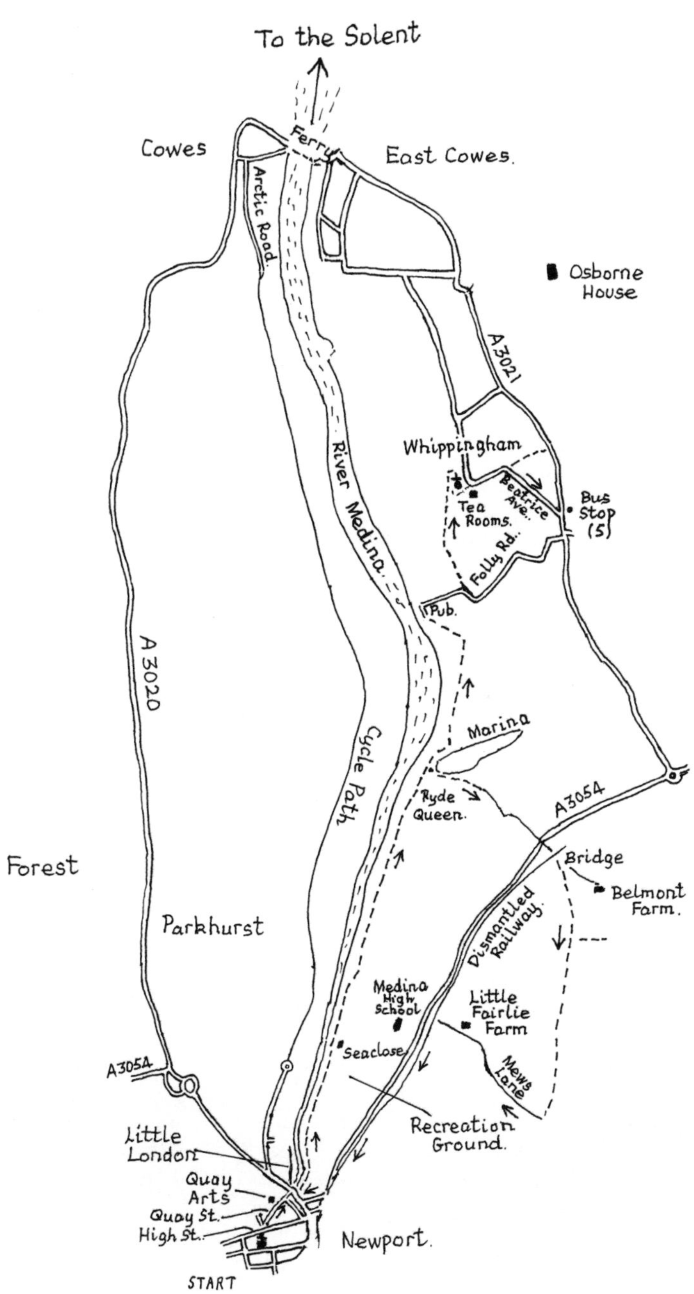

The Walk

From St Thomas Church walk along the High Street to the Tourist Information Office in the Guildhall. Veer left to walk along Quay Street to cross Sea Street to the Quay. Quay Arts Centre is on the left. Walk under the road bridge then follow the path beside the river on your left. On the other side you can see the converted warehouses.

Pass your own warehouses on this side then you can again walk beside the river. Extensive playing fields on the right are open to the public, so you can wander onto the grass and enjoy the scattered trees and return to the river.

Here is a firm path, tree-lined in places and with plenty of gaps to see the view across the river. Footbridges have been provided to cross small inlets.

In 2 miles you reach the Marina, a larger inlet at Island Harbour. The wreck of Ryde Queen is on your right. The control tower is ahead. Pass this to reach the harbour walkway (no need to walk all around the harbour!)

Pass fields on your right as you head for Whippingham Church; the tower can be seen among trees.

First you reach Folly Inn, open for sailors, walkers and drivers. The walk continues along the access road to the Inn. After 250 metres up Folly Lane, turn left into a footpath across fields.

Walk below the Church before turning right into an enclosed path to the churchyard. There are several seats here for you to enjoy the view.

Go to the front of Whippingham Church. A seasonal café is on your right.

Go straight on along Beatrice Ave to the Main Road, A3021. Cross to the bus stop diagonally right opposite for a number 5 bus to Newport.

For the alternative walk back to Newport, *retrace your steps to the Marina and turn left to walk along the access road. In ½ mile cross the main road A3054 to the track opposite. It leads under the old railway bridge.*

Veer right and head south for 1 mile. At a junction of paths, turn right. Pass buildings on the left. Follow the hedge on the right. Bear left between hedges and pass Little Fairlee Farm on the right. You continue on Mews Lane, leading to Holberry Lane and the disused Newport to Ryde line.

Turn left and follow the disused railway line back to Newport.

Whippingham

Walk 5: Gatcombe to Carisbrooke

From a quiet village church tucked away in a wooded corner, climb to upland sheep pastures and wide views over the Island then descend to the famous centre of old battles. Return along rich brook side fields.

Starting Point: The lane in front of Gatcombe Church **GR**492852
Map: OS Explorer OL29 **Terrain:** Moderate hills **Distance:** 7 Miles
Local Information: 1. Carisbrooke Castle, the finest on the Isle of Wight, has defended the nation over many centuries. Roman stones have been found here. The Keep and Curtain Wall are Norman. The bastions are Elizabethan. The gatehouse is medieval. The castle is in the care of English Heritage. Phone 0870 333 1181 or 01983 522107
2. Lukely Brook rises at Bowcombe Farm and runs through Beaucombe Valley. In medieval times the lane here produced the richest harvest on the Island. Roman tiles and glass have been found in a midden at Bowcombe.

The Churches

St Olave, Gatcombe is basically 13th century with original north doorway and south lancet window in the nave. The font of Purbeck marble is medieval. The overbearing tower and the large windows north and south are Perpendicular. One south window contains pieces of 15th century stained glass representing angels. The more modern east window has glass by William Morris and Co. Circles of

Gatcombe

Gatcombe to Carisbrooke

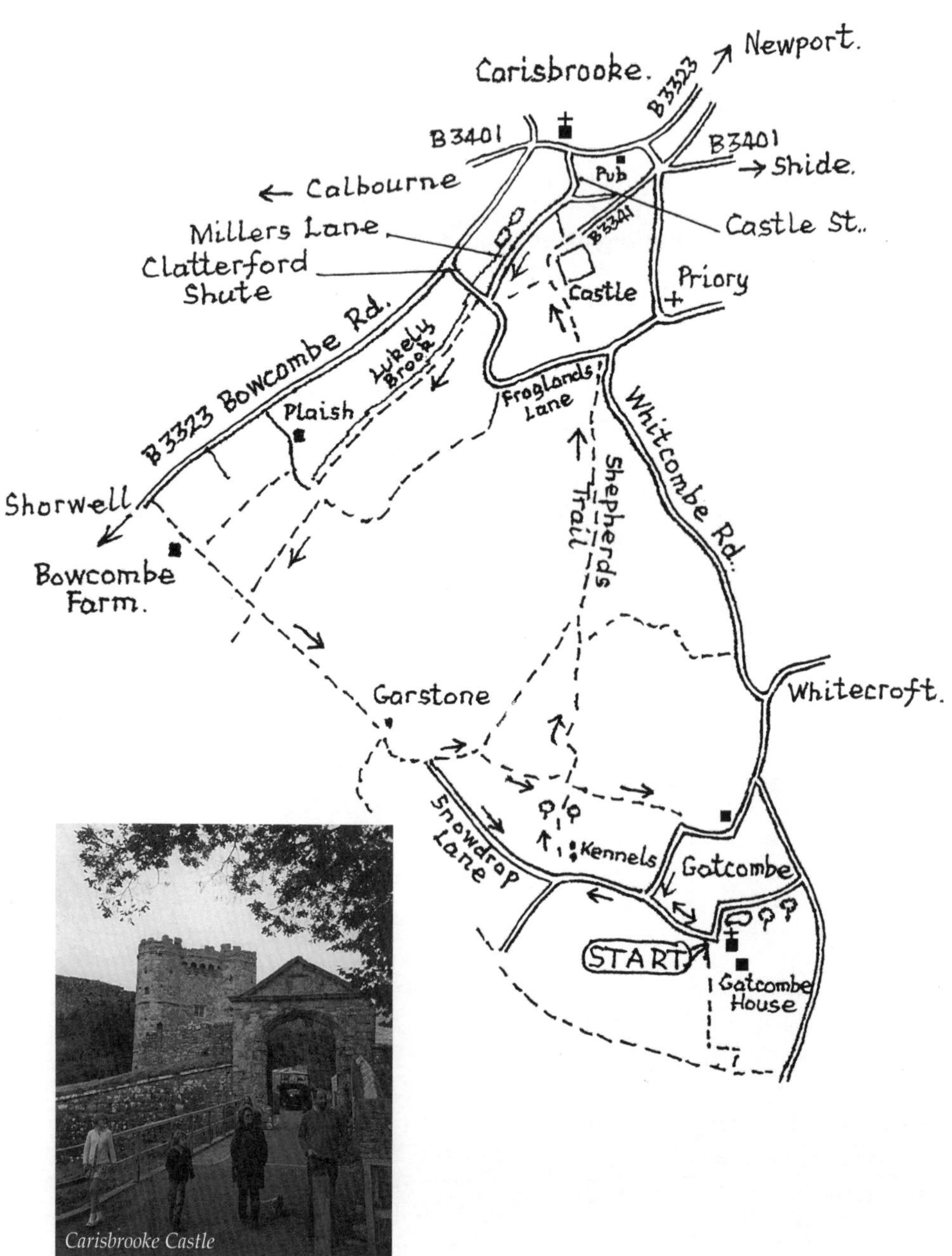

Carisbrooke Castle

various shades of blue enhance the traditional New Testament scenes in these windows. On the north side of the nave the effigy of a crusader lies with his feet on a dog. One legend has it that the dog comes to life every 100 years to dance in the churchyard in the moonlight.

Priory Church of St Mary the Virgin, Carisbrooke was built in 1120. After the Norman Conquest, it is one of six Saxon churches on the Island given by William FitzOsborne to the Abbey of Lyra. The Abbot gained permission to build a priory. Cloisters were added on the north side and an aisle on the south. The line of circular pillars replaced the south wall. Norman windows at the top of the west piers are still there. When Henry V suppressed the priories in 1414, Carisbrooke was put under the control of the priory of Sheen and eventually dissolved. The church survived. The Perpendicular tower, added in 1490, is one of the finest on the Island. It has five stages and a stair turret. In 1570 the chancel was removed and an east window inserted. The east window of the south chapel was then reduced in size to match. Only the chancel arch, circa 1200, is original. The sanctuary was re-designed by Seely and Paget in 1967. The graceful stone Madonna and Child by John Skelton fits beautifully in a niche in the south chapel

The Walk

From Gatcombe Church take the lane straight ahead to the few village houses, some thatched. In nearly ½ mile 'Shepherd's Trail' crosses the road.

Turn right and climb the hill up past kennels on the right, then Copsewood House. The trail heads north for 1½ miles to Carisbrooke. Continue climbing through the copse up to crossways on the down.

A view opens across the Island to Portsdown Hill on the main land. Just below are the red buildings of Whitecroft, the old mental hospital. The tower has survived its conversion to a housing estate.

Keep straight on along the top of the sloping field to find the enclosed path hugging the hedge on the left. Keep on course when views open to the left. Avoid turnings to right and left. Your trail enters a pleasant sunken way. *Ferns grow in the shade of overhanging oak, hazel and beech trees whose twisted roots are exposed on the banks beside you.*

Finally the trail comes gently down to Froglands Lane and you can look across fields to Carisbrooke Castle.

Turn left into the lane and in 50 metres there is a footpath on the right across the field to the castle.

Go to the left of the castle and veer right to find the entrance. *You are free to visit the gift shop. See above for more information.*

The main B3341 ends at Carisbrooke Castle. Cross the road to the bus stops on the other side and turn right. In 50 metres you will find a footpath on the left and a view to the church. Turn left and go down the steep path to Millers Lane. Turn right and walk past a few houses to Castle St on the left.

Turn left and follow the walkway above the water in the street. You come to the

Carisbrooke Priory

main road through Carisbrooke, B3323. The church is diagonally left opposite. *Pub, garden, and public toilets in a car park are down to the right.*

From Carisbrooke Church retrace your steps along Castle St. and turn right into Millers Lane. Avoid the path up to the Castle and continue along the lane to a junction. Clatterford Shute is the road on your right.

Turn right then immediately left into a footpath that runs southwest in the valley of Lukely Brook for over 1 kilometre. After passing Plaish Farm over to the right, you come to a T-junction with a farm track. Turn left on the track. In 25 metres turn right into a footpath across an open field with views ahead to Garstons Down and Chillerton Down. In ¼ mile at the next T-junction *Bowcombe Farm is to the right.* Turn left.

You are heading southeast uphill for ½ mile to Garstons, a lone house. After a bend, you come to Snowdrop Lane on the right, leading southeast for 1 mile back to Gatcombe Church.

If you prefer a field route, pass Snowdrop Lane on the right. Keep on an elevated track avoiding a left turn. Keep heading east until you come to familiar cross paths. Go straight across Shepherds Trail and in ¼ mile you come to a tarmac lane at Gatcombe. You are at a bend in the lane.

Turn right and follow the lane to a T-junction. Turn left for Gatcombe Church.

Walk 6: Shalfleet to Calbourne

Sustained by the agriculture of the Island, two churches have survived from Saxon times to the present day

Starting Point: The church hall car park in Church Lane **GR**414893
Or the Car Park over A3504 on the lane to the Quay **GR**415895
Map: OS Explorer OL29 **Terrain:** Fields and lanes, many stiles!
Distance: 6 ½ Miles
Local Information: 1. Calbourne Water Mill is a 17th century working flour mill. There is a renewable energy centre on the site. Phone: 01983 531227.
Winkle Street, formerly known as Barrington Row, is a pretty row of cottages, overlooking the brook. Only local traffic is allowed to enter.
The name 'Caul' means 'Kale' and 'Bourne' means 'Brook'.

The Churches

The Church of St Michael the Archangel, Shalfleet. The name 'Scealden Fleote' is Saxon for 'shallow creek stream'. In Domesday, the name had become 'Seldeflet'. An early Saxon burial ground has been discovered near the Norman church. The massive tower of this church may have been built first as a fortress against Danes and, later, French invaders, approaching from the creek. The walls are 5 feet thick. The north wall of the nave has Norman foundations and a north door with one of the finest tympanums on the Island. A bearded man in control of two lions is depicted there. In 13th century the church was enlarged. It was then that the fine wide south aisle with its slender pillars was built in Purbeck stone. The Decorated windows have unusual oval tracery in them. In one of these windows are the arms of Isabella de Fortibus, Lord of the Island (1283 – 1293). An arch cut into the tower caused subsidence that had to be rectified. Buttresses were added in 14th and 15th centuries. In 20th century the tower, which has survived without foundations, was underpinned.

All Saints Church, Calbourne overlooks the village from its green slope. Calbourne is mentioned in Domesday. Malgar, Archbishop of Rouen and uncle of William the Conqueror was the first rector. Apart from the font, little remains of the Norman church. The present building is Early English.
The windows in the chancel

Shalfleet

Shalfleet to Calbourne

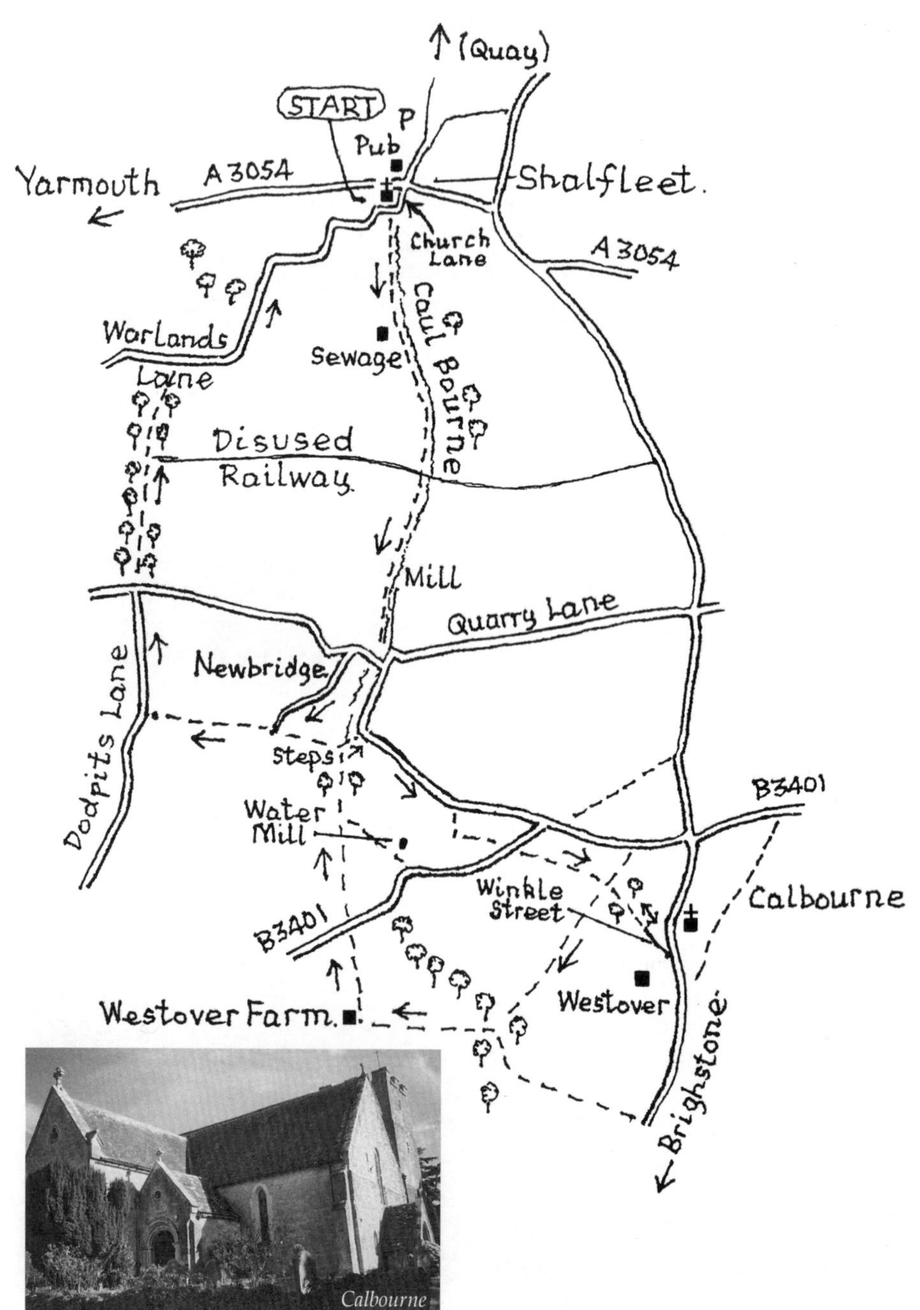

Calbourne

and south aisle are original. Many changes were made during 15th to 19th centuries. The tower was rebuilt in 1752 after a fire. The north transept contains the Simeon Chapel. They were Lords of the Manor of Swainston and rebuilt this transept in 19th century. Another Island family who held the Manor of Westover is remembered in the south aisle. This part of the church is remarkably empty, apart from a fine brass memorial of a 14th century knight, possibly William Montecute.His tragic tale is recounted in the church history. The north porch, built in Norman style, is in fact Victorian.

The Walk

From Shalfleet Church take the footpath opposite. This well worn path crosses two small village greens to farmland – and the first stiles! It heads due south for over 1 mile, following the tree-lined stream on the left. This is the Caul Bourne that has given its name to our destined village.

Shalfleet north door

On the way you pass a well screened sewage works and cross a disused railway line (this section belongs to the farmer!) You join the track south through Homestead Farm and enjoy the view ahead to Brighstone Forest.

Soon after the farm, the track veers to the left. *You have the option of taking the footpath on the right across fields.* I have chosen the track that passes Mill Cottage and the mill pond on the left then follows the tree covered stream on the right.

You come down to Quarry Lane and turn right to nearby B3401. Turn right again towards the village of Newbridge with picturesque old cottages. In 100 metres take the first turning left into Clay Lane. In ¼ mile it ends in a view across fields and a 3-pronged finger post. *Note the turning to Dodpits Lane for the return walk.*

For now, turn sharp left hugging the hedge on the left. The path turns left and crosses a small field towards trees. These trees conceal a deep little valley. There are rough steps and a damp little bridge over the stream to enable you to sink, cross and rise on the other side.

At the T-junction at the top, *note* ***this spot*** *for the return walk.* Meanwhile, turn left through the trees to re-emerge on the B3401 at a bend with a straight stretch in view. Turn right and walk on the verge beside the road for ¼ mile.

Turn right into a footpath enclosed with shrubs. It soon bends to the left and opens onto a high bank above the Caul Bourne below on the right. Keep to the hedge on the left for 200 metres when you come down to the byway.

Cross with care to the steep steps up the bank opposite. Continue southeast following the stream down on the right. Pass a plain stone farmhouse and keep on across small fields and into woodland.

Winkle Street Calbourne

You emerge to well-known Winkle Street where pretty houses, bedecked with flowers, face the flowing stream. At the end, turn left and walk up the road to the Church. *You have to continue for another ¼ mile to find the pub.*

From Calbourne Church go back down the road. *As you enter Winkle Street, you notice a large pond and gates on the left to Westover Mansion.*

Retrace your steps along Winkle Street and the woodland path at the end. When you come out to fields, avoid right turns (including the path that brought you here). Instead, turn left and cross the bridge over the stream to farmland. More stiles are here and ahead.

A clear path heads southeast for 1 kilometre. It starts with a gentle uphill and continues across flat fields to woodland, Withybed Copse. Walk through the copse to a T-junction.

Turn right into a track that leads out of the wood and heads west across fields to Westover Farm. Keep going on the concrete yard through the farm and turn right to walk northwards on another track. In ¼ mile you reach a little thatched place on the right. Go through the gate to the byway.

Cross with care diagonally left to the footpath opposite. Here you continue northwards through uncultivated scrubland for ½ mile. *The willowherb was over when we passed by at the end of September.* When you have battled half way, you pass a footpath on the right, *leading to the working water mill.* Keep going north to enter woodland and walk above the stream in the valley on the left. In 250 metres you reach **this spot.**

Take the familiar path on the left down steps to cross the stream and climb up the other side. Cross the field and follow the hedge on your right now.

At the three-pronged finger post, turn left (not sharp left) and follow the path to Dogpits Lane. You pass Eades Farm on the way. In 500 metres you reach the lane and turn right. You head due north for over one mile and encounter no more stiles, apart from one.

At the end of Dodpits Lane, cross B3401 to the track opposite. On this tree-lined bridleway, a lady in a pony trap passed us and managed to get all the way through to Warlands Lane at the end.

Turn right at this lane and follow it around bends and back to Shalfleet. After the post office turn right for Church Lane.

Walk 7: Niton, St Catherines's Hill and Chale

Two ancient churches lie on either side of this hill, a famous landmark.

Starting Point: Roadside parking on A3055 heading south out of Niton **GR**506763
Terrain: One gentle climb, one steep descent, one very muddy patch, some cliffside walking
Distance: 7 Miles
Local Information: **1.** St Catherine`s Oratory was built by Squire Walter de Godeston in 14th century. He had helped himself to wine salvaged from the shipwrecked St Marie of Bayonne in 1314. His punishment was to endow a chapel with a priest to pray for the souls of mariners. He also had to build a lighthouse. The lighthouse still stands. Let the punishment fit the crime!
2. Foy Monument was built by a Russian merchant, Michael Foy to commemorate the visit of Tzar Alexander in 1814. In 1857 Lieutenant Dawes added a tablet to remember the British dead in the Crimea

The Churches

St John the Baptist, Niton stands in a well tended churchyard garden; flowering shrubs are sheltered by yew trees and paths lead down to various entrances. There is a grand lychgate of 1920. Niton is one of the Island churches built soon after the Norman Conquest, probably on the site of a Saxon church. No sign of the Saxon building remains. It is one of six churches given to the Abbey of Lire in Normandy in 1070. Edward 111 put an end to this connection. In 1414 Henry V gave the church to Charterhouse in Surrey. In 1626 Charles 1 gave it to Queen College, Oxford. The college still holds the advowson. The nave is Norman. The large font with a thick basin carved from one block of stone is probably Norman. Aisles were added in 12th century. The pillars are rounded, wide apart and supporting gently pointed arches. The chancel is 14th century. It has a Victorian Gothic east window. In 15th century the south aisle was enlarged. The south chapel has a wide low arch connecting with the chancel. The Victorian renovation also included the north wall and north arcade. The Perpendicular west tower has a short stone spire.
St Andrew, Chale by contrast is in an open place where sea breezes blow and the Needles are in sight. Among the graves in the churchyard, many hold the remains of shipwreck victims. The captain and some of the passengers from the Clarenden that ran aground near Blackgang in 1836 are buried here. As at Niton, the basic church, nave and chancel was built in 12th century. Later in the same century it was extended; the Manor Chapel and the Walpan Chapel came into being. In 15th century the Manor Chapel east window and the porches were added. The tower is Perpendicular. Victorian restoration has kept the church in good condition. George Arnold Hearn, an American descendant of one of the rectors has donated five windows, the clock, two bells and an organ.

The Walk

Face Niton Church and look for the lane on the right. This is your way up to St Catherine`s Hill. It starts as an access lane to a row of cottages. Pass these on your right. The lane narrows and forms a footpath called Bury Lane. Climb gently for ½ mile on this straight path enclosed by hedges.

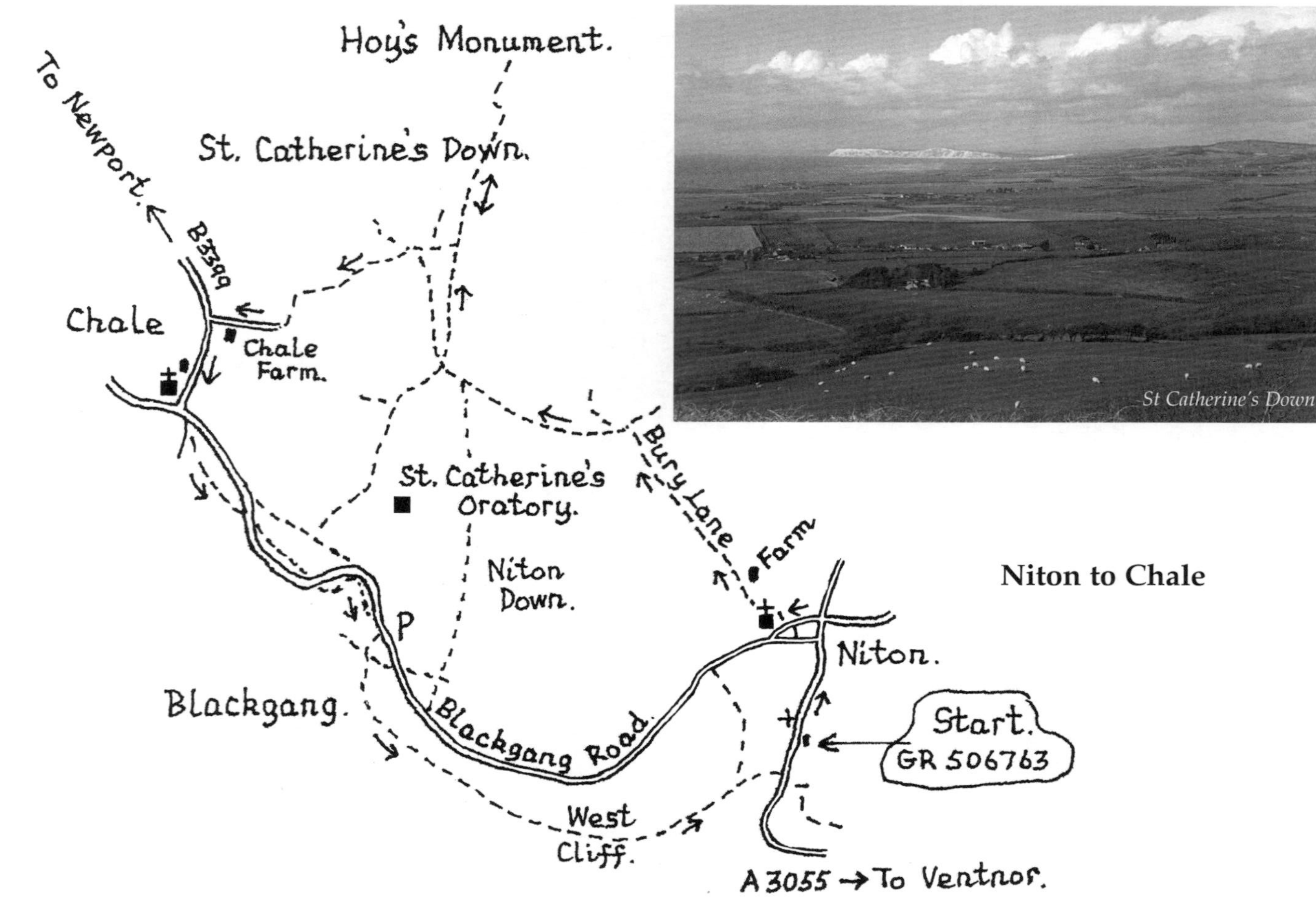

St Catherine's Down

Niton to Chale

Niton

At the top, at a T-junction you are rewarded with fine views ahead over Godshill to the Solent. Turn left and walk along this delightful elevated path. St Catherine`s Oratory is up on the left. *The energetic may be tempted to make a detour up to this highest point.*

Pass the Oratory and turn right to head north along the top of a ridge for ½ mile to Hoy Monument. (See note 2 above). Retrace your steps over halfway back along the ridge. It is now possible to see the waymarked path to your right. Admire the view to the distant white cliff before the steep descent!

When you reach a grassy base below the ridge, avoid the path to the right. You have to find an enclosed bridleway down to Chale on the left. You now have muddy terrain for over ¼ mile and may envy the cows beside you in their grassy field.

At the bottom turn left to go through a farmyard to a welcome lane. It leads to B3399 Newport Road.

Turn left for the pub in Chale and continue to a T-junction with A3055. The church is on the corner.

From Chale Church turn left to cross the A3055 and walk past the Newport Road. Almost immediately on your right you will see a notice for Pedestrians to Blackgang Chine. Turn right here and follow the enclosed path – back to the main road again! Fortunately you can continue along a wide grass verge for almost ¼ mile to a roundabout where the main road curves up to the left. Avoid this left turn and the Blackgang road to the right.

Instead, walk across the middle of the roundabout to the opposite side where wooden steps lead down to trees and a manicured field. Walk up to the right hand corner of the field and enter an enclosed path leading to a car park and lookout point. Once again you can avoid the nearby main road.

Find the Coastal Path on your right. It has a warning notice about the cliffs ahead. To start with the path is quite near the crumbling edge – so walk with care! You are heading southwest with the sea away to your right. The land below you on the right has crumbled and formed a tree-covered ledge. Pass St Catherine`s Lighthouse below. Avoid a path to the left and keep on course for a descent into woodland.

When you reach the road below, turn left and walk up to the A3055 on the south side of Niton.

Walk 8: Mottistone to Brighstone

Walk in the footsteps of Neolithic tribes who cultivated the slopes and buried their dead on top of the downs. Then descend to find two beautiful churches.

Starting Point: The National Trust Car Park, Mottistone Manor, off B3399
GR405837 **Map:** OS Explorer OL29 **Terrain:** Moderate climb to open downland, some paths through farm and woodland **Distance:** 8 Miles
Local Information: 1. Mottistone Manor Garden. The architect and then owner of the manor, John Seely gave the estate to the nation. The National Trust manages the gardens and tea room, open late March to end of October (not Fridays and Saturdays). Phone 01983 741302
2.You pass early Bronze Age barrows on Mottistone Down. In more recent history, the Harborough Barrow was part of the national beacon system.
3. Brighstone Shop and Museum, open all year (mornings only in winter)
Phone 01983 740689

The Churches

St Peter and St Paul, Mottistone is a 12th century church by Brian de Insula of Mottistone Manor. Church and manor have always been closely linked. The Cheke family inherited the estate in 1300. In 15th century Robert and David Cheke enlarged the church. They rebuilt the nave and added the tower and chancel. Outside the east window are carvings of the Cheke shield and the Tudor rose. There are holy water stoops in the south porch and lych gate. In 19th century the church was given a thorough restoration. The broach spire was removed and replaced with a parapet and little spire. The cedar wood in the chancel roof comes from the wreck of the Cedrene that ran aground nearby in 1862. Sailors and convicts waded ashore.

Mottistone

Mottistone to Brighstone

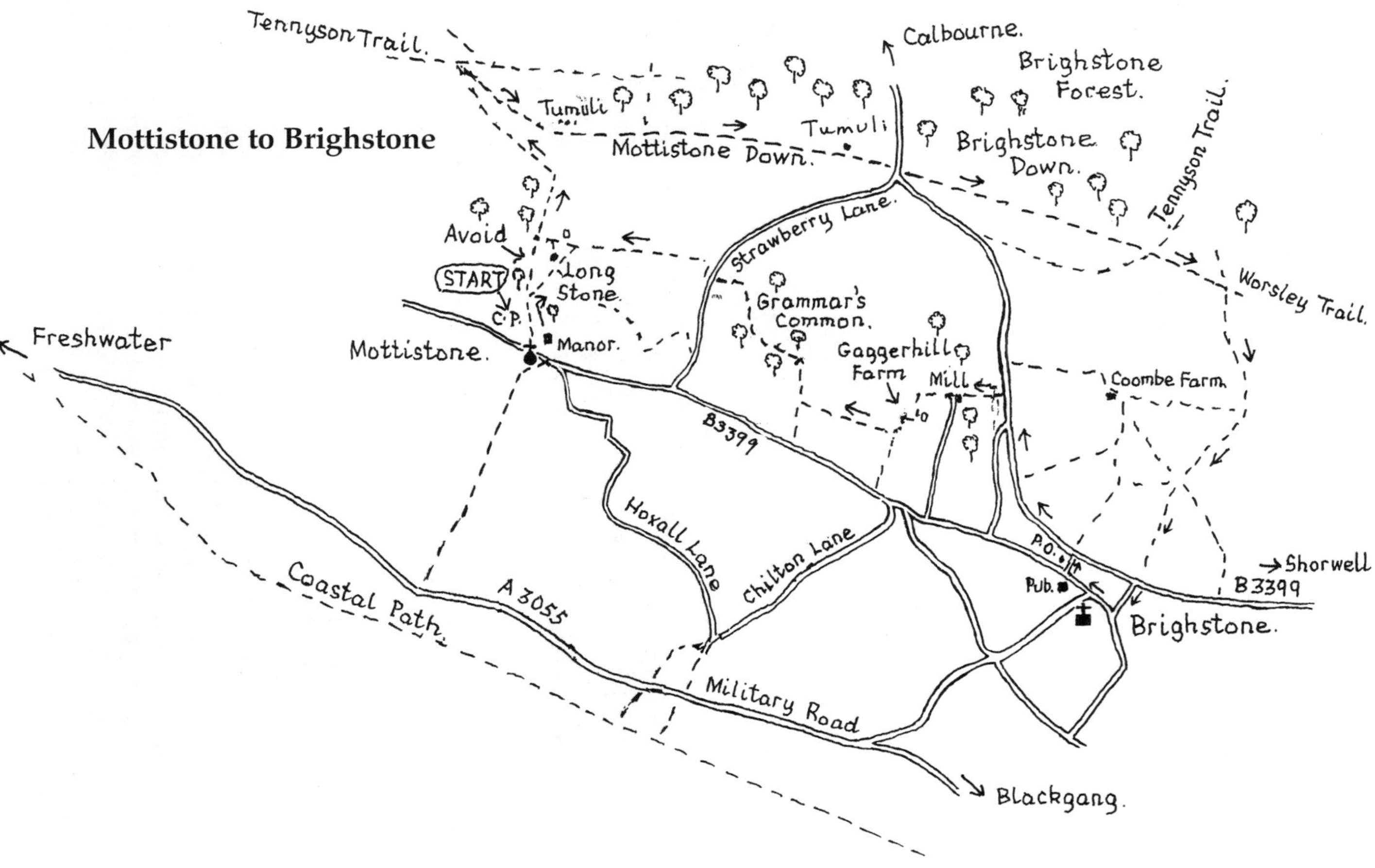

St Mary the Virgin, Brighstone In 1190 the first chapel was built here, witness the Norman arcade on the north side of the nave. Over the ages the huge round pillars have tilted slightly outwards. The octagonal Perpendicular font is large enough to immerse the baby. The south arcade is early 15th century. Tichbornes of Limerstone had an oratory here in 13th century and built the chapel south of the nave. When Limerstone Priory suffered at the Dissolution of the Monasteries, the tenants came to Brighstone. Much of the chancel is late 13th century with lancet windows containing later glass that tells the story of the Passion. In 16th century the Lords of the Manor, the Waytes had the south wall of the chancel pierced and added slender pillars and pointed arches to form the Chapel of the Holy Spirit. The tower is 14th - 15th century with a new spire of 1720 replacing the old one. Rectors of Brighstone and Brook formed the first Isle of Wight lifeboat service in 1860. In 1888 brave men gave their lives to rescue crew of the wrecked Sirenia,

Brighstone

The Walk

From the free car park head towards the Manor but not as far as the entrance gate. Instead turn left into a footpath overhung with trees and bushes. *Naturalists take this sunken path up to find nightjars in the summer.*

In 250 metres the way forks. A signpost indicates the Long Stone to the right. Accordingly, veer right away from the main track and follow a narrow path that winds through the upper reaches of the manor grounds. Cross a track outside the grounds and continue on the path straight on uphill.

Suddenly you emerge to confront the Long Stone set in sandy bumps beside an open field. *This remote spot was once a Saxon meeting place.*

Pass the Long Stone on your left and you see a nearby brick cottage ahead and an old barn over to the right. Avoid these. Turn left onto a stony track.

In 100 metres you reach woodland. Turn right and walk along the edge of the wood, now on your left. The path rises above the wood and veers left on a delightful grassy hillside ledge. There are views ahead to Freshwater Bay and Tennyson Down. As the path curves upwards, views open to the north of the Island and over to Dorset. Keep going as far as crosspaths.

Turn right to join Tennyson Trail. You are striding southeastwards on a wide grassy way for about one mile. The trail rides the top of Mottistone Down here with magnificent views south to the coast and forest. Two radio masts stand on downs ahead. We pass Neolithic tumuli. In ½ mile pass a path on the left. Keep going until you come to the byway, Lynch Lane.

To shorten the walk, turn right here and go down the lane to Brighstone.

For the full walk, cross to the track diagonally right opposite. Tennyson Trail continues here and climbs beside the forest of Brighstone Down on the left. The village of Brighstone is down on the right.

In 1 kilometre avoid a path to the right and keep straight on southeast. Soon after this you say goodbye to Tennyson Trail as it turns left into the forest. Keep on course along Worsley Trail for 250 metres as far as cross paths where you leave the trail at Limerstone Down. *No windmills here yet!*

Turn right, go through a gate and follow the signed path down to Brighstone. *The cluster of buildings you see down on the right make up Coombe Farm.* Avoid side paths to left and right. In 1 kilometre you come to a ridge of heath land. Here is a choice of ways.

Turn right and go through a gap next to a gate. Immediately the path forks, both routes lead to Brightstone. Assuming you take the left fork you come down the side of a field, pass a bungalow on the right and follow the road straight on. It bends right to Brighstone Church.

From Brighstone Church cross to the café opposite and turn right then immediately left. You are on the main road. In 100 metres, turn right and cross with care to North Street. Pass the Post Office and National Trust Museum on the left. Continue to the nearby T-junction.

Turn left and climb the lane for 1 kilometre. On the way you pass a road on the left in a residential area. Take the next turning left along a track to a converted mill. Pass a pond on the right and turn left on the path behind the mill, then immediately right.

The enclosed path takes a zigzag route up to Gaggerhill Farm. We enjoyed a prospect of pigs and goats before turning left to pass the bungalow. Look out for a footpath sign in the trees on the right. *Despite the sign: 'Strawberry Lane', the way ahead is unclear in places. Strawberry Lane is 1 mile away.*

Turn right at this footpath sign and walk through the trees then on the enclosed path up over fields to a large copse of fir trees on a steep slope known as Grammar`s Common.

As soon as you enter the copse, avoid the unofficial path ahead. Instead, veer left and northwest on the path that soon leads to a T-junction. Turn right and head north on a narrow path that climbs through the trees. At a cross track, veer left to take the steepest path opposite. As you climb, you realise that the trees on the left are on a precipitous slope. Keep climbing as your path curves to the right. You come to a natural platform that seems to be an impasse. In the far left corner you will find a hidden path leading out of the wood and into common land, the only area deserving its name!

Head westwards to reach Strawberry Lane – at last! Turn right on the lane then left into an enclosed path that soon leads to familiar open fields and the Long Stone. Go right up to touch the stone. You will then see the sunken way that brought you here. Retrace your steps down to Mottistone Manor. The church is opposite, just across the main road.

Walk 9: Freshwater Bay, River Yar, Farringford, Tennyson Down

Through a new nature trail we find an ancient parish church beside a prize-winning pub and a unique little thatched church. The long walk also includes an ornate brick Catholic church and a stride over Tennyson Down.

Starting Point: Afton Road, A3055 at Freshwater Bay, roadside parking or a nearby car park with pay points. **GR**347857 **Map:** OS Explorer OL29
Terrain: Mud in Afton Marsh can be avoided if you walk on roads.
The Long Walk has a short steep uphill and a gentler downhill.
Distances: Short Walk, 3 Miles Long Walk, 6 Miles
Local Information:
1. Afton Marsh is a Local Nature Reserve. Clearances, planking and a fine wooden footbridge enable it to be open to the public. It follows the River Yar from its source in Freshwater Bay. A Nature Trail Handbook for £1 from Tourist Information Centres and the Coastguard Shop, Freshwater Bay
2. Farringford House was the home of Alfred Lord Tennyson and his family. He bought it in 1856 with the proceeds of his poems, notably 'Maud'. Other poets and writers visited him here including Lewis Carroll and Thomas Carlyle. Prince Albert also made an unexpected call and admired the wild flowers. Two or three families owned the Island at that time.
3. Fort Redoubt was built in 1855 to protect the Solent from the French. It has been a restaurant and is now closed – watch this space!

The Churches

All Saints Church, Freshwater began in early Saxon times as a wooden building to be replaced by a stone church. The whole Anglo-Saxon church probably fitted into today`s central nave. There is some long and short stone work high in the west piers. An early village existed at the river crossing here. Afton Manor belonged to the Saxon Earl Tostig.The church would have been at the centre of this village. The font is 12th century. Members of the Afton family are buried here. Two side chapels of the chancel are the Afton Chantry and the Compton Chantry. They are named after 14th century members of those families. Brasses include one of the Knight, Adam de Compton. It was during the 14th century that the west end of the church was extended and the tower was built. It has an unusual closed pointed arch. The church interior is spacious and attractive with exposed stonework and lively Victorian stained glass. The angel`s face in the glass of the south aisle portrays Lady Emily Tennyson who is buried here. The Tennysons came from Farringford to services in All Saints.
St Agnes Church, Gate Lane, Freshwater Bay is the only thatched church on the Island. The London architect, Isaac Jones, based his design for the church on a painting the Rector, Revd. Robertson made. Local builders used the stone walls of

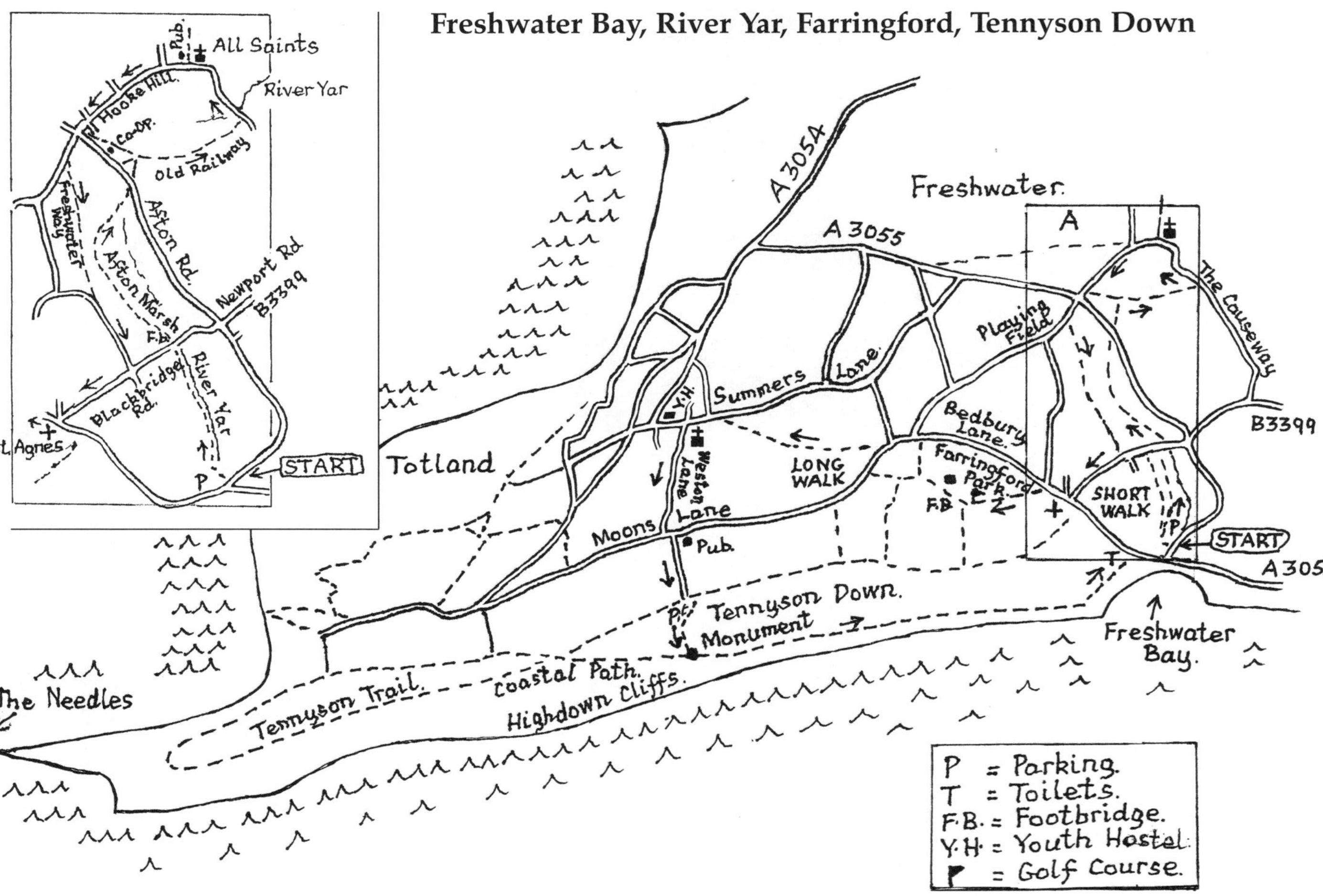
Freshwater Bay, River Yar, Farringford, Tennyson Down
Pub.
All Saints
River Yar
Hooke Hill.
Co-op.
Old Railway
Freshwater Way
Afton Rd.
Afton Marsh
Newport Rd
B3399
F.B.
Blackbridge Rd.
River Yar
St. Agnes
START
P
Totland
A3054
Freshwater.
A
A3055
The Causeway
Playing Field
Summers
Lane.
Y.H.
Weston Lane
Bedbury Lane.
B3399
LONG WALK
Farringford Park
F.B.
SHORT WALK
P
START
A3055
Moons
Lane
Pub.
T
Tennyson Down.
Monument
Freshwater Bay.
The Needles
Tennyson Trail.
Coastal Path.
Highdown Cliffs.
P = Parking.
T = Toilets.
F.B. = Footbridge.
Y.H. = Youth Hostel.
= Golf Course.

a farmhouse where the scientist Robert Hooke once lived. The church was built in 1908 on land donated by Hallam, eldest son of Alfred Tennyson. It is a delightful single cell rural church with plain windows, looking out on the wild life of the nearby field. Martins nest each year in the porch roof.

St Saviour`s R.C. Church, Totland. In stark contrast with the romantic idylls above, this church was built entirely of red brick in 1923. The wide assortment of patterns in brick must have been a challenge to the architects, James and Wilfrid Mangan and the builder Frank Privett. This spacious church with its wide entrance may hark back to Italian Romanesque style. The octagonal Martyr`s Chapel at the front contains paintings of saints. The rounded windows and square tower suggest they took their inspiration from Osborne House. A parshioner told me that Catholics worshipped in nearby Weston House before this new church was built.

Freshwater

The Walk

Cross the Afton Road to the entrance to Afton Marsh Nature Reserve, quite passable when I was here at the end of September. *If the ground is too muddy, you can walk for 1 mile along Afton Road, away from the Bay, past the Newport Road on the right. Continue to the 'End of the Line'* ***café****, a conversion of the old railway station. It is next to a plant nursery and Co-Op stores. Alternatively, just do the long walk from St Agnes Church, below.*

The narrow path through the Nature Reserve starts behind buildings then swings to the right above reedbeds. Avoid the path up to the left and keep on course through trees for about ¼ mile to Blackbridge Road. Turn right.

In 50 metres turn left to re-enter Afton Marsh. Cross a new wooden footbridge over the Yar. You then have a choice of ways, leading to the same place. The path to the left is described as less muddy. It is quite wide and passes through birches beside a branch of the river. You rejoin the other path just before the exit onto Afton Road. Turn left and walk a short way.

On your right a path leads behind the **café**, plant nursery and Co-Op. It joins the disused railway line, a wide firm causeway heading east. Trees on the right screen Afton Manor. At the byway, pause to admire the view across the River Yar then

Freshwater

turn left and walk with care over the old stone bridge and up to All Saints Church just past the bend.

The Red Lion Pub is next to the church. Pass the pub and continue along Hooke Hill, avoiding Copse Lane on the right. In ¼ mile, you come to busy crossroads, the Co-Op is on your left. Cross to Stroud Road opposite. Pause.

Playing fields are on your right. When you come to the finger post marking Freshwater Way on your right, turn sharp left into a private garden.

Well concealed here is the southern section of Freshwater Way. It leads through a small field to a succession of kissing gates, passing lawns then scrub land and continues, after a stile, along a quiet residential Easton Lane.

At the end of the lane, turn right into Blackbridge Road. This brings you to the busier Bedbury Lane. St Agnes thatched church is diagonally right opposite.

For the Short Walk, after visiting St Agnes Church, go **down** Bedbury Lane, passing footpaths to Tennyson Down and toilets on the right. At Freshwater Bay at the bottom, pass the car park on the left and return to Afton Road.

For the Long Walk, after visiting St Agnes Church, walk **up** Bedbury Lane for 70 Metres. Before you reach the corner shop, turn left into a footpath along a traffic free lane. A rough hedge screens the golf course on the right. Avoid the path on the left. As you keep on course, you pass Tennyson`s house, Farringford Park on the right. Only the tall trees show the spot, unless you are cheeky and open a wooden door in the hedge!

You go under the little footbridge he took to reach the downland that now bears his name. The lane sinks between hedges and, on the right, holiday chalets can be seen. At a junction with a farm track, cross diagonally left to the footpath that now enters a field. Hug the hedge on the left until you come to a finger post. Veer slightly to the right here and cross the field sloping down to Moons Hill (a continuation of Bedbury Lane). Turn right.

Walk along the road for 100 metres. Beware of traffic at this picturesque corner of thatched cottages. One of them is on the site of the Briary, where Tennyson had friends. Turn left here into a track that is both a bridleway and driveway. It starts under trees then emerges to pass country homes and Stonewood Farm. After the farm, avoid the track to the right. Instead, keep straight on across a small field to a copse. The clear path continues northeast through the copse and another small field to a lane.

Turn left and walk along Summers Lane, past a cemetery, then a few houses and a school. St Saviours Church is on the corner at crossroads. The Island`s last remaining Youth Hostel is on the corner diagonally opposite.

Turn left into Weston Lane, passing the church on your left. You now have nearly ½ mile of road walking. At the bottom, you come to crossroads with a pub on the corner. Cross to the track opposite so that you pass the pub on the left. At the end of the track a small car park is inside a stone pit, cut into the Downland. Tennyson Trail, the long distance path runs past the pit.

Do not enter the pit. An information plaque is on the right. Our footpath is on the left of the pit. Turn sharp right onto a narrow footpath that climbs up above and around the pit. *Here you have a view back to Hurst Castle.* The path then turns left and, with the aid of rough steps, takes you through trees to the top of Tennyson Down.

Tennyson Down

Go straight to the stone cross that is a monument to Tennyson then turn left and follow the delightful open path over turf with the sea on your right and views across to Compton Down. This is the Coastal Path. After one mile of gentle descent, you come to a gate and a steeper path down into Freshwater Bay. Return to Afton Road.

Totland

Long Distance Paths or Ways encountered on walks in Hampshire:

On the mainland nearly all trails lead to the old capital, Winchester

South Downs Way 100 Miles, is both the longest and the oldest. Stretching across the south country, east – west from Eastbourne in Sussex to Winchester in Hampshire, it is a prehistoric upland path.

St Swithun`s Way 36 Miles from Winchester to Farnham in Surrey where it joins the North Downs Way to Canterbury in Kent – a total of 112 Miles. It recalls the ancient pilgrim route between the two Cathedrals. It takes a country way avoiding the A31, part of which covers the actual route.

**Pilgrim`s Way** 28 Miles from Winchester southeast to Portsmouth. It follows the River Itchen then passes south of St Catherine`s Hill and across fields and woods to go over Portsdown hill and descend through Portsmouth to the Ferry Port. Here a ship to Cherbourg will enable pilgrims to continue their walk to Mont Saint Michel in Normandie.

Clarendon Way 24 Miles from one great cathedral to another, Salisbury in Wiltshire to Winchester. Most of the walk crosses hills in Hampshire.

Solent Way 60 Miles, follows the Hampshire coast from the little harbour town of Emsworth in the east to Milford-on-Sea and the New Forest in the west. Mid-way it follows the shore of Solent Water.

Avon Valley Path 34 Miles, on the western edge of Hampshire, follows the River Avon from Salisbury Cathedral in Wiltshire to the Norman Priory of Christchurch in Hampshire. Here the Rivers Avon and Stour meet and enter Christchurch Harbour. On route the path passes through rich meadows with wetland flowers and rare birds, also calling in at villages in the New Forest.

Test Way 44 Miles, follows the River Test from the heights of Inkpen Beacon in Berkshire to become one of Hampshire`s finest chalk streams. It passes famous places, Romsey and Mottisfont on its way south to enter Southampton Water at Eling Wharf near Totton.

Itchen Way 32 Miles, follows another chalk stream, the River Itchen from Alresford to pass pretty villages before flowing through the east side of Winchester and south over meadows to enter the Solent at Southampton.

Oxdrove Way 25 Miles takes cyclists, riders and walkers along old drove roads for cattle north of Alresford.

**Wayfarer`s Walk** 70 Miles, is Hampshire`s first long distance path and follows some tracks first used by stone age man. From Inkpen Beacon in the north it crosses the heart of Hampshire to the harbour town of Emsworth.

Allan King`s Way, in memory of a Hampshire rambler, is 45 miles long from Porchester then north of Portsmouth to Winchester.

Staunton Way almost 21 Miles, from one country park near Petersfield, Queen Elizabeth Country Park it crosses the Downs to another park, Staunton Country Park near Havant.

Hangers Way 21 Miles takes a remote route along hill slopes known as 'hangers'. From Alton it heads south via Selborne, Hawkley and Petersfield to join the South Downs Way above Buriton.

Strawberry Trail 16 Miles in the Hamble Valley makes two circular routes; 1 around Royal Victoria Country Park and north to Bursledon, 1 around Manor Farm Country Park and north to Botley.

Long Distance Paths or Trails on the Isle of Wight:

Coastal Path 67 Miles around the whole Island. We do a small part of it in Walks 1,2,7 and 9

Yar River Trail 19 Miles (The Eastern Yar) from source in the Downs near Niton to the sea at Bembridge). Walks 1 and 3 see some of it.

Tennyson Trail 14 Miles from Alum Bay to Newport. Walks 8 and 9 touch it.

Worsley Trail 13 Miles from Brighstone Forest to Shanklin. Walks 3 and 8 encounter it.

Stenbury Trail 10 Miles from Newport to Ventnor. Walk 3 sees some of the middle part of it.

**Shepherd`s Trail** 7 Miles from Newport to Shepherd`s Chine. Walk 4 follows part of it.

Freshwater Way 5 Miles from Yarmouth to Freshwater Bay. Walk 9 uses part of it.

Bibliography

Hampshire and the Isle of Wight - by Nicholaus Pevsner and David Lloyd *Yale University Press*

England`s Thousand Best Churches - by Simon Jenkins (1999) *Penguin Press*

The King`s England Hampshire and the Isle of Wight - by Arthur Mee (1939, New Edition 1967), *Hodder and Stoughton, London, E.C. 4*

A History of Hampshire by Barbara Carpenter Turner (reprinted 1988) *Phillimore, Shopwyke Hall, Chichester*

Hampshire and the Isle of Wight, Ordnance Survey Historical Guide By David Hinton and Dr A.N. Insole (1988), *George Philip, Ordnance Survey*

The Church in Anglo-Saxon Society - by John Blair (2005) *Oxford University Press*

Pastoral Pilgrimage – A Sketch Book of Walks and Churches on the Isle of Wight by Victor Vivian (1994), *Coach House Publications, Freshwater, Isle of Wight*

The New Forest – A Personal View - by C. A. Brebbia (1997) *Computational Mechanics Publications, Ashurst, Southampton*

The Green Roads of England - by R. Hippisley Cox (1924, reprinted 1948) *Methuen and Co.*

The Itchen Way - by Richard C. Kenchington *Walk The World Ltd, Fair Oak, Hampshire.*

Our Village - by Mary Russell Mitford *Macmillan and Co. (1893)* (Out of print at time of writing) *Prentice Hall Press*

Notes